# SINGLE-CAMERA VIDEO PRODUCTION

*Barry J. Fuller* is President of Media Works of Arizona, a media production firm specializing in education and training materials. He has completed the course work for a Ph.D. in Educational Technology and has produced numerous presentations, including a 30-minute videotape that illustrates in detail how to use the techniques in this book.

*Janyce Brisch-Kanaba* and *Steve Kanaba* are co-owners of Media People, a firm specializing in the production of audio-visual materials for business, industry, education, and medicine. In addition to co-writing a regular column for *Media Digest,* they have produced numerous audio-visual programs.

# SINGLE-

Techniques, Equipment, and
Resources for Producing
Quality Video Programs

A SPECTRUM BOOK

Prentice-Hall, Inc., Englewood Cliffs, New Jersey 07632

BARRY J. FULLER
STEVE KANABA
JANYCE BRISCH-KANABA

# CAMERA VIDEO PRODUCTION

*Library of Congress Cataloging in Publication Data*

Fuller, Barry J.
    Single-camera video production.

    A Spectrum Book.
    Bibliography: p.
    Includes index.
    1. Television cameras.   2. Television—Production
and direction.   I. Kanaba, Steve.   II. Brisch-Kanaba,
Janyce.   III. Title.
TR882.F84   1982        778.59        82–13323
ISBN 0-13-810762-9
ISBN 0-13-810754-8 (pbk.)

A SPECTRUM BOOK

Printed in the United States of America

10   9   8   7   6   5   4   3   2   1

ISBN 0-13-810762-9

ISBN 0-13-810754-8 {PBK}

This book is available at a special discount when ordered
in large quantities. Contact Prentice-Hall, Inc., General Publishing Division,
Speical Sales, Englewood Cliffs, N.J. 07632.

Production coordination and page layout by Inkwell
Manufacturing buyer: Barbara A. Frick
Interior design by Maria Carella

Prentice-Hall International, Inc., *London*
Prentice-Hall of Australia Pty. Limited, *Sydney*
Prentice-Hall Canada Inc., *Toronto*
Prentice-Hall of India Private Limited, *New Delhi*
Prentice-Hall of Japan, Inc., *Tokyo*
Prentice-Hall of Southeast Asia Pte. Ltd., *Singapore*
Whitehall Books Limited, Wellington, *New Zealand*
Editora Prentice-Hall do Brasil LTDA., *Rio de Janeiro*

# CONTENTS

x

# PREFACE

Now you can be an educational, industrial, or independent video producer. This book covers all the basic and intermediate information that anyone needs to know to begin producing video programs with a single-camera video system. Covered in this book is information relating to effective, creative, inexpensive single-camera production techniques in the field, as well as in the studio. Fully portable and semiportable, black-and-white and color, single-camera systems are all discussed. All the information presented is based on the personal experience of the authors—some of it humorous and some hair-raising. This book has everything from battery-acid spills to loose mountain lions—from bursting tungsten-halogen lamps to the creature from Xena. It has the latest on:

1. the make-up of single-camera systems,
2. the interconnection of single-camera and related video systems,
3. audio,
4. lighting,
5. shooting,
6. editing,
7. using other audiovisual materials in video production,
8. graphics,
9. set design, and
10. the business of video.

Single-camera video production techniques have become more important than ever due to the big move to shooting video presentations "film style"—with one camera. The technology is within reach of everyone. Low-cost, lightweight, single-camera systems now enable you to produce high-quality educational, industrial, artistic, and documentary presentations at prices that schools and corporate training facilities can afford. The single-camera video revolution is coming into the home as well, with many hobbyists and artists turning to the new VHS and Betamax ½-inch formats.

For the first time a large number of students and aspiring producers—as well as seasoned media producers, educators, and trainers—can personally own the equipment that gives them the means to communicate with thousands of others through the medium of television. The market for such video presentations is increasing geometrically, as the need for programming in the fast-growing cable and satellite-television systems becomes more critical. Seemingly limitless commercial possibilities are opening up in corporate video and in the industrial field as a whole. Many progressive companies are turning to video for the creative change of image that the video format offers for their training and marketing presentations.

Besides being an up-to-date, informative text on the "how-to" aspects of video, this book devotes an entire chapter to the business of video—how to get into video production and how to make it profitable. Unlike any other text of its kind, it is supplemented with a 30-minute videotape, which shows specifically how to produce video presentations using the techniques taught in this book. (See Media Works educational materials, p. 000.)

You'll find whatever you want to know about the newest forms of video production in *Single-Camera Video Production.*

## ACKNOWLEDGMENTS

We would like to express our deeply felt appreciation to all the individuals and organizations who helped us make this book possible. *Thank You!*

BARRY J. FULLER
STEVE KANABA
JANYCE BRISCH-KANABA

# SINGLE-CAMERA VIDEO PRODUCTION

# 1

# THE SINGLE-CAMERA
# SYSTEM

Ever since May 1, 1939, when the opening ceremonies of the New York World's Fair were televised by RCA–NBC, the television industry has undergone a virtual literal explosion of technology and software. With the improvement and increased availability of hardware, it has become relatively commonplace for anyone to own a video camera and recorder. In recent years, terms like "electronic news gathering (ENG)," "electronic field production (EFP)," and others reflect the fact that equipment has become easily portable, allowing for use outside the studio situation.

Everything was "live" in television until the mid-1950s, when the first practical videotape recorder was used. Then CBS developed the first "minicam" for the 1968 political conventions. Weighing 51 pounds, its portability was determined by the strength of the camera operator. It was refined and adapted for electronic news gathering in 1971. From then on, United States broadcasters had the money and the technical clout to influence equipment manufacturers to develop more portable cameras, recorders, and support equipment. Some of the quickest to respond were the Japanese, who developed cameras for broadcasters, as well as for industrial and educational users. The development of the "portapak" allowed anyone with about $2,000 to produce television programs electronically in the field. The cameras were small and lightweight, and the black-and-white signals they produced were recorded on reel-to-reel recorders using half-inch videotape (Figure 1-1). This clearly marked the beginning of an era for institutional users.

Electronic news gathering (ENG) became widely accepted by broadcasters in the early 1970s with the development of hardware by independent manufacturers. Sony is credited with the development of the ¾-inch U-matic videotape recorder. This design overcame many of the shortcomings of the ½-inch

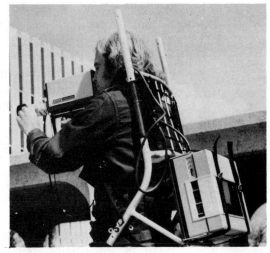

FIGURE 1–1. The lightweight, black-and-white portapak opened up the world of television to a wide range of users.

machines already in use by the educational and industrial markets. The portable ¾-inch recorder was battery powered, reliable, low cost, and capable of recording in color. The design of the ¾-inch cartridge made tape loading easy, and the cassettes could be taken to the station or studio, where they could be edited on ¾-inch editors allowing for assembly of out-of-sequence footage. This single-camera style of shooting was further supported through the development of time-base correctors, which allowed broadcasters to use the ¾-inch footage on the air. In 1973 another Japanese company, Ikegami, introduced its first generation of cameras specifically developed for on-location production.

On the American scene, RCA released a broadcast-quality portable soon after. Since then, manufacturers from around the world have continued to flood the market with cameras, recorders, editors, signal processing equipment, and other peripheral gear. The wide acceptance and use of these cameras, as well as the related operational techniques, continue to affect approaches to television program production.

## THE LIMITS OF A SINGLE-CAMERA SYSTEM

Prior to the wide use of single-camera, portable, videotape recorder systems, television-style shooting was (and still is, in many cases) a multicamera situation. A typical television studio has anywhere from two to five cameras, all synchronized and in a controlled situation. A great deal of physical space—with special provisions for floor surface, ceiling height, electrical fixtures, acoustics, intercommunications, lighting, and air conditioning—is required. The cameras, monitors, videotape recorders, switching apparatus, and audio controls are only part of the total equipment system necessary to "get on the air." It also takes people and a great deal of money to keep such a system operational. This complex array of equipment, facilities, and people is especially necessary when producing "live" television, which is, of course, how television programming started and which has left us today with many of those original methods, designs, and approaches to studio design and production.

By comparison, our single video camera and recorder seem pretty limited. In some respects, though, the large studios and broadcasters have their limits as well. For them to stay ahead of their competition, they must invest in the latest state-of-the-art equipment, and this huge expense can be viewed as a limitation. Broadcasters must also consider unions, sponsors, ratings, standardized program lengths, and many types of legal problems. These considerations also limit them in what they can do.

So perhaps individuals like you, who are either independent producers or responsible for developing television programs for an institution or agency, cannot expect to duplicate the "slick" style of the large multi-camera studios with a single-camera system. You can, however, strive for a creative approach to fit your particular needs, which may more than compensate for your lack of equipment. Using the facilities at hand and incorporating interesting techniques into your programs will go far in achieving your communication goal.

When a single-camera system simply will not do, cameras, recorders, editing time, and entire teleproduction facilities can be rented. And they should be considered if your budget allows and if your project calls for something you can't do in-house. (This alternative is discussed further in Chapter 10, "Supporting Your Video Habit.")

Regardless of the limitations on the type of equipment you have, the techniques in this book will allow you to use your single-camera system to its fullest capability, since all video cameras and recorders work basically the same way. So for our purposes, we will define a "single-camera system" as consisting of any video camera and any compatible videotape recorder, whether they are studio or portable models. All the techniques and all the peripheral gear discussed are based on this simple system.

## STUDIO EQUIPMENT

As a general rule, studio equipment is usually larger, heavier, and more complex than portable equipment. Since the studio is a controlled and permanent facility, little attention is paid to the size, weight, and power requirements of equipment. Conventional studio cameras, bulkier than portables, sit on large tripods or on tripods and dollies and they have large, top-mounted viewfinders. As trade-offs for their lack of portability, studio cameras offer a number of advantages. They usually have large viewfinders, which permit easier viewing and thus make framing the subject matter on camera easier. When mounted on a heavy-duty tripod or dolly and head, they move more smoothly and accurately than lightweight equipment. They are also usually connected to a camera control unit (CCU), which contains the electronic circuitry and controls allowing the adjustment of color (if the camera is color), contrast, brightness, and many other parameters (Figure 1-2).

FIGURE 1–2. Typical studio camera. (Photo courtesy KPHO TV5, Phoenix)

In fact, the key characteristic of a studio camera is its capability to be interconnected with a system comprised of other cameras and/or video sources. In this multi-camera system, a number of cameras and other video sources are fed through various switching and/or mixing devices. The final signal is then routed to a videotape recorder, transmitter, closed-circuit system, or any combination of the three (Figure 1-3). Since each studio camera in such a system is assigned a control unit, it is usually monitored, controlled, and adjusted at a central location such as a control room or engineering area. Remote trucks and teleproduction vans are also designed using this approach, which allows for "tighter" control over the output of each camera and results in closely matched images. Advances in microprocessor control of cameras are allowing for incredible speed and accuracy in the setting-up and matching of multiple camera systems.

Actually, the name "studio camera" is somewhat misleading because in many cases studio cameras are used for such on-location shooting as sports events, conventions, pageants, and other "nonstudio" events. In addition, more and more camera manufacturers are utilizing modular designs so that their cameras can be used in different situations without having to purchase additional

units. In such cases, the basic camera is a completely portable self-contained unit. In this configuration, the camera contains all the necessary electronics to generate a black-and-white or color signal in the field. This type of camera is called a "ENG camera" (electronic news gathering), because this term describes their original application—gathering news footage. Such totally self-contained cameras grew in sophistication and popularity due to the influence of broadcasters, who typically use such cameras to "gather" news footage. From there, a camera control unit (CCU) can be added; which allows the camera operator to hand-hold the camera while an engineer is at the CCU watching levels, making adjustments and communicating to the camera operator. This configuration, although less portable, provides for more accuracy in recording. In the studio configuration, the basic portable camera and CCU are taken a couple of steps further: A top-mounted viewfinder and rear-mounted lens controls are added, and the camera is mounted on a tripod or dolly. So the general term "EFP (electronic field production) camera" describes the portable camera either with the CCU or in the studio configuration. As opposed to ENG, EFP is a more controlled situation warranting the use of a CCU (Figure 1-4).

**FIGURE 1–3.** Studio cameras are usually tied into a system in which many other sources of video are switched and/or mixed for eventual recording or transmission.

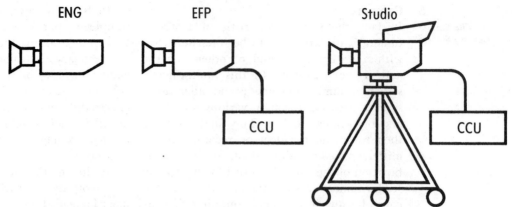

ENG          EFP          Studio

CCU          CCU

FIGURE 1–4. Many cameras are designed with a modular approach. The basic portable can be transformed into an EFP and/or studio camera with the addition of a camera control unit (CCU) and top-mounted viewfinder.

## VTRs

Videotape recorders (VTRs), designed for use in studio situations, vary in their size and sophistication as much as television cameras. In general, they are installed as permanent fixtures in either a studio control room or a tape room. Many times, they are also installed in a remote van. A typical studio VTR that uses 2-inch tape is about the size of two refrigerators. Newer, 1-inch machines are smaller in size and offer equal quality. In many cases, smaller ¾-inch VTRs are used as an alternative to the more expensive recorders, but in broadcast situations they require time-base correction to approximate broadcast quality. Again, studio VTRs are designed to be used with other equipment and incorporated into a system. They are not very portable due to their weight and size, but they offer a greater amount of control over the signal being recorded and/or played back (Figure 1-5).

FIGURE 1–5a. 2-inch quadruplex VTR.

FIGURE 1–5b. 1-inch VTRs. Photo courtesy KPHO TV5, Phoenix)

## PORTABLE EQUIPMENT

Lightweight, portable, and battery-powered equipment—at the urging of broadcasters—was designed to allow operators to place a camera on their shoulders and carry the videotape recorder separately, very much as 16-mm motion picture operators do. As videotape replaced film in broadcast news coverage, shooting "film style" became very popular. Just as in film production, the footage was edited into a finished piece, but it was edited by electronic means, rather than by physically cutting up the footage. So the time to produce a finished piece, was dramatically decreased and so electronic news gathering was born. The fantastic demand for electronic news gathering equipment drove the price of the basic shooting system down to the point where people in industry, in schools, and in hospitals could all shoot film style. The development of relatively low-cost videotape editing equipment allowed practically anyone to get into producing television programs for a wide variety of audiences and purposes. Shooting film style requires a good deal of planning, as we will see in Chapter 5.

## Cameras

Portable cameras are generally self-contained in that all the controls (and sometimes the power supply) are incorporated into a one-piece unit. From a production standpoint, the portable camera and VTR combination offers incredible flexibility. Footage can be obtained from the air, in remote locations, or on water. The same camera can then be taken indoors to shoot talent, graphics, projected images, or whatever other elements are needed for a finished program. Portable cameras can also be used in specialized situations. Due to their light weight, they can be hooked up to a microscope allowing for real-time display and/or videotaped footage of highly magnified images. Medical instruments often have adapters that permit the attachment of the camera to endoscopes and surgery lights; the resulting images help medical practitioners to make accurate diagnoses.

When we examine the various ways of adapting the video camera and recorder for use in many situations, we begin to understand how the single-camera system can offer a great deal of creative flexibility and thus find solutions to communication problems.

When purchasing or specifying a particular camera, you should consider the available options, such as a camera control unit (CCU), a top-mounted viewfinder, and the like. For example, in a studio configuration a portable camera becomes more useful when mounted on a tripod: Operating the camera smoothly is easeir, especially when executing camera movements.

## VTRs

The same forces that prompted the development of the portable camera also hastened videotape recorder technology. The early and mid-1970s saw the development of new cameras with incredible features and versatility. At the same time the introduction of the ¾-inch U-matic format allowed broadcasters to use the easy-loading videocassette and reliable ¾-inch portable recorders in the field. These machines were low in cost, lightweight, and easy to use, and they produced higher-quality images than the open-reel ½-inch portables of the late 1960s and early 1970s. Recent years have seen the use of the many ½-inch portable videocassette formats for less exacting location production (Figure 1-6).

Perhaps the most important consideration, when shooting or recording with a single-camera system, is image quality. In general, portable videotape recorders of all types are used more as a means to a end than for producing finished material. So the general approach in ENG, EFP, or shooting film style is to take the footage obtained in the field or on location back to the studio, or to a postproduction facility, where it is edited into a finished piece. While low-cost portables, in-

FIGURE 1–6. Typical ENG portable camera and ¾-inch VTR in use. (Photo courtesy KPHO TV5, Phoenix)

cluding the popular ½-inch and ¾-inch formats, offer adequate reproduction of the recorded images, they come nowhere near the quality offered by broadcast-compatible portable system costing ten times as much. When selecting a videotape recorder or camera, the most important technical consideration is that the quality of the finished product can be only as good as the equipment used to record it.

## HOW CAMERAS WORK

Besides being classified as either "studio" or "portable," cameras can also be categorized according to whether they produce an image in black-and-white, in color, or in both. In the United States, all broadcast quality color cameras must be able to produce color images that can be received and converted into a black-and-white image on a monochrome television receiver. As you might suspect, color cameras are more expensive than black-and-white models due to the additional circuitry necessary to produce color images.

## BLACK-AND-WHITE CAMERAS

A typical black-and-white television camera works by focusing light onto a photosensitive surface (the pick-up tube). The amount of light entering the camera is controlled by a lens, which also focuses the image on the photosensitive pick-up tube. That image in the tube is scanned by an electron beam, which produces a very weak current that varies depending on lightness or darkness of the different areas in the image. These varying pulses of electricity are amplified and

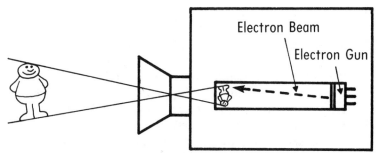

**FIGURE 1–7a.** The image focused on the pick-up tube is scanned by an electron beam.

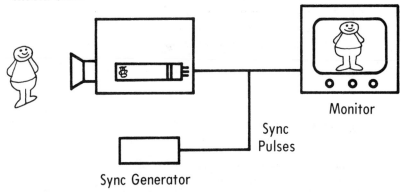

**FIGURE 1–7b.** Synchronizing pulses are added to stabilize the signal.

combined with synchronizing pulses as the signal leaves the camera. This combined signal can be routed by coaxial cable to a monitor, videotape recorder, or switcher, if more than one camera is being used (Figure 1-7).

In 1941, the Federal Communications Commission (FCC) approved the *National Television Systems Committee* (NTSC) recommendations for a standard of monochrome television transmission. In this system, 30 frames are flashed on the TV screen every second, creating the illusion of motion. Each frame consists of 525 horizontal scanning lines, divided equally between two interlaced fields. So the first field has 262.5 "odd-numbered" lines, and the second field has 262.5 "even-numbered" lines. To complete the first field, the odd lines start at the upper left-hand side of the screen and stop at bottom center. The scanning beam then returns to the top center of the picture, and it "fills in" with the even-numbered lines the areas not scanned in the first field. The two fields take one-sixtieth of a second each, giving us the one-thirtieth of a second for each frame (Figure 1-8).

**FIGURE 1–8.** Each frame of video information is comprised of the interlaced fields.

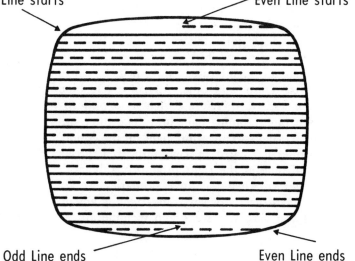

Odd Line starts

Even Line starts

Odd Line ends

Even Line ends

This 525-line, 30-frame-per-second NTSC scanning system is used in the United States, Japan, and South America, all of whom have alternating current of 60 cycles per second. Two other major standards are used in other parts of the world. Britain and parts of Europe use the *phase alternate by line* (PAL) system, which is a modified form of the NTSC system. It utilizes 625 scanning lines and 25 frames per second. Other parts of Europe, France, and the USSR use a 625-line, 25-frame-per-second scanning system, which was designed in France and called SECAM, or *sequential with memory.*

## COLOR CAMERAS

These three major world standards differ not only in their basic scanning rates, but also in how they encode color information from its primary red, green, and blue components. When producing television programs for use outside the United States, you must be able to supply tapes that conform to these other systems (as we will discuss in Chapter 6).

In 1955, NTSC standards for color television transmission were approved by the FCC. By means of this system, color information is interleaved with the black-and-white signals. In this way, a black-and-white receiver can still receive a color signal, since the composite signal contains the basic black-and-white information. Color images are produced in a number of ways, depending on the camera design, optics, and the pick-up tubes used.

### Color Theory

From basic color theory, we know that all colors in the visible spectrum of light are made up of a mixture of three primary colors —red, green, and blue. All color television cameras are therefore designed to optically separate incoming light into these three primary colors. While white light (or the "color" white) is created by combining red, green, and blue in the right proportions, black is obtained when the three primaries are absorbed—that is, when white light is absent. If you look at a scene and imagine all the

light and dark areas separated into three separate color elements of the scene, you have a good feel for how a color video camera works.

In video, two basic elements are assigned to color information. The first is *chrominance,* made up of the hue (tint) and the saturation (amount of color). The second is *luminance* (intensity). Mixing the three primary colors in differing quantities of luminance and chrominance, the color camera creates any color in the visible spectrum.

### Pick-Up Tubes

This process begins with optical arrangements and pick-up tubes of the camera. As in the black-and-white camera, images are focused by a lens. Then the incoming light is passed through and/or directed by filtering devices, such as prisms, dichroic filters, and mirrors. The filtering devices divide the incoming light into the primary colors. The light is thus split into two, three, or four beams of light, and each beam is focused onto the surface of a corresponding pick-up tube.

Color cameras have four different tube configurations, as necessitated by their filtering systems:

1. In the *four-tube camera,* three tubes are assigned to red, green, and blue respectively, with the fourth tube reading black-and-white information. (Although there aren't many four-tube cameras around any more, they are a good starting point in understanding color video.)
2. In the *three-tube system,* each tube is assigned one primary color. The black-and-white signal is derived from the green signal.
3. *Two-tube cameras* have one tube reading all three colors and another reading black-and-white.
4. In a *one-tube camera,* the pick-up reads both color and black-and-white information.

In all cases, the images focused on the face of the pick-up tube(s) are scanned by a beam of electrons much in the same way the black-and-white image is formed in black-and-white cameras. (Figure 1-9).

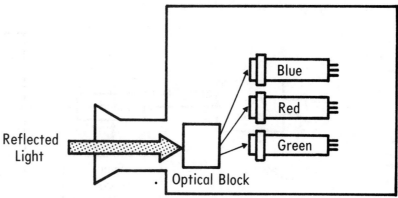

FIGURE 1–9a. A filtering device splits incoming reflected light into the primary colors of light.

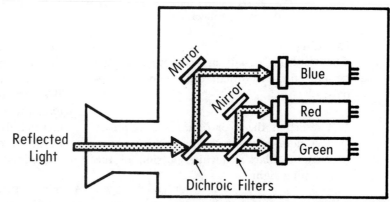

FIGURE 1–9b. In a three-tube camera, filters direct light to each tube.

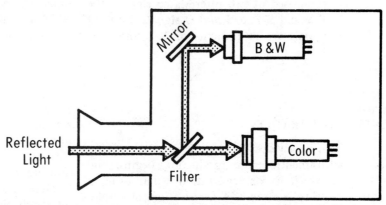

FIGURE 1–9c. A two-tube camera uses one tube to read black-and-white signals and the other to read all three primary colors.

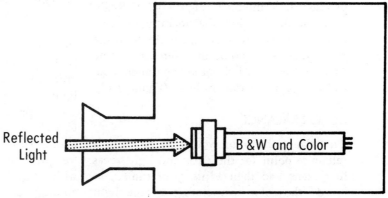

FIGURE 1–9d. A single-tube camera reads both color and black-and-white information.

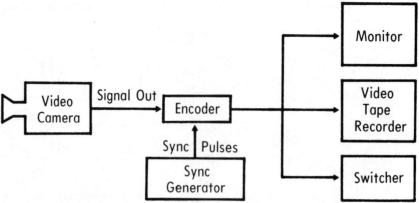

FIGURE 1–10. Color signals are combined with syncronizing signals at the camera encoder. The encoder may be built into either the camera head or a camera control unit, or it may be a stand-alone unit. The same applies to the sync generator.

### Encoding

The resulting signals are combined at the camera encoder, which forms two new signals:

1. The first is the $Y$ or *luminance signal* (it does not stand for yellow), which represents the black-and-white portion of the incoming light.

2. The second is the *chrominance,* which is comprised of two interrelated signals, the R-Y and B-Y, or I and Q signals. I and Q signals are refinements of R-Y and B-Y.

Both sets of chrominance components have to do with the level of sophistication of the camera encoder. Although R-Y and B-Y are compatible with the NTSC system, the I-and-Q format is the preferred method. In fact, all cameras that use an I and Q encoding system are legally of "broadcast quality."

Various synchronizing signals are added to the Y, I, and Q signals, forming one final signal called the *composite video signal,* which contains all the necessary elements for transmission and/or recording (Figure 1-10).

## COLOR CAMERA ADJUSTMENTS

### REGISTRATION

The color video camera needs several routine adjustments before production begins, one of which is for registration when using a multi-tube camera. A *registration,* or *resolution, chart* is used to determine if the filtered images coming from the pick-up tubes are precisely superimposed (Figure 1-11). Registration controls allow the operator or technician to adjust the images, usually with the green tube as a point of reference. These controls are located either at the camera control unit or at the camera head (Figure 1-12).

### COLOR BALANCE

To balance the color, you must establish a reference point for the dark and light areas in a scene and then adjust your camera to "read" the color temperature of the light source used for the scene. In other words, you may find yourself in a situation that has a number of light sources, such as daylight, fluorescent, and/or tungsten. In such a case, you can adjust your camera to "see" this mixture of light as white light.

Here's how that is done. In many cameras, filter wheels behind the lens compensate for certain colors inherent in different sources of light. The different filters on this wheel can be dialed into place behind the lens depending on the type of light available. With the chosen filter in place, the camera is then pointed at either a white card or a grey scale *chip chart,* so that the reflected light the camera "sees" can be mixed in the proper proportions of red, green, and blue to yield white. Many cameras have an automatic white balance circuit, which allows for push-button adjustment when using a white card. The main idea is to vary the amounts of red, green, and blue to accommodate different sources of light falling on the particular scene (Figure 1-13).

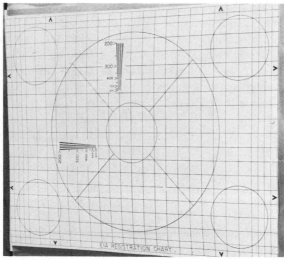

FIGURE 1–11. The camera is set up using a registration chart, which visually shows whether the images from the pick-up tubes are precisely superimposed.

FIGURE 1–12. An example of a camera control unit. The module on the extreme right has front panel adjustments for registration.

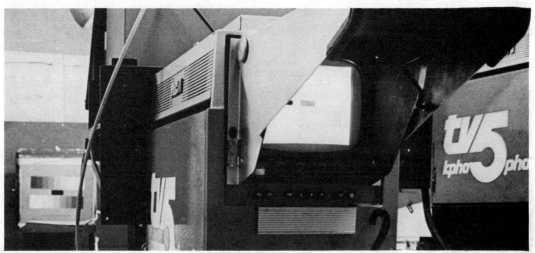

FIGURE 1–13. A chip chart is used to color balance cameras. (Photo courtesy KPHO TV5, Phoenix)

The electronic tolerances and specifications involved in producing the video image differ from one piece of equipment to another. Correspondingly, the cost of a particular video component usually reflects its level of technology and refinement, which in turn determines the quality of the image it produces.

## IMAGE QUALITY

Image quality is a highly personal and subjective issue. Some people swear that the quality of an image generated by a $5,000 camera is as good as the image from a $50,000 camera. To the uninitiated, the actual electronic creation of a picture is such "magic" that image quality goes unnoticed. Upon closer examination, however, you can find that all the elements comprising a particular camera design are associated with built-in limitations.

Generally speaking, the more the camera costs, the better the image quality. Although many lower-priced cameras meet minimum technical requirements, they usually require higher amounts of light and work at their best only in ideal situations. Higher-priced cameras usually offer sophisticated automatic circuits, sport a number of mechanical features, and work at peak performance even under adverse conditions.

How much image quality do you need? The type and quality of camera used depends on your application. A typical broadcast-quality camera is intended for through-the-air transmission. In this case, the signals generated must maintain established engineering standards, as written by the EIA (Electrical Industries Association) and the FCC. They must also follow the NTSC television transmission standards which we have already covered. A nonbroadcast camera, for which there are no standards, may be used in closed-circuit applications. *Closed-circuit television* (CCTV) simply means that the signal is never sent through the air like broadcast television. Examples include surveillance, institutional television (such as in hospitals, business, and schools), and community antenna television (CATV). In CATV, the signals are fed to homes via cable from a central studio.

The single-camera system and film style shooting are adaptable to all these situations. Although broadcast-quality equipment costs a great deal more than its nonbroadcast counterpart, producing with broadcast-quality gear is often desirable because it is compatible with set standards. Since budget is often a limiting factor, however, it is necessary to apply the resources you have to fit the application. Although getting the message across is far more important than technical quality, it is helpful to keep quality in mind when planning equipment purchases. Knowing what to look for when seeking the best possible quality helps to avoid problems.

## RESOLUTION

The primary criterion is the camera's resolving power—its ability to reproduce a sharp, crisp image in all its fine detail. Resolution can be measured objectively by focusing the camera on a resolution chart (the same one used to register a multi-tube camera). The resolution test pattern on this chart is a numerical standard against which the performance of the camera can be measured in lines of horizontal and vertical resolution. The chart has horizontal and vertical wedges at the center and at each corner. The point at which the camera no longer distinguishes between lines in these wedges is the limit of its resolving power. Standard black-and-white cameras resolve between 400 and 500 lines. (Figure 1-11). Low-cost color cameras resolve between 250 to 300 lines, and some broadcast-quality, three-tube cameras can resolve up to 600 lines. For color cameras, resolution is usually measured in terms of two values:

1. The black-and-white, or luminance, value for resolution is always higher in rating than color, due to the difficulties encountered in registerng the multple color images.
2. The camera is also measured with a recommended amount of light, in footcandles or lux, and at a certain f-stop setting on the lens.

It is wise to operate your camera with the manufacturers' recommendations in mind. The specification sheet or operation manual supplied with your camera tells you this information. Once again, expensive cameras are able to produce a high resolution at lower light levels.

Light sensitivity is a function of the:

1. optical system (the lens, filters, and mirrors),
2. the pick-up tubes, and
3. the associated electronic circuitry (discussed in the following section on Noise and Stability).

## Optical Systems

A high-quality lens can focus an image accurately and without distortion, permitting a relatively great amount of light to pass through. Usually, the camera manufacturer supplies a lens that matches the performance of the camera. Many high-priced cameras, however, are sold without lenses and in many cases without pick-up tubes, so as to allow users to select these items to match their

needs and budget. Lenses and pick-up tubes vary in cost, specifications, and capabilities. Once again, you get what you pay for. Since lens types are covered in Chapter 5, "Shooting," let's focus our attention on the rest of the optical system.

The rest of the optical system can include:

1. dichroic mirrors and filters, or
2. prism optics.

In the *dichroic system,* the light gathered by the lens is separated by a series of dichroic filters and mirrors (Figure 1-14). Dichroics are relatively inexpensive, which may be (a consideration when buying a color camera), and they work well. Yet since this type of system absorbs a considerable amount of light before the colors reach the pick-up tubes, its design is not well suited to low-light situations. Also, in a dichroics system, the tubes are positioned parallel to each other. Hence the alignment is critical, and the system is not capable of sustaining the shocks and bumps of location production.

The *prism optic system* incorporates prisms bonded in one solid block, thus allowing the pick-up tubes to be attached directly to the optical block and in turn cuts down the overall weight of the camera. So this type of system is more efficient and stable than dichroics, and it allows more light to pass through, which makes it suitable for low-light situations. In the (more expensive)

FIGURE 1–14a. As we saw in Figure 1–9, dichroic mirrors were used to split up the incoming reflected light.

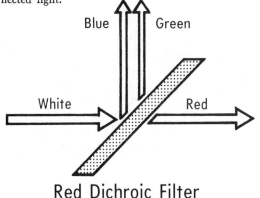

Red Dichroic Filter

FIGURE 1–14b. Prism optics are one solid piece and offer the ability to pass more light and fewer registration problems, since the pick-up tubes are mounted directly to the optical block.

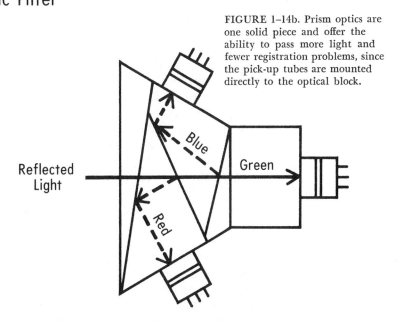

Prism Optic System

prism optic system, registration problems are also kept to a minimum (Figure 1-14).

The quality of both dichroic and prism optics can be measured by their associated f-stop ratings. For example, two cameras may have prism optics, but one is capable of passing light down to f-1.8 and the other, to f-1.4. The optics that pass light at f-1.4 is considered "faster," and it probably costs more.

### Pick-Up Tubes

The many types of pick-up tubes now in use all work pretty much as explained in the section on how the black-and-white signal is produced, except for the new, solid-state charged-coupled devices, which are still under development (Figure 1-15). The major difference among pick-up tubes is in the chemical formulation of the target material on their faces. As you might suspect, each

FIGURE 1–15. Various pick-up tubes.

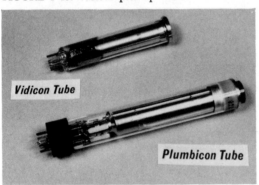

has particular characteristics, and manufacturers design camera's electronics to match the type of pick-up tubes it uses. The diameter of the tubes also differ, that is, $\frac{2}{3}$-inch, 1-inch, and $1\frac{1}{4}$-inches (18 mm, 25 mm, and 30 mm). The larger tubes are usually found in studio cameras, whereas $\frac{2}{3}$-inch and 1-inch tubes are found in ENG and EFP cameras.

Popular pick-up tube names such as Vidicon, Plumbicon, Saticon, and others are all basically the same, but let's discuss them separately anyway and briefly:

Generally, *Vidicons,* although the least expensive, are capable of very high resolution. The drawback is that they are susceptible to "burn-in," "lag," or "comet-tailing." These conditions plague all camera tubes, but some designs are more susceptible than others. When the camera encounters a bright light or extreme contrast difference, such as a light area surrounded by a dark

area, the tube cannot respond quickly enough to compensate for the change in brightness. On the monitor, the bright image "smears" or "lags," especially if either the object is moving or the camera is moving in relation to it. If the image is held on camera long enough, it can actually "burn-in" on the faceplate of the tube. That is, of course, why you should never aim a camera at the sun or at bright lights. Some very expensive cameras are specifically designed to handle these situations, but avoid them as a general rule, if possible. Since the Vidicon is susceptible to lag and burn-in, it usually has to be replaced sooner than other types of tubes.

*Plumbicon* tubes, an improved version of the Vidicon, have less lag and burn-in problems, but they are designed for each primary color. In other words, there is a different Plumbicon for red, green, and blue.

*Saticons* are interchangeable, which means that if one tube in a multi-tube camera needs replacement, it can be done easily since there are no red, green, or blue Saticons.

The ability of a pick-up tube to detect changes in each scan line is a function of its frequency response: the higher the frequency response, the higher the resolution. Most of the pick-up tubes we have mentioned come in "grades," a term that refers to their resolving power or their frequency response. For example, some Plumbicons may cost more than others because they are a higher-grade tube, capable of reproducing images with higher resolving power.

### NOISE AND STABILITY

Signal-to-noise is another good indicator of quality. Any electronic device that generates a signal of some kind has an inherent amount of noise, or random energy, associated with the system. The amount of noise generated is related to many factors such as temperature, the frequency of the operating system, harmonics, and the resistance within the system. The ratio of the signal generated by the system to the inherent noise in the system is called the *signal-to-noise ratio*. In the case of the video camera, a high signal-to-noise ratio results in a clear, sharp image, and a low ratio results in a low resolution—a muddy picture with irresolute reproduction. Low-cost color cameras with one pick-up tube may have a signal-to-noise ratio of 45 dB, and high-cost three-tube cameras may have a signal-to-noise ratio as high as 60 dB. The signal-to-noise ratio, always specified with the information supplied with a camera, relates directly to the camera's overall ability to produce quality images.

The stability of a camera refers to how well it maintains its specified ratio under various operating conditions. In this respect, stability can affect not only the camera's overall image quality but its use in production as well. A highly stable (and high-cost) camera allows for lengthy operation under a wide variety of environmental conditions. For example, from a mechanical point of view, a camera with dichroic optics would be less "stable" (from an alignment point of view) than a prism optics camera. A single-tube design eliminates this problem, but it does not have the resolving power of the multi-tube designs.

From an electronic viewpoint, all the elec-tronic components in a camera have certain percentages of fluctuation or tolerances in accuracy. For example, the resistor or capacitor that has a plus-or-minus 1-percent value is better (and more expensive) than one with a 5-percent or an even greater percentage value. So inasmuch as all the electronics associated with generating the video signal affect the final output, the camera's ability to produce low-noise signals, to reproduce colors accurately, and to hold accurate registration depends on the stability of the electronics. Since the amount of noise increases with temperature, frequency, and resistance in the system, the built-in tolerances and refinements of all the components built into the circuitry in a camera design combine to affect its stability. Better cameras are designed with finer tolerance electronic components and optics.

## SUITING THE TECHNOLOGY TO THE APPLICATION

Video technology has advanced a great deal since its beginning. New cameras, recorders, and peripheral equipment are continually being upgraded to provide increased capability for producers. Although video producers should not necessarily be concerned with technology as such, they should be aware of what is out there and what it can do. Just as artists must know the characteristics of their medium, video producers must be familiar with what technology has to offer.

### NONBROADCAST EQUIPMENT

Increased competition has pushed cameras, recorders, and support equipment into many new markets. Just as the portapak of the late 1960s and early 1970s started the growth of nonbroadcast video, the small-format color camera and VTR of the 1980s are allowing more and more individuals to produce video on a small scale. "Small-format" video equipment—specifically designed for nonbroadcast applications—has penetrated the home consumer, business, industry, educational, medicine, and cable television communication markets, among others. In general, the bulk of the equipment used in these areas is relatively low in cost as compared to broadcast quality gear. Nonbroadcast, or small format, VTRs include ½-inch, ¾-inch, and some older 1-inch format machines. These small format machines can often be adapted for broadcast use by passing the output signal through various signal processing devices such as the digital time-base corrector.

The main point is that the small format user can cross over into many areas with the help of some basic equipment. And there is a great deal of such crossover in all areas, whether home, CCTV, or broadcast. For example, a hospital or business that is interested in developing training materials may start out with a low-cost, consumer-type video camera and VTR. As its demand for higher quality grows, budgets increase, and eventually equipment of broadcast quality may be purchased. An example of small-format video used in a broadcast situation is a locally produced documentary shot with nonbroadcast equipment. The artistry of the delivery, as well as the excellence of the message, far surpasses the technical quality. A local broadcaster may choose to make the necessary technical changes to get the program "on the air."

Another common approach is to use a broadcast-quality camera with a small format (½-inch or ¾-inch) VTR. The rationale is that since the camera can deliver high-quality images under a wide variety of lighting conditions, the edited videotapes will also retain a high degree of quality since the original signal was as sharp and noise-free as possible. In this case, a common practice is to transfer the resulting footage (from the small format machine) to broadcast-quality studio recorders for editing purposes and/or transmission. This technique is used extensively in news gathering and in limited commercial work since originating footage on small-format machines costs much less than on broadcast-quality gear.

## BROADCAST EQUIPMENT

Even though broadcast cameras—and specifically camera encoders—must be designed to meet NTSC television transmission standards, more and more equipment manufacturers are building cameras to meet only minimum standards. So resolution, light sensitivity, noise, and stability, all of which affect overall qualty, vary widely from camera to camera. Thus some cameras cost more than others. In general, while nonbroadcast cameras range from $1,000 to $15,000, broadcast cameras start around $15,000 and reach as high as $100,000.

Broadcasters and serious commercial producers must rely on their equipment to give them top-quality results because their respective audiences demand it. They must use top-quality gear because it performs consistently under heavy use. Studio and portable VTRs are available in every format, and each has unique features and accessories related to its intended use.

Serious producers therefore need to purchase or to rent equipment based on their production requirements. All producers—broadcasters and nonbroadcasters alike—should also carefully consider the features on a VTR under consideration. For example, are there separate inputs for video and audio for use with different sources? How about multiple audio channels with manual override for mixing and tight control over audio sources? Picture quality, editing capabilities, operational controls, and many other variables all require deliberation.

The important thing to remember is that all video cameras are put to use by people. Those people, with their technical skills and creative abilities, determine the results. No matter how good the camera is, it cannot compose a shot or pick an angle for you.

## VIDEOTAPE RECORDERS

Is a studio or portable VTR what you need? Should you use a 2-inch, 1-inch, ¾-inch, or ½-inch tape format? How does each of these popular formats affect the image quality of your production?

Let's start answering these questions by explaining what a VTR does. The job of the videotape recorder (VTR) is to transfer the video signal (with or without audio) to magnetic tape so that the information recorded can be retrieved. The VTR transfers this information to the videotape by sending pulses of energy to video heads, which are tiny electromagnets. When the VTR is in the *record* mode, audio and video signals enter the VTR and create varying magnetic fields in the audio and video heads. These varying magnetic fields are recorded on the moving videotape. The *video erase* and *audio erase* heads eliminate any video or audio information previously recorded; thus videotape, like audio tape, is reusable. In the

*play* mode, the information recorded on the magnetic videotape is fed back through the heads and the related electronics. The video signals are retrieved from the videotape and sent out to a monitor, to another VTR, to a switcher or mixer, to a transmitter, or to some other component (Figure 1-16).

## VIDEOTAPE

Videotape corresponds to the film in a camera. Even if you use an expensive still camera, as long as you use old, dated, or "off-brand" film, your chances of getting optimum results are reduced. The same principle applies to videotape. Old, worn-out, or poor-quality videotape can result only in poor reproduction, and it can even result in no recording at all or in damage to the delicate video heads.

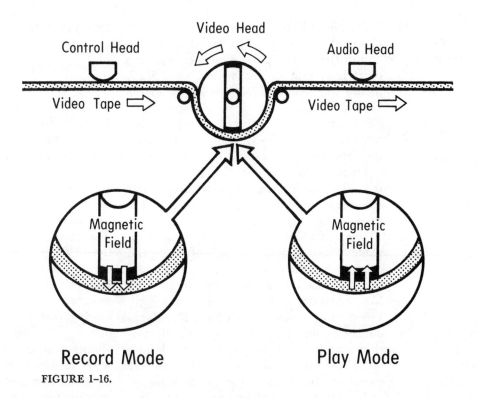

Record Mode        Play Mode

FIGURE 1–16.

## Physical Properties

Videotape is much like audio tape in that a metal-oxide coating of particles is bound to a polyester (plastic) base. The magnetic properties of the metal-oxide particles determine the videotape's sensitivity, frequency response, and signal-to-noise ratio. The back of the tape is usually coated with an anti-static carbon, which reduces static electricity generated by any friction caused as the tape rubs against the tape guides on the VTR. As a general rule, use the tape recommended by the manufacturer (Figure 1-17).

Since tape is a polyester-based material, it is prone to a small amount of stretch, especially if reused again and again. A tape stock with a highly rated, tensile-strength backing cuts down on this problem.

Videotape is also prone to losing some of the magnetic material, which causes a tiny portion of the recorded signal to *dropout*. Since there is a blank space in the tape, the picture information is lost (for a short duration) when viewed on a monitor. A drop-out looks like a small white speck, or flash in the picture. To avoid drop-outs, before recording critical information, record something on the whole length of a new reel of tape to check for drop-outs, wrinkles, and edge damage. If the playback is satisfactory, then bulk erase it and use it for the master recording.

FIGURE 1–17.

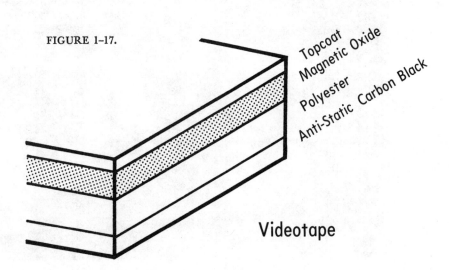

Topcoat
Magnetic Oxide
Polyester
Anti-Static Carbon Black

Videotape

Usually name-brand videotape has few, if any, flaws and provides excellent results. Nonetheless, you should wind new cassettes or reels of tape in fast-forward on a VTR to the end, then rewind them back to the beginning. Doing so breaks up any static electricity charges on the tape backing, and prevents *clinching,* and helps to cut down the incidence of drop-out.

Since the first and last few feet of a tape reel are handled in manufacturing, start recording a few feet into the reel, rather than at the very beginning.

Keep in mind also that videotape is capable of recording both black-and-white and color information. Videotape recorders are built to meet technical specifications and, like cameras, meet NTSC guidelines as well. When using videotape, VTRs, and players, do not smoke. Keep the tape and the machines as dust-free as possible, avoid high humidity, and minimize handling of the videotape. It is also important to store all reels or cassettes in their appropriate packages vertically and at room temperature.

Videotape is one of the least expensive elements of the recording process. It is also the most important link in the retrieval of the video signal. The electromechanical design of a VTR and/or videotape player determines which types of tape can be used. These design parameters in turn determine image quality and, like video cameras, reflect this by what they cost.

## TYPES OF VTRs

There are two popular systems of videotape recording:

1. the transverse or quadruplex scanning system, and
2. the helical scan system.

### Transverse Scanning

The transverse scanning system, developed in the 1950s, proved to be a practical method of recording video and audio information. Four small rotating heads rotate at high speed across 2-inch videotape, which is also moving past the heads at either 7½ or 15 inches per second. This pioneering design allowed a great amount of information to be recorded on a reasonable length of tape. As the heads scan the tape, the information goes onto the tape at right angles to the direction in which the tape is moving. The tape also passes through a vacuum assembly to curve the tape as it approaches the rotating head assembly (Figure 1-18). The quadruplex VTR was and still is used as a standard format of the broadcast industry. Since a 2-inch, or "quad," recorder can easily cost $100,000 and run up large costs for maintenance and tape stock as well, the search for a less expensive system was initiated.

FIGURE 1–18. The head assembly on a 2-inch quadruplex machine. (Photo courtesy KPHO TV5, Phoenix)

## Helical Scanning

Helical scan, or "slant track," refers to the path of the heads (as they rotate) with relation to the tape. Because the scan of each portion of the video signal takes up a relatively long section of tape, the tape width and tape speed can be decreased. This is why there are so many different helical scan machines using different widths of tape. Two or more recording heads are mounted on a rotating drum, called the "head drum." These rotating heads put the video information onto the tape in a slanted, rather than in a transverse, manner. As in the case of the quad design, the video information is "written" into the center portion of the tape. Audio and other tracks are recorded near the edges of the tape. The tape, which is available in a number of widths, is wound around the head drum in a helical pattern. The tape comes off the supply reel, is slanted as it wraps around the head, then loses contact with the head drum as it is wound on the take-up reel.

The size of the head drum and the width of the tape, as well as the positioning of audio, control track, and other heads, are determined by the format or design of the particular machine. Generally speaking, wider tape stock and faster "writing" speeds result in higher frequency response, stability, and signal-to-noise ratio. Since quad, 2-inch, and many different 1-inch helical VTRs are capable of recording higher frequencies of video information, they are referred to as *highband VTRs*. Most high-quality color recorders and players are high-band, and they provide higher-quality pictures with less video noise and better resolution than low-band VTRs.

The way the tape wraps around the head is another design function. Manufacturers use either the alpha or the omega "wrap." In the alpha, the tape is wound once completely around the head drum (360 degrees). In the omega wrap, the tape covers only a portion of the head (Figure 1-19).

Helical scan machines are the most popular because they have many advantages over quad VTRs. Except for some top-quality helical VTRs that use 2-inch videotape, most helical machines are less expensive due to their simpler design. The better-quality helical machines use 1-inch tape, with the latest 1-inch machines offering quality equal to quad. The $10,000-to-$75,000 price range of the many different 1-inch VTRs accounts for their popularity. (The broadcast-quality helical scan machines are in the upper price range.) Most of these 1-inch VTRs use reel-to-reel tape rather than cassettes.

Helical scan is also used on the extremely popular ¾-inch videocassette recorder/players. Since they offer good-quality reproduction, are so easy to use, and cost relatively little, ¾-inch helical scan videocassette recorder/players have gained acceptance in nonbroadcast applications, becoming the

FIGURE 1–19. Two popular methods of tape transport in helical scan machines.

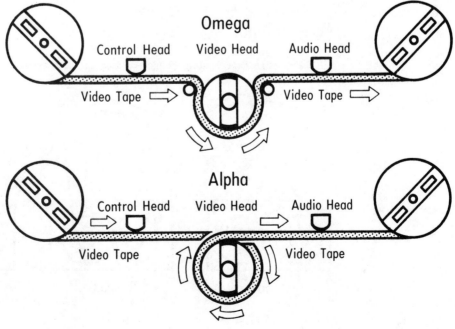

most popular type of VTR for schools, industry, business, and medicine. Although the ¾-inch format was originally supposed to be marketed for home use, by the time it was released, its price tag was over $1,000. As a result, it was marketed instead to education and industrial users. (The ¾-inch U-matic format is unique because it is the only VTR that uses ¾-inch tape).

VTR manufacturers, however, continued to develop machines for consumer use. Two systems for high-density recording were developed, both based on the helical scan design: Beta and VHS. Both use a technique called *azimuth recording,* which allows the information to be packed onto the videotape in a much denser configuration (Figure 1-20). The two systems eliminate the space, or guard bands, between scanning tracks by recording each video track alongside each other, but at a slightly different angle: In Beta format, the angle is seven degrees; in the VHS design, the angle is six degrees. Both systems use different-sized videocassettes loaded with ½-inch videotape. The Beta uses a tape loading system similar to the ¾-inch U-matic and threads the tape around the head in an alpha-wrap configuration. The VHS uses an omega wrap and offers a shorter tape path. In addition, they differ in head drum sizes and in the positioning of audio and control track head (Figure 1-21). These machines, which generally cost under $1,000, offer the consumer a wide range of options to choose from. Industrial versions of either Beta or VHS cost a few hundred dollars more and offer more features and better quality.

Another popular ½-inch format is the EIAJ format, which comes in open reel and cassette. "EIAJ" refers to the standardization in design that allows for the interchangeability of tapes. These machines, most commonly found in schools, range in price from $800 for black-and-white to $1,200 for color. Many other ½-inch machines exist, but they are not compatible with other VTR's.

**FIGURE 1–20.** The azimuth method of recording eliminates guard bands between scan lines for recording each track at a slightly different angle from the other.

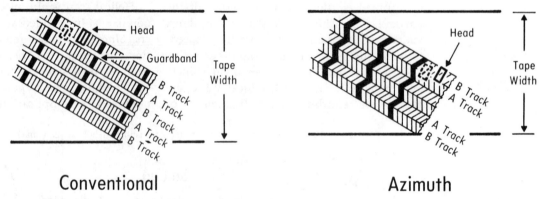

Conventional                    Azimuth

**FIGURE 1–21.** Tape loading designs as seen in three popular videocassette formats.

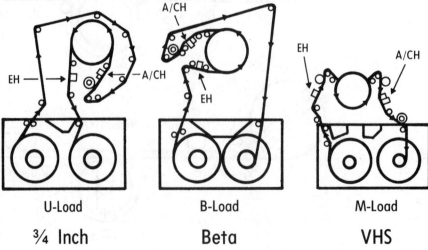

U-Load            B-Load            M-Load

¾ Inch             Beta               VHS

## TAPE WIDTHS AND COMPATIBILITY

Some machines use the same width tape—2-inch, ¾-inch, and ½-inch—but they record and play back the signal differently. The electromechanical design also varies from one machine to another, depending on the application: Broadcasters, for example, use 2-inch and 1-inch VTRs of all brands and types extensively. Sometimes ¾-inch and ½-inch machines are used for broadcast news and limited commercial production, but they are primarily used in nonbroadcast situations. In recent years, however, newer 1-inch and ¾-inch systems have been upgraded to meet stringent standards of quality and reflect state-of-the-art technology.

Compatibility refers to the ability to play a videotape on one machine that was recorded on a different machine. For example, a 2-inch tape, recorded on a quad machine, will not play back on a 2-inch helical machine. The two formats are incompatible. That same tape, however, will play on any other quad machine, because the manufacturers of the two quad devices have agreed to follow certain specifications with regard to tape, to head-drum speed and size, and to the physical position of audio and other heads. Technical standards of the reproduced signal also follow guidelines set by NTSC, IEEE, and SMPTE (Standards for Motion Picture and Television Engineering).

The same sort of limited compatibility applies to all of the other formats as well:

1. One-inch machines are presently available in many different formats, while many more outdated formats are still in use.
2. Half-inch VTRs also come in different formats. The EIAJ, Beta, VHS, and other formats are not compatible, but tapes recorded on a machine of a given format can generally be played back on a machine of that same format regardless of its brand name. We say "generally" because, to further complicate the issue, Beta and VHS can record at different speeds to allow for different lengths of record/playback time. For example, a 4- or 6-hour recording made on one VHS machine can be played back, but it will probably not interface well on another VHS machine because of stability problems. The independent producer must know which tape format is used to fit a particular application and whether it will be compatible with the format of the end-user.
3. Three-quarter-inch machines are unique, because of the wide acceptance of the U-matic videocassette format. Although world standards differ—PAL, SECAM, NTSC—some manufacturers have designed ¾-inch machines to play on all three world standards and to operate on different voltages.

## DIGITAL APPLICATIONS

"Digital video" is a relatively new catch phrase in the industry. Although many new VTRs and cameras incorporate digital electronics for mechanical control functions such as tape shuttle, editing, and camera set-up, this type of control does not have anything to do with the way the video signal is recorded or retrieved. All the VTRs mentioned so far employ an *analog approach,* that is, they record and play back continuous streams of amplitude changes to produce variations of brightness (and color) on a monitor or a TV screen. Their color signal is interleaved with the luminance in accord with NTSC specifications.

An analog signal can be converted into a stream of numbers or discrete bits of information. This "digital" numbering system changes much like the fluctuating analog system. An analog-to-digital converter changes the incoming "analog" information to either high or low numbers, corresponding to the fluctuation of the incoming signal. Digital time-base correctors and frame-storage devices—examples of analog-to-digital converters—will be discussed further in Chapter 6, "Editing" (Figure 1-22).

The advantage of a digital video system lies in the tie-in between it and computers, which "speak" digital languages and which can lend expanded versatility and creativity to video technology. A digital VTR and camera system would also offer a higher degree of quality and storage density then current analog systems. Consequently, numerous manufacturers are pouring much research and development into this area. Yet broadcasters world-wide have not committed

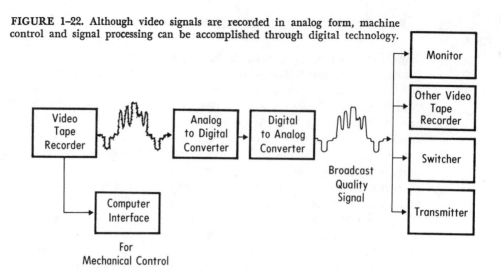

FIGURE 1–22. Although video signals are recorded in analog form, machine control and signal processing can be accomplished through digital technology.

themselves to any particular design. Until a practical system is designed with a common world standard, format, and compatibility, broadcasters are not prepared to invest in any one design. Nevertheless, the mid- to late 1980s should see total digital systems in use.

**VIDEO DISCS**

Video discs do not record on tape, but on a magnetic disc. Used by broadcasters to record and to play back slow-motion sequences in sports coverage, most discs used in such applications can handle only a short (20- to 40-second) amount of information. They can, however, record single frames of video and short segments to be used for instant replay at any speed from slow motion to high speed, as well as in reverse.

Playback-only video discs are currently available for home use. Large amounts of money have been spent in developing different systems, and even more for marketing. Two major systems exist:

1. The first uses a light beam that reflects or passes through a disc.
2. The second uses a needle-type pick-up device, much like an audio turntable stylus.

The advantage of the video disc lies in its capability to store a great deal of information in a relatively compact space. Making copies costs less than videotape, especially in large volume. Their low weight and smaller size allow discs to be shipped and stored at a fairly low cost. Although home users are not able to record on their video disc machines, the projected lower cost of available software will determine the success of either type.

**MARKET APPLICATIONS**

VTR and disc technology are in competition for all markets, but especially for the consumer dollar. Since the market is potentially so large, constant improvements in technology continue to offer the consumer more and more advantages. The ½-inch VHS, Beta, and other machines—outgrowths of the ¾-inch format—allow home-users more control over what they view. Tuners, timers, and pre-recorded materials increase program sources and options. The addition of a camera enables consumers to produce their own "home tapes." Thus portable VTRs and cameras offer a flexible and low cost means of "getting into video." Video can offer a convenient method of preserving and viewing home movies and slides, not to mention a creative outlet.

Professional video production techniques, when applied to consumers' situations, can open up the world of video to them even more. More and more nonbroadcast applications offer an expanded market for production of all types. Whether you're involved with making "home tapes" to entertain family and friends, or responsible for training new employees in a large corporation, the message always overrides the method. It is the creativity of the individual that puts the technology to use.

24

**THE EDITING PROCESS**

The single-camera system user depends heavily on the editing process. Since electronic video signals are encoded on videotape, editing is done electronically rather than by physically cutting the tape.

When shooting single-camera style, however, much of the editing is based on the producer's ability to plan the shots in advance and to edit them into a planned order. Planning, which includes both technical and nontechnical considerations, offers creative coverage of an event. Footage obtained at several different shooting sessions can be edited into a finished production. Using this general approach, it is important to pre-plan to save on editing time. (As we will see in Chapter 5, "Shooting," the more you plan, the more efficient you can be.)

To edit videotape, you play back your original footage on one machine, while a second machine records selected segments from this original material. The creative editor can thus build a logical sequence of audible and visual events. Either the original sequence can be pre-planned so that raw footage can be cut down in length, or it can be rearranged to tell a story. Pre-planning and organization become critical, since changes and missed shots can be costly to reshoot.

## EDITING SYSTEMS

The machines involved in the editing process can be costly additions to the basic single camera/VTR system. Here is what such a system can involve:

1. The simplest editing set-up requires two VTRs, one to play back and one to record. The player is usually called the *slave* and the editor/recorder is called the *master*. Mastering machines vary in their sophistication.

2. Basic edit controllers are often added to make editing a very quick and easy task. The more sophisticated edit controllers add capability and functions, which require additional slave machines and other sources of video.

3. Other peripheral gear must be used with even the simplest editing systems. At least one monitor is needed to view the playback of the original material, as well as the edited version. Audio mixers, audio tape decks, video signal processors, switchers, and other sources of video can be interfaced offering maximum flexibility to the editor.

The most popular editing systems utilize ¾-inch videocassette format machines and an edit controller (Figure 1-23). These systems can be purchased from a number of manufacturers. They offer good-quality, low-band color video, a good deal of creative and operational flexibility, and low cost. The latest developments in Beta and VHS editing machines have also brought low-cost, non-broadcast video production within reach of an even greater number of consumers. Such access to video is within the reach of the average person and offers a means of expression and communication.

FIGURE 1–23. ¾-inch editors with controller. (Photo courtesy KPHO TV5, Phoenix)

**SUMMARY**

The production techniques discussed in this book can help single camera/VTR users realize the full potential of their systems, regardless of their personal levels of sophistication. These techniques will demonstrate that a well-planned and edited videotape can be a tremendously powerful way to communicate a message.

To know how the camera, VTR, and other pieces work together, however, you have to start with a basic knowledge of how everything is "hooked up." So our next chapter is about the INs and OUTs of video hookups.

# 2
2
2
2
2
2

**THE INS AND OUTS
OF VIDEO HOOKUPS**

At your first encounter with the array of cables, connectors, and adaptors used in video production, you may be confused and somewhat intimidated—especially if you have little or no experience in the audio-visual field. Even those who have some experience mistakenly believe that making a small error in interconnecting equipment will necessarily damage it. This belief prevents many individuals from even trying to set it up or from experimenting with it. The truth is that most equipment manufacturers have designed their equipment components so that making mistakes when interconnecting them is nearly impossible. This is not to say that mistakes never occur, but you almost have to try to do it wrong. Usually the worst thing that happens is that the equipment doesn't perform as expected.

**CABLES,**
**CONNECTORS,**
**AND ADAPTERS**

## POWER CABLES

Let's begin with the easiest cable to identify—the power cable (Figure 2-1). Power cables used in video should always have three prongs. The third prong, which is rounded and slightly longer than the other two, provides a ground for the equipment. Older electric systems may have only two-prong outlets. If the wall outlet is of this type, you should use a three-to-two-lead adaptor with a ground wire or ground lug, to adapt the power plug to the wall outlet (Figure 2-2). When the adaptor is plugged in, the ground wire or lug should be slipped under the screw on the wall outlet and tightened down. If the wall outlet is grounded, this connection protects the equipment and the operator from electric shock, and it also eliminates interference in the video image during recording and playback.

FIGURE 2-1. Typical VTR/VCR power cable.

FIGURE 2-2. Three-lead to two-lead power cable adaptor. Lug or ground wire should be grounded.

Many times the wall outlet is not grounded. The only way to find out whether it is grounded is to take off the outlet cover and find out if a ground wire is connected to the box. Many people fail to do so because it sometimes takes time to find a suitable ground in the event that the box isn't grounded. Some people even cut or break off the ground prong on the power cable to avoid having to use adaptors. Both of these practices are potentially dangerous and are categorically discouraged. It's a good idea to carry several adaptors with about twenty feet of No. 12 wire attached to the ground wire or lug. The wire can be stripped on one end so that it can be clamped to a water pipe, entry box ground, or some other suitable ground. Grounding takes only a minute, and it really should be done for the protection of the operator and of the equipment, as well as, in some cases, for quality of the recording.

## AUDIO CABLES

The next most easily identified cables are the audio cables. The audio cables used in video production are the same as those used

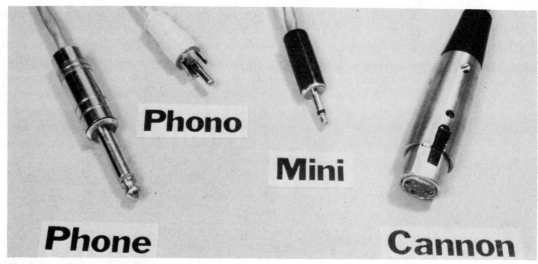

**Phono**

**Mini**

**Phone**

**Cannon**

FIGURE 2–3. Frequently used audio plugs.

in audio production. So the audio buff or the person experienced in audiovisual work will probably have very little problem getting used to recording the audio portion of a video production.

The audio plugs most frequently used in video are:
1. the Standard Phone plug,
2. the RCA or Phono plug,
3. the XLR or Cannon plug; and
4. the mini plug (Figure 2-3).

These audio plugs fit into "jacks" of the same size on the VTR, monitor/receiver, mixer, or other audio equipment used with the video system. Frequently, several different types of plug are used at the same time. For example, a microphone may be attached to an audio mixer with a Cannon or XLR plug (Figure 2-4), and then an audio cable with a Cannon or XLR plug on one end and a mini plug on the other may be used to connect the mixer to the videotape recorder (Figure 2-5). We should also mention that recent ½-inch cassette equipment, typified by the VHS format, uses the RCA (Phono) plug to carry the video signal as well as the audio signal. So it's not safe to make the blanket assumption that the plugs mentioned are used only for audio applications.

However they are used, when these plugs are attached to one another, in any combination, the resulting cable is called a *patch cord*. Very often you'll run into situations calling for a different combination of plugs from that on the available patch cord. For example, you may have a patch cord with a Phono (RCA) on one end and a Mini on the other, and you really need a Standard Phone plug in place of the Mini.

FIGURE 2–4. Cannon or XLR plug from mike to mixer.

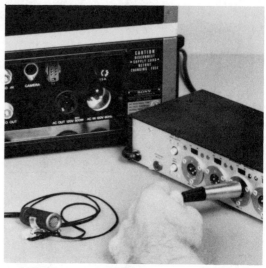

FIGURE 2–5. Mini plug from mixer into VTR.

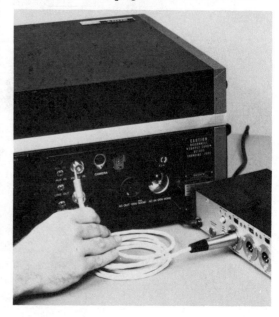

## Audio Adaptors

By reason of the patch cord problem, various adaptors are available, which, when connected to the plug you have, change it to the one you want (Figure 2-6). Using more than just a few adaptors is not recommended since every adaptor adds to the potential for problems due to loose or dirty connections. Using a great number of adaptors increases the risk of low-quality or intermittent recordings.

## Special Patch Cords

Once in a while no patch cord or adaptor combination gives you what you need. So you either have to make a custom patch cord yourself, or have it made. If you do either, always use shielded cable to avoid interference from AC line humming or RF interference. (Figure 2-7).

There are plugs for sale with solder connections on them for just this purpose. These adaptors and plugs with solder connections are available at electronic supply outlets such as Radio Shack. Comprehensive Video Supply Corporation (see Source Index) also carries a very broad assortment of adaptors, connectors, and patch cords.

In addition, a special patch cord, like the "Y" cord (Figure 2-8), is handy for going

FIGURE 2–6. Audio adaptors.

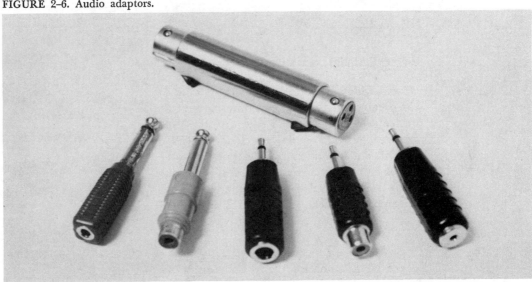

FIGURE 2–7. Do-it-yourself adaptors. Use shielded cable to avoid noise and hum in your audio.

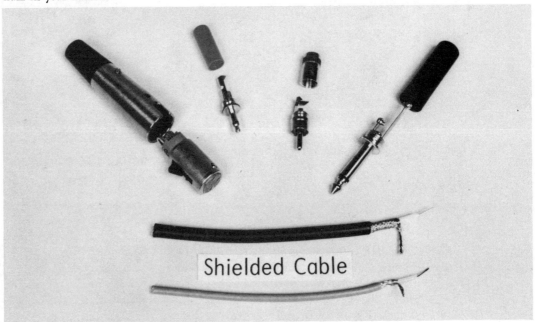

from one output to two inputs. It also can be used for going from a television monitor/receiver to the inputs on a stereo amplifier and through the speakers. This arrangement provides much more sound "presence" than the sound coming from the little speaker in the monitor/receiver.

FIGURE 2–8. Y cord for going from output to two inputs.

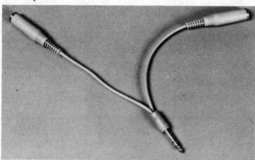

## VIDEO CABLES

Novice video producers usually find the video cables to be the most unusual of all the cables used in video production. Like audio cables, video cables, which are typically coaxial, are identified by the types of connector or plug attached to the end of them. Also, like audio plugs, video plugs fit into corresponding jacks on the VTR monitor/receiver or camera. The common video plugs are:

1. the UHF connector,
2. the BNC connector, and
3. the F connector (Figure 2-9a).

FIGURE 2–9a. UHF, BNC, and F connectors are always connected by coaxial cable.

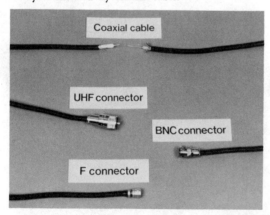

The UHF connector is pushed onto its jack (Figure 2-9b), and then the sleeve around it is turned clockwise until it is tight (Figure 2-9c). The BNC connector is pushed onto its jack (Figure 2-9d), and then turned clock-

wise about one-half turn (Figure 2-9e). The F connector's center conductor is lined up with the hole in its jack (Figure 2-9f), and then its sleeve is tightened clockwise (Figure 2-9g).

FIGURE 2–9b. Connecting UHF connector to its jack.

FIGURE 2–9c.

FIGURE 2–9d. Connecting BNC connector to its jack.

FIGURE 2–9e.

FIGURE 2–9f. Connecting F connector to its jack.

FIGURE 2–9g.

Video connectors and jacks are prone to certain problems. The UHF connector's sleeve is often very difficult to turn onto its jack, sometimes simply as the result of misuse. Somebody may have dropped the connector, stepped on it, or rolled something heavy over it. Any such treatment knocks it out of round and makes it difficult to push it onto its jack. But sometimes the sleeve or jack are cross-threaded and simply will not tighten up. In an emergency, the connector can be pushed into the jack and taped in place with electrical tape.

The BNC connector is fairly reliable. Its jack is, however, sometimes damaged because it protrudes out away from where it is anchored, and it isn't as structurally sound as the UHF or F jacks.

The F connector is relatively fragile—certainly more delicate than either of the other connectors. The small wire protruding from its center is subject to bending and breaking (Figure 2-10).

**Video Adaptors**

A number of video adaptors are used to interconnect equipment components when the available jacks and plugs are incompatible (Figure 2-11). For example, the L-shaped UHF adaptor in Figure 2-11 is used when space behind a piece of equipment is cramped or when the cable has to make a right-angle turn. With a UHF "T" adaptor, you can send the video signal to two locations simultaneously (Figure 2-12). Or, with one type of adaptor called a *barrel*, which has identical receptacles on both ends, you can extend the length of the video cable (Figure 2-13). UHF, BNC, and F barrels are available.

Also available is a wide variety of other adaptor combinations, consisting of mixed video adaptors and hybrid video and audio adaptors. For example, a mixed video adap-

FIGURE 2–10. Small delicate wire in center of plug is F connector conductor. It can be bent and sometimes broken quite easily.

FIGURE 2–11. Video adaptors.

FIGURE 2–12. UHF T adaptor.

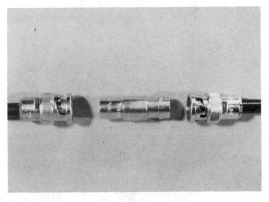

FIGURE 2–13. BNC barrel adaptor.

tor would be an adaptor with a UHF plug on one side and a BNC plug on the other. An example of a very handy hybrid video and audio adaptor is one with a UHF plug on one side and an RCA (phono) plug on the other.

31

If you need to customize your cables or junction boxes, you can purchase video plugs, cable, and jacks from video supply houses. Solderless crimp connector kits are also available for those who do not like to solder. All these materials are available from Comprehensive Video Supply Corporation and other local vendors.

## MULTI-PIN CABLES

In many cases, the power, the audio signal, and the video signal are all conducted through separate leads inside one multi-pin cable (Figure 2-14). The shape of the connector, the number of leads in the cable,

FIGURE 2–14. A multi-pin camera cable that carries audio (intercom), video, and power.

and what each carries (audio, video, power, or some combination thereof) vary among multi-pin cables (Figure 2-15). For instance, the 8-pin cable in the center in Figure 2-15 conducts audio and video signals to and from

FIGURE 2–15. Typical multi-pin cables.

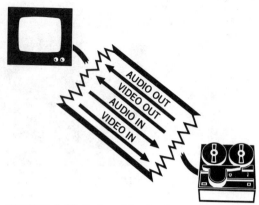

FIGURE 2–16. 8-pin cable circuit.

the VTR and its monitor/receiver. In other words, audio and video signals can be sent both ways through this single cable (Figure 2-16). Most multi-pin cables have special applications such as connecting a portable camera to a portable VTR. Sometimes the plugs on either end of the cable look different, and they may even have a different number of pins, but they perform the same function in the hookup. (See the cable on the right in Figure 2-15.)

### Multi-Pin Adaptors

Standard adaptors are available for multi-pin cables, such as the 8-pin barrel used to extend the length of 8-pin cables, but custom multi-pin cables have to be made to order. Individuals with greater-than-usual electronic talent can buy multi-lead cable and connectors to custom-build their own. Again, local electronic parts suppliers and Comprehensive Video Supply Corporation are about the only places to get the parts.

### Problems

The two problems with multi-pin cables are that (1) they are great dirt catchers and (2) if just one pin gets bent, trying to connect them to their jack becomes an exercise in patience. If you have to force a multi-pin connector on its jack, the chances are very good that something is wrong. Either the connector is bent out of shape, one or more pins are bent or broken, or the sleeve, if there is one, is cross-threaded. If so and if there is no immediate way to repair or replace the cable, you may be able to patch the power, audio, and video some other way using separate leads and operating the deck by hand.

Which brings us to our next subject: interconnecting a single-camera system.

To operate correctly, as well as to record and play back a picture and sound, all single-camera systems must be fed:

1. power to run the motors that spin the video heads, move the tape, display the image, and play the sound,
2. a video signal to be recorded and displayed, and
3. an audio signal, if sound is desired, for recording and playback.

While both portable and studio equipment have these requirements, portable single-camera systems are generally interconnected in a somewhat different way from studio equipment. The reason is that studio systems are generally designed to interface with more components than portable systems, and portable systems are designed to be used by a smaller crew than studio systems. Many newer portable systems can be interfaced with studio systems with the addition of optional equipment like a larger studio viewfinder, an AC adaptor, and special controls to regulate zoom and focus from a standing position behind the camera. Even though there are differences in the ways both types of single-camera systems are interconnected, there are also similarities.

### THE POWER HOOKUP

All single-camera systems, whether portable or studio type, must have a source of power. In portable single-camera systems, the power is supplied by batteries, some of which are small enough to fit into a battery compartment in the VTR or on a camera (Figure 2-17). Since powering the deck and camera quickly exhausts most such batteries, however, the industry designed battery belts to run the camera which have a longer running life and which can be recharged by plugging them into an AC outlet for a few hours. The batteries designed to fit into the VTR can be recharged by plugging them into the AC converter that comes with the VTR and that is also used to run the deck when AC power is available. The same is true of the batteries that come with the camera. They can be recharged by plugging them into the camera's AC converter.

But VTR and camera batteries fail to offer a long enough running time, so many people

**33** have resorted to using 12-volt car batteries

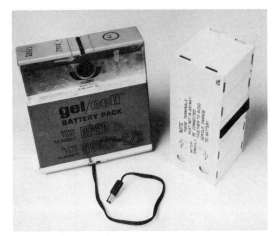

FIGURE 2-17. Typical VTR/VCR batteries.

to power the VTR and the camera. Since car batteries are relatively inexpensive compared to VTR batteries, camera batteries, or battery belts, and since they can power a single-camera system for several days between charges, they have become very popular. Since the disadvantage to car batteries is their weight, almost everyone using car batteries has designed a cart to carry the complete single-camera system including the battery, the VTR, the camera and VTR, AC converter, a color monitor, microphones, extra cables and, in the case of older cameras, the camera control unit. These carts are designed to fit through standard doorways and to lie down in a trunk or on the back seat of a large car.

While the batteries that fit into the deck have either a wire connection or contacts to fit snugly against the VTR contacts (Figure 2-17), a car battery requires a special hookup (Figure 2-18). In this case the power from the car battery is sent through a custom-made Y cord to both the VTR and the monitor. Since car batteries used with video equipment are moved around a great deal, it's really important that they be the maintenance-free type. So-called "maintenance-free" batteries have a plastic strip covering the cap on each cell so that they are less likely to leak. They will leak, however, if turned over or jostled a great deal. Spilled battery acid is extremely corrosive, and it will damage anything it touches. So keep them upright at all times. Unfortunately, sealed maintenance-free batteries are not meant to be discharged and recharged over and over again, especially if fully discharged in each cycle. So don't run these batteries down "flat" before recharging them.

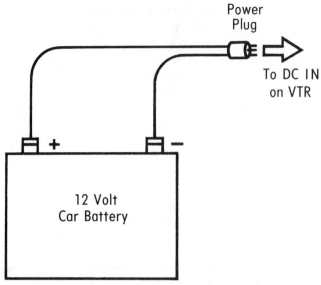

**FIGURE 2–18.** Hookup to 12-volt car battery. Make sure that polarity is correct at the plug or you may damage your video equipment.

## THE BASIC SIGNAL PATH

No matter what the source of power, everyone should remember a couple of basics about interconnecting a portable single-camera system for recording.

First make sure that all power switches are turned off before beginning to hook components together. This prevents arcing and sudden voltage surges, which can damage the equipment. The same rule applies when disconnecting the equipment for transportation or storage—turn it off first.

Next, remember the basic underlying principle of how a video system works (Figure 2-19). After entering the camera through the lens, reflected light is focused on the faceplate of the pick-up tube. Once it is processed and amplified by the camera's front end

electronics and CCU (camera control unit), which may be part of the camera or a separate unit, it is finally sent to the videotape recorder (VTR). At the same time, the audio signal enters a microphone—which may be permanently mounted on the camera, designed to be removed from the camera, or plugged directly into the VTR or first into a mixer which itself is plugged into the VTR. If the microphone is permanently mounted on the camera, the audio signal reaches the deck through the same multi-pin cable that carries the video signal, but on a different circuit in that cable. If the microphone is detachable but still plugs into the camera, the same is true. If the mike is plugged into the VTR, either directly or through a mixer, the signal path is different. It travels from the mike, down its cable, and then

**FIGURE 2–19.** Basic signal path. Audio and video signals may be sent to the VTR along different conductors within the same multi-pin cable.

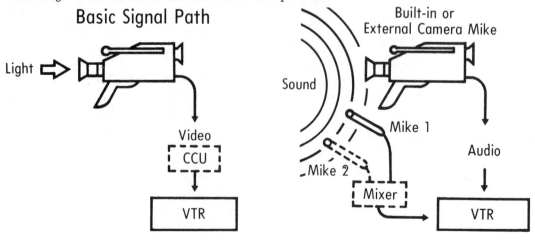

either directly into the VTR or through a mixer into the VTR for recording on the videotape. Keeping the basic path from camera to VTR in mind makes it a lot easier to figure out how any single-camera system has to be hooked together for recording.

## RECORDING

Here is a primary recording principle: On a piece of video equipment, any jacks marked "IN" are used to feed a signal "IN" to it; any jacks marked "OUT" are used to feed a signal "OUT" of it. Some of the common INs and OUTs are listed in Figure 2-20.

Sometimes the words "IN" or "OUT" are not used on a jack. For example, a multi-pin jack on a deck or CCU may say just "Camera." But, since almost all inexpensive and medium-priced cameras for portable use have a camera cable attached to them permanently with only one plug on the other end, it seems fairly evident that this plug should be connected to the "Camera" jack on the deck. Why wouldn't the jack be labeled "Camera OUT" or "Camera IN"? The reason is that during recording the video signal automatically travels from the camera into the VTR and during playback it travels from the VTR into the camera to the camera's vewfinder. So manufacturers consider it safer and more accurate to label the jack just "Camera."

If the camera you are using has a built-in control unit, and if you have connected the camera cable to the VTR, the system is ready to be operated. If your camera has a separate CCU, like the Sony 1600, you must connect the camera to the CCU and the CCU to the VTR.

FIGURE 2–20. Common INs and OUTs.

| INS | OUTS |
| --- | --- |
| Video In | Video Out |
| Audio In | Audio Out |
| AC In | AC Out |
| Line In | Line Out |
| etc. | etc. |

## PLAYBACK

Once you've recorded what you want, you may wish to play it back right away to make sure everything worked correctly and to check picture stability. Checking the playback is especially important in the field to make sure that you don't have to return to a location because something malfunctioned. Usually playback in the field is done by rewinding the tape and playing it back through the camera's viewfinder. In this case all hookups are the same as in recording. The only difference is that a switch somewhere on the VTR, camera, or camera control unit is thrown to reroute the signal from the VTR to the camera's viewfinder.

The only drawback with this set-up is that the image played back is in black and white, because camera viewfinders do not have color picture tubes. This limitation is acceptable if you're using a black-and-white recording system, but a black-and-white image doesn't tell you much about a color image. For instance, you may not be recording color at all. That could be disastrous. So if you're lucky, you will have a small battery-operated portable color monitor. In this case, you can hook the video and audio OUTs or their equivalents onto your VTR to video-and-audio IN on the monitor. If you are confident that the audio portion of the recording is okay, or if you don't need the audio, you can just hook up the video. This procedure tells you whether the image is stable and whether color is being recorded. If your color monitor has been set for the proper color balance, and not readjusted since then, it also tells you whether your camera is properly color-balanced. To better judge the color balance of the signal, it's handy to have a five-minute cassette with color bars to set up the monitor for comparison to the camera output. If your camera can generate a color bar pattern, you can set up your color monitor by adjusting the monitor's controls with the camera switched to "bars."

At a location with a source of AC power, playback is done for the same reasons as in the field. The only difference in hookup is that, instead of running the VTR off the battery, you can use the VTR's AC converter, which "converts" the outlet voltage (about 110 volts AC) to the DC voltage of the battery source (usually about 12 volts). The converter is plugged into a wall outlet and

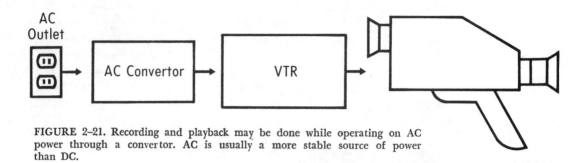

AC Outlet → AC Convertor → VTR →

FIGURE 2-21. Recording and playback may be done while operating on AC power through a convertor. AC is usually a more stable source of power than DC.

then connected to the video deck; the hookups from the deck to the monitor remain the same. When AC is available, the monitor can be plugged into an AC outlet to save its battery. It needs no converter. Whenever possible, run off AC since it is usually a more stable source of power than DC (Figure 2-21). Just remember to interconnect everything before turning on any power.

## SEMIPORTABLE
## SINGLE-CAMERA SYSTEMS

The portable camera, which is primarily designed to be used where AC power is not available, can frequently be used with other types of studio equipment when hooked to a camera adaptor (Figure 2-22). Usually, however, when the single-camera system is used

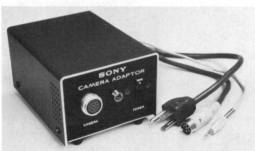

FIGURE 2-22. A camera adaptor enables you to operate some cameras on AC power that are normally operated on DC battery power.

in a studio or on a location with AC power, it is semiportable, that is, it is rolled from location to location on dollies and carts (Figure 2-23). The semiportable single-camera system—camera, VTR, and monitor/receiver—must be hooked to an AC power supply. Because they are only semiportable and depend on an AC power source, these systems tend to be used in controlled situations more than portable systems.

Usually, the video and audio are fed to the VTR separately, and a monitor/receiver

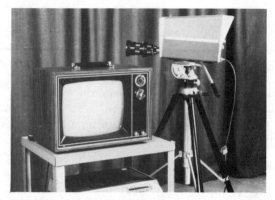

FIGURE 2-23. Semiportable single-camera system.

is connected to the VTR with an 8-pin plug for monitoring the recording or playback. If, as is frequently the case, a television receiver is used, instead of a monitor or combination monitor/receiver, the receiver is fed both audio and video from the RF (radio frequency) OUT jack on the VTR (Figure 2-24).

FIGURE 2-24. An RF OUT jack. An RF (radio frequency) unit produces a composite audio and video signal, which, when sent to the VHF terminals of a home TV receiver, makes it possible to see the video image and hear the accompanying audio. The advantage to using RF is that a more expensive monitor/receiver is not needed to display the video image and hear the sound.

The cable used to connect the RF jack to the TV receiver is unusual. It has a plug on one end that fits into the RF jack. Connected to it somewhere, usually on the other end, is a small cylindrical or square object called an *impedance-matching transformer,* which makes the signal coming out of the VTR compatible with the television receiver. This transformer has either Y-shaped clips (that connect to the VHF and UHF terminals on the receiver like an antenna lead), an F connector, or sometimes both (Figure 2-25).

FIGURE 2–25. Impedance-matching transformer.

If neither an 8-pin cable nor an RF cable is used, or if neither is available, and if a monitor/receiver is available, hook separate cables for audio and video between the VTR and the monitor/receiver. Two separate video cables are needed to conduct video signals both to and from the VTR if you intend to record off the air and play back without repatching the calls. You need the same for the audio hookup—two cables to conduct audio signals both to and from the VTR (Figure 2-26). Recording and playback of recordings made with the camera can be done with only one set of cables, but if, for some reason you wish to record off the air from the monitor/receiver to the

FIGURE 2–26. Audio and video IN and OUT of monitor/receiver.

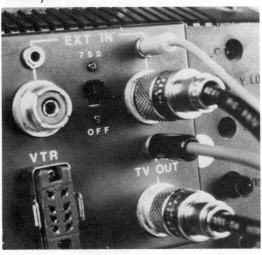

VTR), you have to repatch the cables. When using the camera, the video and audio are fed OUT of the camera or VTR to the IN jacks of the monitor/receiver. When recording off the air, the video and auditor come OUT of the monitor/receiver to the IN jacks of the VTR.

Semiportable systems are also frequently accompanied by more complex audio systems than in portable systems. The reason is that, although portable battery-operated mixers are available for field use with portable video systems, they are not frequently seen in actual use. Yet less expensive mixers, which run off AC power, are often seen used with semiportable systems. The audio hookup is fairly simple. The microphones are plugged into the mixer, and the mixer is in turn plugged into the VTR usually from AUX OUT (high-level output) to Line IN on the VTR. (Figure 2-27). In this way individual microphone volumes can be controlled, as well as the mixer's total output to the VTR.

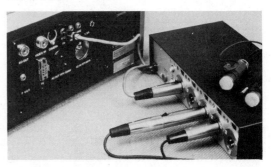

FIGURE 2–27. A semiportable, single-camera system audio mixer hookup.

Note that the microphones in Figure 2-27 are connected to the mixer with a Cannon (XLR) plug and to the VTR with a mini plug. Mini or RCA (Phono) plugs are used for getting audio into many VTRs. In audio terminology, this hookup is called an *unbalanced line,* because it is prone to picking up electrical and RF disturbance. Here's why it's called "unbalanced." The Cannon or XLR plug contains three leads, as opposed to the two found in the other types of plug. One of these three leads is connected to a wire shield which surrounds the other two. When any electrical or RF disturbance enters the shield, it is immediately conducted to ground or "attenuated" before it can build up a disturbance in the leads carrying the signal being recorded. The mini or Phono plugs do not shield against such disturbance. Unfortunately Cannon or XLR plugs are not installed on inexpensive VTRs, despite the fact that, to work at all, the line must be balanced all the way through to the VTR. (For more on balanced and unbalanced lines, see Chapter 3, "Audio for Television.")

### HYBRID SYSTEMS

Hybrid systems take on importance in relation to interconnecting single-camera systems. Many people think that a certain manufacturer's camera must be used only with that manufacturer's VTR or playback system—in other words, that single-camera systems are "manufacturer-specific." With some exceptions, however, this assumption is simply not correct. For instance, a Panasonic 3200 camera, manufactured principally for the ½-inch home consumer market, can be hooked directly into a more expensive ¾-inch JVC 4400 VTR, which is designed for the industrial and broadcast market. The advantage of this particular combination is that the camera has very good low-light sensitivity. Using this camera to record directly onto ¾-inch tape not only saves a generation in the transfer from ½-inch tape to the final tape, but also allows the editing to be done on ¾-inch equipment, which is more accurate than ½-inch equipment. Conversely, very expensive, broadcast-quality cameras can be used with ¾-inch and ½-inch decks with excellent results. Usually this footage is transferred to broadcast format 1-inch or 2-inch tape for editing and transmission.

### Compatibility Problems

Sometimes equipment in compatibility may pose a problem. For instance, a Sony 1600 camera and its CCU can be hooked to a JVC 4400 deck, but you have to modify the deck so that it can be triggered by the camera. You also have to match the 1600's microphone output impedance with the 4400's audio input impedance. When you are in doubt as to whether certain pieces of equipment will work together, the best idea is to try them out. A little experimentation now saves a lot of headaches later. Just remember that, although pieces of equipment used together may vary, the basic signal path remains the same, and so do the basic interconnections.

## PLAYING BACK VIDEO TO A LARGE GROUP

No matter what type of single-camera system is used to record a production, sooner or later it has to be played back to a large group. When such is the case, the playback method depends on the number of people in the group and on the amount and type of equipment available. As a general rule, one 21-inch monitor can easily handle an audience of 50 to 75 people depending on how the seats are arranged. Larger groups require a greater number of monitors or a larger viewing screen, such as a video projector.

### THE LOOP-THROUGH METHOD

When several monitor/receivers are available with jacks for audio and video IN and OUT, the audio and video signals from the VTR can be "looped through" one monitor/receiver to the second. To do so, connect the audio and video OUT from the VTR to the audio and video IN of the first monitor/receiver. Then connect the audio and video OUT jacks of the first monitor/receiver to the audio and video IN jacks of the second monitor/receiver (Figure 2-28). If the monitor/receiver available has only audio and video INs, use an audio Y adaptor and a video T adaptor to feed the signals to another monitor/receiver (Figure 2-29).

FIGURE 2–28. Loop-through method of hooking several monitor/receivers to one VTR for playback to large groups or at several different locations.

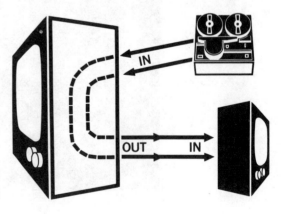

FIGURE 2–29. Hooking up several monitor/receivers that have only audio and video INs can be done by using an audio Y adaptor and a video T adaptor.

## Termination

When several monitor/receivers are hooked together like this, the video on the last monitor/receiver in the line must be terminated so that there is no signal loss to any of the other monitor/receivers. Look for a switch on the back of the end monitor/receiver labeled "75-ohm and Off" (Figure 2-30), and move it to the "75 ohm" position. It might also read "Hi Z and Term," in which case switch it to "Term." If any other monitor/receiver in line has this switch, be sure that it is in the "Off" or "Hi Z" position. If none of the monitor/receivers has a built-in video termination switch, use a video connector of the appropriate type, with a 75-ohm resistor soldered across it, as shown in Figure 2-31. Commercial terminators can also be used (Figure 2-32). Remember that only the last monitor/receiver in line should be terminated. Terminating any other results in signal loss to the remaining units in line (Figure 2-33). Audio can be looped through also, but it does not require termination due

FIGURE 2–30. Video termination switch.

FIGURE 2–31. Home-made video terminator.

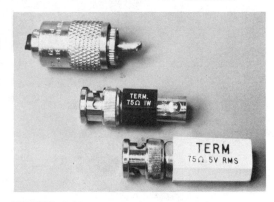

FIGURE 2–32. Commercially produced video terminators.

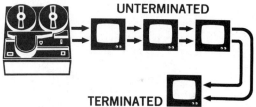

FIGURE 2–33. Terminate the video of the last monitor/receiver in line.

to the impedance characteristics of the audio signal.

Just how many monitor/receivers will work together in the loop-through method at any one time? Since so many factors are involved, it is really difficult so say, but, given that the equipment is in good shape, four is the recommended maximum. With four units, some signal loss begins to appear. Extensive signal loss results in a degraded image and, to some extent, in picture break-up.

## DISTRIBUTION AMPLIFIERS

To avoid the signal loss resulting from sending the signal through one monitor/receiver to another, a device called a *distribution amplifier* (DA) may be used (Figure 2-34). The video signal coming from the video player is sent to the DA, amplified, and then conducted directly to a monitor/receiver (Figure 2-35). In this way, the signal to each monitor/receiver is stronger than it would be in the loop-through method. If one video distribution amplifier is not enough, several of them may be hooked together to feed more monitor/receivers. This technique is called *stacking* or *cascading* (Figure 2-36).

FIGURE 2–34. Typical video distribution amplifier.

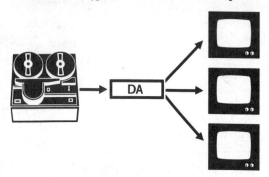

FIGURE 2–35. Video distribution amplifier to monitor/receiver hookup to send the video image to many locations simultaneously.

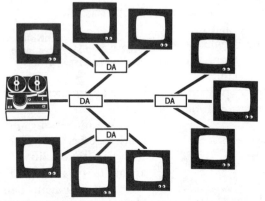

FIGURE 2–36. Stacking video distribution amplifiers for sending the video image to a great number of monitor/receivers.

Since distribution amplifiers handle only the video signal, the audio signal must be conducted to each monitor/receiver using the loop-through method or dealt with separately. To do so, you have to connect the audio or line OUT of the VTR to an audio amplifier, and then connect the amplifier to a number of speakers (Figure 2-37). The location of the speakers in relationship to the video image is important. Whenever feasible, the video image and the amplified sound should be as close as possible to one another —unless some special effect is desired. Normally, it's really distracting to hear sound from one direction and see the image somewhere else.

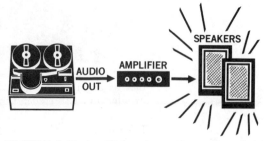

FIGURE 2–37. Amplifying the audio portion of the video presentation for playback to a large group.

## RF SPLITTER

RF OUT can be used as a combined source of video and audio, thus carrying both the audio and video signals on only one system and using TV receivers instead of the more expensive monitor/receivers. To feed more than one TV, however, you have to "split" the RF cable with a device called, appropriately enough, an *RF splitter*. Common RF splitters can be used to supply the combined video and audio signal to as many as three TV sets (Figure 2-38). Any splitter outlet not used should be terminated with a home-made or commercial 75-ohm terminator. Also available are other types of RF amplifiers that function similarly to video DAs in that they amplify the RF signal and feed it to individual receivers. The advantage, once

FIGURE 2–38. RF (radio frequency) splitter.

FIGURE 2–39. The RF signal is affected by many types of interference.

again, is that only one system is needed; the audio does not have to be handled separately. When using RF, all receivers must be provided with an impedance-matching transformer.

Using RF should be avoided in high-interference situations such as near TV or FM radio stations, or around electrical equipment or traffic. The RF signal is much more vulnerable to such interference than the video and audio OUT (Figure 2-39). This is especially true in places like New York City, where high buildings with steel frames act like antennas, and electronic emanations are too numerous to mention.

## VIDEO AND RF

Another handy way to feed several images simultaneously is to use both a monitor and a conventional TV set at the same time. The monitor is supplied audio and video signals from the deck's audio and video OUTS, while the TV set gets its signal simultaneously from the RF OUT section of the deck. When only one monitor/receiver and one TV set is available, this set-up makes it possible to feed two images without looping and without a lot of extra patch cords and equipment (Figure 2-40).

FIGURE 2–40. A VTR with an RF unit can send audio and video to a monitor/receiver and to a TV set simultaneously.

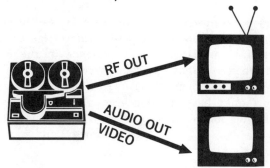

## VIDEO PROJECTION

When a video projection system is available, interconnection problems are minimized. The VTR is simply hooked to the projection console in the same manner as hooking it to a monitor/receiver. The outgoing audio and video signals from the VTR are hooked to the video and audio IN jacks on the video projector's console. The video image is then seen on the projection screen, and the audio is heard through the projection system's speaker.

The audio amplification system in a video projector system frequently leaves something to be desired, as far as clarity and power output are concerned. So if the viewing audience is especially large, you can hook the audio from the VTR to an external amplifier and speaker system. Although hooking an external amplifier and speakers to a VTR player usually presents no problem, there may be a slight impedance mismatch. If so, it causes level problems or distortion in the sound at high volumes. Usually the distortion is minimal and not noticeable enough to warrant any attention. Sometimes, however, especially when amplifying audio from the speaker OUT of a monitor/receiver, the distortion may be great enough to justify the use of a device called a Teledapter available from the Rhoades National Corporation (see Source Index). The Teledapter matches the output impedance of the monitor/receiver more closely with the input impedance of the audio amplifier (Figure 2-41a). It

FIGURE 2–41a. Front of Teledapter. (Photo courtesy of Rhoades National Corporation)

FIGURE 2–41b. Rear view.

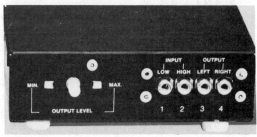

comes built into a little box with RCA (Phono) jacks and a level control for the input signal (Figure 2-41b). Probably its nicest feature is the simulated stereo effect it produces. Audiophiles find this gadget's improved audio quality very beneficial for video and television viewing.

CARE OF CABLES AND CONNECTORS

Regardless of the type of system or its interconnections, you must pay attention to certain things to avoid cable damage. Such damage almost always results in frustrating delays, and it may even result in more expensive damage to the video system as well. Both problems can be avoided by very simple preventive maintenance.

1. Keep connectors clean and dust-free. If a little dust or dirt gets into a connector, especially a multi-pin connector, it can interfere with the signal, or, worse yet, it can cause the connector to jam or bend a pin when it is pushed onto its jack. Usually the offending dirt can be blown out with canned air. If it's packed in the connector so tight that it won't come out with a burst of canned air, use a small sharp object like a jeweler's screwdriver to get most of it out, and then the rest can be cleaned out with a cotton swab.

2. Be careful not to bend the pins and, of course, to disconnect the other end of the cable from equipment which is turned on before doing anything. Never force connections. Chances are that if more than nominal force has to be exerted, something is wrong. Either something foreign is in the connector or jack, or something is physically wrong with it. A pin in the connector may be bent. Or the connector or jack housing may be either out of round, or cross-threaded. Usually the cross-threading takes place when a damaged or bent connector is forced onto its jack.

3. Naturally, don't drop or throw a connector on the floor. Don't step on it, and don't roll something else over it. Rolling heavy equipment over or stepping on any part of a cable can cause internal leads to separate or to break and short together.

4. Don't bend cables excessively, especially near the connector. Too much bending can weaken internal leads and sometimes cause them to separate from the connector internally where the break cannot be seen. This is one of the most common causes of a lost or intermittent signal.

5. Observe the proper "wind" of the cable. Every cable comes from the manufacturer wound a certain way. When the cable is coiled up for transport or storage, it should be wound in the direction that it "wants" to go. Forcing it to wind up a different way will probably crimp it, thus making it hard to handle and putting unnecessary stress on its internal lead.

6. If connectors are damaged, replace them with "strain-relief" connectors. These connectors look the same as normal connectors, and they do the same thing. But they have a "strain-relief collar" attached to them, which absorbs some of the bending stress near the connector and which cuts down the frequency of lead separation near the connector.

7. Number or color code all the cables that belong with a particular system. There is no standard way to do this, so just use some type of durable colored adhesive tape to keep equipment and cable matched. Identification marks are also a good idea from the standpoint of ownership. They make it possible for you to easily distinguish your cables and equipment from others. And, of course, they can be used to help the uninitiated match a given connector with the correct jack.

TROUBLE-SHOOTING: C.C.Eq.

Although treating your cables and connectors with care goes a long way toward preventing equipment downtime, cables and connectors are only part of the breakdown scene. Inasmuch as malfunctioning video equipment can be so frustrating, you should have a general strategy for locating the source of equipment problems.

The strategy we suggest does not presuppose a knowledge of electronics or even any experience in the field. It is not all-encompassing. It will not make you a technician. It is just a way to isolate a malfunction through a process of deduction. The approach is called the *C.C.Eq.* (pronounced "seek") strategy, and it stands for *Controls,*

*Cables, and Equipment.* We feel that this sort of general, organized approach to locating malfunctions can be of benefit to anyone taking the time to study and to use it. For this reason, we also feel that you should read this section more than once.

The approach, it must be noted, does not tell you what to do once you locate the problem. If the trouble is relatively minor, some people prefer to tackle it themselves. In fact, with C.C.Eq., you might very easily and quickly find that the "problem" is nothing more than "pilot error," requiring the flipping of a switch or the pressing of a button.

Other times, the problem turns out to be something fairly easy to repair. As you become more familiar with the operation of video equipment, you will want to repair and adjust it yourself—assuming you have the necessary technical background. If not, it takes very little training to adjust tape tension, to change belts (if your equipment has them), and even to replace heads. Knowing how to perform basic adjustments and repairs saves you an immense amount of time and money—and a lot of headaches, especially in the field. The only thing you need is someone to show you how it's done and a good set of tools. A hammer, a set of pliers, and bailing wire do not work for video repairs. You need good-quality, well-designed tools to do the job. Marshall Industries (see Source Index) carries a broad selection of tools and accessories for repairing video and computer equipment. Their EZE series of tool kits are specifically designed for working in tight quarters like inside computer terminals or camera heads (Figure 2-42).

We do feel, however, that video users without the necessary technical knowledge should never attempt to do more than the routine maintenance, as outlined in the owner's manual. So, to know precisely how much you should try to do yourself, you should not only read the manual as closely

as this section, but you should also keep the manual handy whenever you are using the equipment.

One last note: We put videotape into the equipment category. Actually, many people feel that videotape is more a type of material than equipment, but, for the benefit of this division, videotape is equipment.

## MALFUNCTIONS THAT AREN'T MALFUNCTIONS

Before learning the C.C.Eq. strategy, you should be aware of several frequently occurring problems that are really not malfunctions but that may appear to be to someone unfamiliar with video equipment.

### Dirty Heads

One of the most frequently occurring problems with almost any type of video equipment is dirty or clogged "heads." The heads on a videotape recorder are small electromagnets on the opposite ends of a spinning bar located inside the head drum (Figure 2-43). The tips of the electromagnets, which have a small gap in them, protrude very slightly from a horizontal slit in the head drum (Figure 2-44). On reel-to-reel VTRs, the head drum and heads can be seen. On videocassette recorder/players, the head drum is inside the VTR, out of sight. As the heads spin during routine recording and playback, they come into physical contact with the videotape. Depending on the quality of the videotape and on the time since the heads were cleaned, the gap in the video heads may pick up some tape oxide, which interferes with their ability to record or play

FIGURE 2–42.

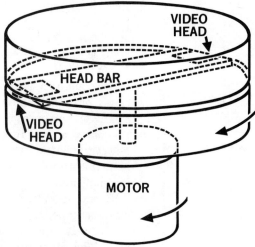

FIGURE 2–43. VTR/VCR heads protrude slightly from a horizontal slit in the head drum.

**FIGURE 2-44.**

back a signal. The resulting image looks like a snow storm—lots of interference either partially or totally obscuring the video image. Since this is a condition of the video heads, the audio, since it originates from a different head in most cases, will probably be unaffected.

A thorough cleaning of the head—following the instructions in the owner's manual—should eliminate the snow. Be sure to read your warranty carefully before doing any work, since sometimes just removing a panel for cleaning the heads can void your warranty!

Several cleaning techniques can be used:

1. The most common is to rub the heads in a back-and-forth horizontal motion with a cotton swab dipped in alcohol. But cotton swabs tend to fray and come apart, leaving little wisps of cotton fibers in the head gap.
2. Better implements are available, and they look like popsicle sticks or tongue depressors with a piece of cloth wrapped around the end. This cloth doesn't fall apart as easily as a cotton swab.
3. Freon-propelled sprays are also available, which some people recommend highly because only the spray touches the very fragile and expensive video heads and it evaporates almost instantly. Some people, however, feel that the spray doesn't clean as well as rubbing the heads with a cleaning implement.
4. Still another method is to use a head-cleaning tape, which is simply installed in the deck just like a normal recording tape. The difference is that the cleaning tape is apparently just abrasive enough to

rub the oxide off the heads. Some people feel that the excessive use of a cleaning tape can shorten head life.

The best approach, again, is to follow the recommendations in your owner's manual.

If a thorough cleaning according to the manual's recommendations doesn't eliminate the snow, look further for the problem. If you are sure that the cleaning was thorough, you might suspect the tape itself. Try a different tape that you know is of good quality, but make sure you clean the heads again before trying the tape you know is good. The reason is that the first tape may have been in such bad shape that it clogged the heads during the retrial after the first cleaning. This has been the case before. If the second tape plays back normally, you know that the first tape is bad. Although tape itself is not very often at fault, it can be.

Remember that new tape is not immune to problems. Once in a while a bad batch manages to escape the watchful eye of the tape manufacturer's quality controller. Usually the owner's manual makes tape recommendations, naming the best types of tape to use with the machine you have. Following those recommendations is better than a good idea.

If you are sure that you've cleaned the heads well, and that the "good" tape is also snowy, the problem is *probably* in the **VTR**. The word "probably" is italicized since something as simple as badly misadjusted vertical and horizontal hold controls on the monitor/receiver could also result in a scrambled image, which the inexperienced producer might mistake for snow. Actually, once you've seen what dirty heads do to the video image, you aren't likely to mistake it for anything else.

**Misthreading**

Another condition that looks like a malfunction but isn't happens once in a while with reel-to-reel machines: They can be misthreaded. Little guides keep the tape properly positioned as it travels over the head drum. On some reel-to-reel machines, the tape can slacken during threading just enough so that it gets caught under one of these guides (Figure 2-45). If you try to play back something from a misthreaded tape, you get very little intelligible information.

FIGURE 2–45. Misthreaded tape hooked under tape guide instead of resting on top of it.

If you suspect misthreading, just rethread the tape following the tape-threading diagram, which you can find somewhere on the deck or on its cover, and try again.

A test tape is helpful in this situation too, since it may be compared with the tape in question. In fact, whenever playback seems to be malfunctioning, playing a "good" or test tape is one way to narrow down the possibilities.

## Skew

If the skew control is misadjusted, the top of the video image *pulls* or *hooks* to one side or the other during playback (Figure 2-46). The solution is simply to adjust the skew control until the "hook" stabilizes and disappears. Sometimes, due to problems during recording or with bad tape, the unstable condition does not disappear no matter how much you play with the skew control. If so, the problem may be inherent in the recording, and there is no remedy for it. Again, the way to find out is to check the playback of this tape against a tape that you know is in good condition.

FIGURE 2–46. If the skew control is misadjusted, the video image hooks to one side or the other during playback.

## Tracking

The tracking control, if not adjusted correctly during playback, causes the video image to "tear." A *tear* is a horizontal band of distortion, which is unstable on the screen and which tends to move slowly upward or hover in one area of the image. (Figure 2-47). When the tracking control is adjusted slowly in one direction or the other, the tear usually disappears. Again, instability of this kind can result from recording problems or from bad or stretched tape, so isolation by comparison is a good idea.

FIGURE 2–47. If the tracking control is misadjusted, the video image shows a horizontal band of distortion called a tear.

## Standardization

This last apparent malfunction is rarely encountered now, but it used to happen quite a bit with old ½-inch black-and-white reel-to-reel machines. Someone lends you a tape. When you attempt to play it back, the monitor/receiver shows a scrambled pattern that does not change despite your correct threading, cleaning the heads, and adjusting all the controls properly. Other tapes play back fine. When you return the tape to the lender, that person threads it up on his or her own VTR, and the image looks great. What happened is a standards mismatch or a *standardization problem,* as it came to be known. The first deck, even though it uses the same tape and looks the same as the second one, doesn't electronically record the signal the same way.

Presently, similar problems arise among incompatible ½-inch consumer formats like Betamax and VHS. Fortunately the videocassettes for the two formats *look* physically different. Tapes recorded on Betamax cannot be played back on VHS. But, within the Beta and VHS formats, a number of recording times or speeds can be selected. If you expect to lend someone a tape, use the shortest recording time (the fastest recording speed) to guarantee the greatest possible quality and stability.

## C.C.EQ-ING THE PROBLEM

Due to the number of variables in a video system, the best troubleshooting approach involves the process of elimination, starting with the most obvious problems. This process of elimination not only helps to locate the problem quickly, but also cuts down on the time that it would take a technician to do the same thing, thus saving money. Many times when something looks wrong, we tend to overlook the obvious in favor of something less visible. In other words, we make the problem more complicated than it is, which necessitates coming up with a more complicated answer. Perhaps because solving a complicated problem is obviously much more appealing than solving an obvious one, we often have no pattern, no procedure, no strategy to lead us to the obvious answers.

Once, when I was trying to play back examples of my work to potential clients, I could not get the cassette moving in play mode. I was convinced that I had a jammed cassette, until after considerable agonizing and embarrassment, I realized I hadn't flipped the mode switch on the AC converter from "Battery Charge" to "VTR." In other words, I didn't have the VTR turned on. After this harrowing experience, the C.C.Eq. strategy became an idea whose time had definitely come.

C.C.Eq. is such a strategy. It stands for Controls, Cables, Equipment, which more often than not is the order in which problems occur. In other words, either the *controls* are not set properly, or something is not hooked up correctly *(cables)*, or something is really wrong with the system (the *equipment*). So the next time something seems to malfunction, try C.C.Eq.-ing the problem.

### Controls
First check the controls. Are all the switches in the correct position?

### Cables
Next, check the cables. Is everything hooked together? If so, are the correct INs and OUTs interconnected?

Then check the equipment. First try substituting a good videotape for the one you are trying to use. Find out if the tape or something else is the trouble source. If your good tape won't work, and if you are sure it is not a problem with dirty heads, try systematically substituting pieces of equipment for those you think may be malfunctioning.

To demonstrate the strategy more clearly, let's assume that a piece of video equipment does not seem to be working at all. After setting up your single-camera system in the studio and recording a segment for playback, you notice that the monitor/receiver is dead. Everything else seems to be working.

The first step in the C.C.Eq. strategy is to check the Controls. Check the power control. Is it turned on? Sometimes, when you're shooting on location, the power cables get plugged into switched wall outlets that are turned off. To make sure the outlet is hot, plug the monitor/receiver into one that you know is working. Check the volume control. Is it up high enough to be heard? If the audio is on but the screen is black, is the brightness control turned up high enough?

Next are the cables. Is the video cable connected to the VTR? Could the power cable be damaged? If power reaches the monitor/receiver when you gently raise or lower the cable, or when you move it in a circular pattern, chances are one of the leads inside the power cable is broken or loose. If you are using lights on the location, as well as several other pieces of equipment, you may have just blown a fuse or popped a breaker, which are built into many pieces of video equipment to protect their electronics from overload. So if you have had other problems with electricity, there is a chance that the fuse or breaker in the video equipment itself has blown out.

### Equipment
If everything else has failed, try a different monitor/receiver. If the second one does the same thing as the first, you know that you missed something in the "Controls" or "Cables" stage of the C.C.Eq. strategy. If the second monitor/receiver does work, you know that the problem is in the first monitor/receiver. If neither works, you might want to try the owner's manual for clues—or just call a video equipment technician.

## C.C.EQ-ING CAMERAS

What about a dead camera or one that is operating but seems to be recording badly? Start with the controls. Make sure all the switches are in the correct position. Make sure the power switch or trigger, if the camera has one, is turned on. If you are running from a battery and getting an unstable recording, check the battery indicator in the camera's viewfinder or on the VTR. If the battery is undercharged, you may get an unstable recording or no recording at all.

Next check the cables and connections for tightness or damage. If the camera gets its power from the VTR's battery but isn't getting power, the power leads in the cable may be loose or broken.

Check the equipment itself next. If the camera is being powered from an AC converter, make sure the converter is turned on and look at the fuses and breakers. All else failing, substitute a different camera. As a last resort, there is always the owner's manual and repair technicians to fall back on.

Since the video signal originating at the camera can be sent directly to a monitor for display, you can in most cases bypass the VTR to find out whether the VTR or the camera is malfunctioning. Depending on the system's set-up, power for the camera may be supplied from the battery in the VTR. Sometimes, when the battery runs down, everything operates sluggishly and doesn't record correctly, if it records at all. If, in this case, you can switch the camera over to its own battery or to an AC converter, you can find out if there is really anything wrong with the system or if the battery just needs a recharge. There is usually a battery indicator on the VTR which will tell you whether or not the VTR's battery needs recharging.

One last example. Suppose that you are getting good audio but bad video in record mode. First the controls. If the problem is off-hue colors, start by checking the camera's color correction filters and white balance. You might also check the contrast, brightness, and color controls on the monitor/receiver that you are using. If your camera produces its own color bars, you can adjust your monitor's contrast, brightness, and color controls to best reproduce the color bars put out by the camera.

If the video signal has a lot of interference or break-up, or if the problem is intermittent, the cause could be the cables. Trace the path of the cables, looking for worn sections, broken spots, or bad connections. If you're getting no video at all, make sure that the cables carry the video signal from the video OUT or CAMERA jack on the camera to the video IN or CAMERA jack on the VTR, and from video OUT to video IN or its equivalent on the monitor/receiver (if one is being used).

## C.C.EQ-ING AUDIO

If you have an audio problem, start with the controls. Is the level control turned up far enough? If the deck has AGC, is it on and working properly? If an audio mixer is being used, are the controls properly set? If a condenser microphone is being used, is its battery charged up?

Next, cables. Starting from the mike, trace the audio path to the deck. Are the proper INs and OUTs hooked together? Is there a gap anywhere in the path? Are all the connections tight and intact?

Equipment. If the signal is muddled, is the audio head clean and demagnetized? Substitute a different microphone, then a different mixer if one is in use. Or patch the microphone straight into the VTR to see if the problem is in the microphone or the mixer. Then perhaps try a different VTR or a different audio channel on the VTR if there is one. If you follow this procedure, you will eventually find the problem.

**SUMMARY**  The C.C.Eq. strategy to solve video problems is a process of substitution, isolation, and elimination. But if you find a definite electronics problem, you have to decide whether or not you have the technical background to handle the problem. Just knowing the source of the problem is a positive step forward. Most problems are found in the Controls and Cables steps of the procedure.

# 3

**AUDIO FOR TELEVISION**

Almost everything ever written about television audio starts out with a few denigrating remarks about how shabbily audio has been treated compared to video. These remarks are generally followed by the assertion that, if audio is not immediately restored to an eminent place in the mind of all producers, the whole of video art shall suffer. Actually, a great deal of attention is given to audio, but since recording audio is comparatively simple, not as much time is spent agonizing over it as over video. Hence the false assumptions that audio has taken a back seat to video, that more energy and research are being channeled into the field of video, and that not much is happening in audio. Yet just look at the recent improvements in audio technology and at the present plans to improve audio quality, as well as to encode stereo audio in the broadcast signal. The truth is that good audio and good video go hand-in-hand, and that astute producers pay attention to both. Just as a well-produced video segment cannot make it without good audio, a superior audio track won't work without high-quality video.

## THE NATURE OF SOUND

Producing a good audio track begins with a basic understanding of the nature of sound. What we hear as sound is radiating pressure waves produced by a vibrating body. In air, these pressure waves travel at about 1,130 feet, or 344 meters, per second. When these pressure waves strike our eardrum, they cause it to vibrate. These vibrations are conducted through the inner ear to the brain, which interprets them as sound. The brain is sensitive to two aspects of sound: frequency and intensity.

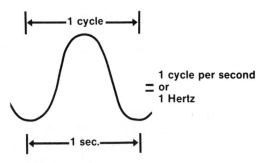

FIGURE 3–1. The Hertz.

### FREQUENCY (Hz)

The frequency of sound is determined by the number of pressure waves striking the eardrum in a given unit of time, usually per second. The brain interprets frequency as tone or pitch. As the frequency gets higher, so does the sound of the pitch or tone. Conversely, as the frequency gets lower, so does the sound of the pitch or tone.

Since all sound has frequency, and since frequency is cyclical (it happens again and again and again), frequency is graphically represented as a sine wave undulation. If one undulation of an air pressure wave (or one cycle of frequency) is produced in one second, the frequency is said to be "one cycle per second" or "one Hertz" (Figure 3-1). (The name "Hertz," abbreviated "Hz," comes from the nineteenth-century German physicist, Heinrich Hertz.) A person with good hearing can perceive sounds of from about 16 to 16,000 Hz, or in other words, sound varying in frequency between 16 and 16,000 cycles per second. Many people cannot perceive sound over this great a range, while a few can hear more. The ear is most sensitive to sound between 1,000 and 4,000 Hz—a fairly narrow range.

Audio technology, of course designed around the physical characteristics of the average ear, fares well as far as frequency is concerned. The audio track of a good ¾-inch videotape recorder can record and reproduce frequencies from about 50 to 15,000 Hz, thus effectively covering the entire audible range. The best microphones cover about 20 to 20,000 Hz. Good microphones usually have a frequency response of about 50 to 15,000 Hz.

### INTENSITY (dB)

Sound intensity is roughly speaking the loudness of a sound, and it is measured in decibels (dB). (The decibel is named after

Alexander Graham Bell, which is the reason for capitalizing the B after the lower-case d.) The decibel is a comparison of one sound to another. One dB difference in intensity is about the smallest change in loudness that the human ear can detect. Loud sounds have a much greater decibel rating than soft sounds: A quiet whisper has an intensity of about 20 dB, while an airplane taking off may be as loud as 120 dB.

An important thing to remember about decibels is that relatively small increases on the decibel scale require large increases in power. For example, a 3-dB increase requires twice the power; a 6-dB increase, four times the power; and a 20-dB increase, 100 times more power. Thus, as shown on the dB scale in Figure 3-2, it takes 100 times more power to produce "very soft music" than to produce the sound coming from "rustling leaves."

The human ear has an incredible range: It can accept sound over a 120-dB range—from near 0 dB to about 120 dB—without damage. Audio technology, however, doesn't do as good a job here as with frequency response. The finest recording equipment available has a range of only about 60 dB, and so it is limited to only about one-half the ear's ability to discern the very softest sounds and the very loudest. The reason you should be familiar with the decibel scale is that it is frequently used not only in referring to levels of sound intensity and to signal strength, but also extensively in equipment specifications. For example, when setting recording levels, a VU meter, usually calibrated in decibels, serves as a visual reference of signal strength (Figure 3-3).

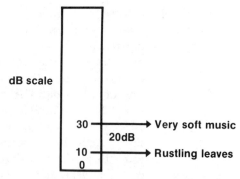

FIGURE 3–2. The dB sound intensity scale.

FIGURE 3–3. A dB scale from −20 to +5 on a VU meter. The percentages below the dB scale indicate signal strength. Zero dB equals 100 percent signal strength. Exceeding 0 dB for an instant does not cause problems, but if the needle is consistently in the 0 to +5 dB area, the record level is too high.

## SIGNAL-TO-NOISE RATIO

The equipment specifications for a good VTR, as an illustration, typically list its audio system's signal-to-noise ratio as about 45 dB. This ratio is a measure of how strong or "clean" the audio signal is compared with background noise and distortion.

## MAGNETIC RECORDING AND REPRODUCTION

Let's take a look at audio recording and reproduction as it pertains to the video medium.

### VIDEOTAPE AS MAGNETIC TAPE

Videotape is fabricated much like audio tape. Both are types of magnetic recording tape manufactured in layers. The two most important layers are the base and the magnetic oxide coating, which is very easily magnetized by an external magnetic field.

On top of the oxide coating is usually a very thin topcoat for protection, and on the

FIGURE 3–4. The structure of videotape.

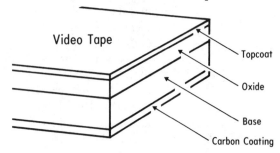

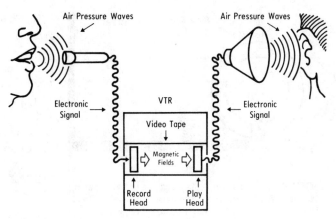

FIGURE 3–5. Recording and playing back audio from video tape.

back of the tape is usually a carbon coating, which reduces static electricity (Figure 3-4).

## HEADS

In the process of recording audio on the tape, the microphone changes sound waves—from vibrating air pressure waves—into an alternating electronic signal, which is then converted into alternating magnetic fields by a recording head. These alternating magnetic fields are recorded on the moving videotape. When the tape is played back, the magnetic fields are changed back into an electronic signal by the playback head, amplified, and played back through a speaker, which converts the signal back to air pressure wave, which the ear and brain perceive as sound (Figure 3-5).

### Record Head

The record head functions as a miniature electromagnet. When a microphone or another piece of audio or audiovisual equipment sends an alternating current (the elec-

FIGURE 3–6. The record head transforms a weak electrical signal into alternating magnetic fields.

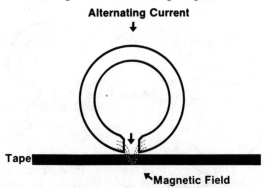

**RECORD HEAD**

tronic signal) to the record head, it turns the signal into alternating magnetic fields (Figure 3-6). As the tape moves past the head, the alternating magnetic fields magnetize the oxide particles on the tape into line-like patterns with north and south polarity (Figure 3-7).

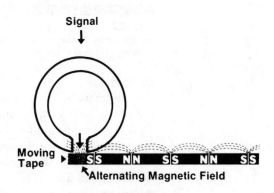

**RECORD**

FIGURE 3–7. The alternating magnetic fields align the oxide particles on the videotape into line-like patterns with north and south polarity.

### Playback Head

During playback, when these stored magnetic fields come into contact with the playback head, the reverse process takes place. The magnetic fields on the moving tape induce an alternating signal in the playback head, which is amplified and sent to the speakers (Figure 3-8). Magnetic fields that are close to one another produce a high-frequency or high-pitch sound; as the space between fields becomes greater, the frequency or pitch gets lower. So, it's easy to see that, to get both high-frequency or treble pitch and low-frequency or bass sound, the magnetized pattern on the tape has to be extremely varied (Figure 3-9).

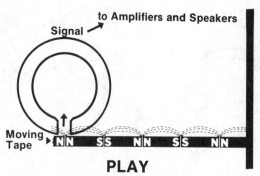

PLAY

FIGURE 3–8. During playback, the alternating magnetic fields on the videotape induce a weak alternating electrical signal in the play head.

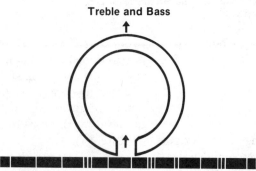

FIGURE 3–9. For high-frequency treble and low-frequency bass, the magnetic pattern on the video-tape is extremely varied.

### Erase Head

To understand how the audio track is erased, as well as how audio insert editing works, you must understand how the erase head functions (see Chapter 6, "Editing"). Actually, calling the erase head an "erase" head is misleading. The erase head does not really erase the magnetic fields on the tape, it just restructures them.

To understand how the erase head works, let's first take a look at the function of the *head gap*. The width of the head gap determines the highest frequency that a head can play back. A head with a very narrow gap can play back high-frequency information, but a head with a comparativey wide gap is capable of playing back only lower-frequency information (Figure 3-10). This limitation

FIGURE 3–10. The width of the head gap determines the head's frequency response.

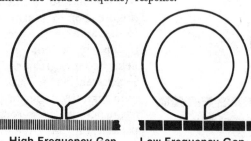

High Frequency Gap    Low Frequency Gap

arises from the fact that the magnetic field from a high frequency cannot touch both poles of the head with a wide gap at the same time, and so it cannot induce a play-back signal in the head (Figure 3-11). In fact, most audio playback heads installed in video recorders have gaps that can't play back frequencies higher than about 15,000 Hz or so.

FIGURE 3–11. A head with a comparatively wide gap does not play back high frequencies.

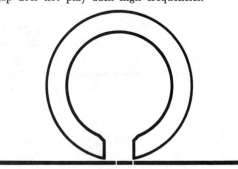

The erase head works by laying down a signal of a much higher frequency than the playback head can play back. The signal, which is generated by an electronic device known as an oscillator, usually has a frequency of about 100,000 Hz, although it varies from VTR to VTR. So you can easily see that, when blank tape or tape with prerecorded information passes the erase head and picks up a 100,000-Hz magnetic pattern, nothing is played back by the play-back head because the gap of the playback head is too wide. Thus, if any pre-recorded information is on the tape, it is "erased" (Figure 3-12).

FIGURE 3–12. The erase head generates such high frequencies that the playback head cannot play them back, thus precorded information is "erased."

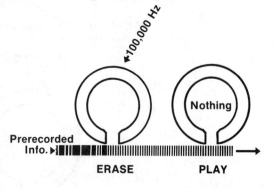

ERASE    PLAY

The erase head works well in theory, and, in reality, it does an adequate job. But it's best, if you're recording new audio and video information, to use a bulk eraser if possible. The *bulk eraser* has a much stronger magnetic field than the erase head on the video deck so it can "erase" the tape much more thoroughly. It's also not a bad idea to bulk-erase new tape before recording on it. Some bulk erasers are table-top models while others are hand-held (Figure 3-13).

FIGURE 3–13. Table top bulk eraser. Similar erasers are used for disgaussing (erasing) videotape.

### Location of Heads
Although we've been talking about erase, record, and playback heads as though they were physically separate from one another, on VTRs this isn't so. There is usually a combination video/audio erase head, along with a combination audio record/playback head. (The record/playback head often also houses a control head, but more on that in the chapter on editing.) The record/playback head is a record head when the video deck is in record mode, and a playback head when the deck is in play mode. The erase head is

always located "upstream" from the record/playback head on the deck. This arrangement makes sense since old material has to be erased before new material is recorded.

### TRACKS

The path on the videotape on which the audio information is recorded as the tape passes the heads is called the *audio track*. On ½-inch video tape, the audio track is usually laid down along the top edge of the tape. Three-quarter-inch tape has enough physical width for two tracks, both along the bottom edge of the tape; this double track makes recording and playing back in stereo possible (Figure 3-15). However, since audio track number one is so close to the edge of the tape, it sometimes falls victim to edge damage. So, especially if recording something extremely important, most producers rely on track two, or they use a Y cord to record the same audio information on both tracks at once. These precautions reduce the possibility of missing important audio either due to a malfunction in the electronics of one or the other of the tracks, or due to missing or imperfect tape oxide.

Some new ¾-inch, 1-inch, and 2-inch broadcast-quality machines have a third audio track called a *cue track* for recording time-code information. With this system, each video frame gets its own number so that searching for a given frame on a tape to

FIGURE 3–14. The audio erase and record/playback heads of the VTR/VCR should be as close as possible to one another to avoid audio lag when editing.

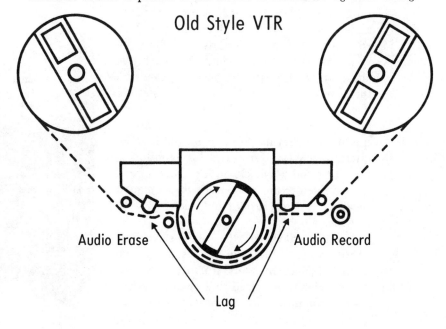

Old Style VTR

Audio Erase

Audio Record

Lag

## Audio and Video Tracks on Tape

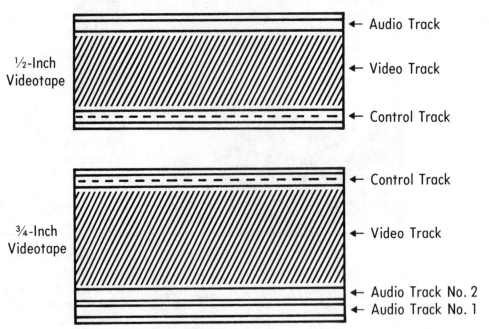

½-Inch Videotape

← Audio Track

← Video Track

← Control Track

¾-Inch Videotape

← Control Track

← Video Track

← Audio Track No. 2
← Audio Track No. 1

FIGURE 3–15. ¾-inch videotape has room for two audio tracks, which makes it possible to record and play back in stereo.

perform manual or computerized edits becomes less time-consuming. Notice that, regardless of the track arrangement, both audio and video are recorded on the same tape at the same time, and so they are always synchronized with one another.

### SPEAKERS

One of the most striking things about video production is how easy it is to forget that the audio track is part of it. Many video studios, with hundreds of thousands of dollars invested in video equipment, play back the audio track through the 3-inch speaker in the monitor. Frequently this sort of speaker doesn't do the audio track justice, and it even allows producers to overlook problems in quality that they might have noticed if good-quality speakers were used in monitoring recording and playback. So it's really a good idea to listen to the audio track through good speakers during production, editing, and viewing.

Using speakers of the highest possible quality also enables you to detect any excessive changes in sound quality over successive generations of editing or duplication. Sound Dynamics Corporation (Source Index)

produces a particularly good speaker for video production. The model 10S (Figure 3-16) is well suited to reproducing the frequency response range of all video recorders. The interesting thing about this particular speaker is that the speaker components used in its design are part of the same company's much more expensive professional speaker monitor systems. In other words, you can get professional-quality speakers at a consumer speaker price, which is very important to most independent videographers.

FIGURE 3–16. The model 10S speaker for monitoring audio playback of video recordings. (Photo courtesy of Sound Dynamics Corporation)

**MICROPHONES** If you get very far into video production, you'll likely find it necessary to use a microphone other than the one that is attached to or a permanent part of your camera. The several different types of microphones are all designed to function in much the same way. The sound-pressure waves that strike and physically vibrate the microphone's diaphragm are turned into a weak electrical signal by the mike's generating element or transducer (Figure 3-17). This weak signal is then amplified and recorded on the moving videotape next to the video information.

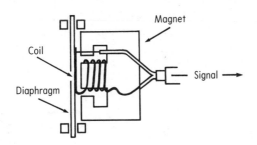

Dynamic

FIGURE 3–17. The dynamic transducer.

TRANSDUCERS

Microphones are often referred to by their transducer types, which also determine to some extent how the mikes are used. So you should know a little about each widely-used type:

1. dynamic (moving coil) mikes,
2. condenser microphones,
3. ribbon microphones, and
4. crystal (ceramic) mikes.

**Dynamic Transducer**
The diaphragm of the transducer in the dynamic or "moving coil" microphone is attached to a coil that moves in a magnetic field between the poles of a permanent magnet. When sound pressure waves strike the diaphragm and move the coil, a weak electrical signal is produced (Figure 3-17). Dynamic microphones withstand rough treatment and very high sound levels extremely well. They are also dependable and relatively inexpensive, having a good smooth frequency response range.

**Condenser Transducer**
The condenser microphone has a light, flexible membrane for a diaphragm, along with a rigid backplate. As the diaphragm moves

first closer to and then away from the backplate, the capacitance is changed between the diaphragm and the backplate. These changes produce a fluctuating electrical signal in the voltage supplied from an external source (Figure 3-18).

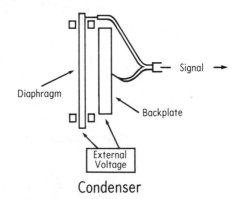

Condenser

FIGURE 3–18. The condenser transducer.

Condenser mikes were originally expensive, and some required an external power source that wasn't portable. The cost of condenser mikes eventually came down, however, to make their price range fairly comparable to that of the dynamic types. In addition, although the power source is still required, it is now built-in in the form of batteries. Many of the latest cameras come with built-in condenser microphones, which are powered from the battery in the deck. This arrangement eliminates having to worry about batteries.

**Ribbon Transducer**
In the ribbon microphone, a light, corrugated-foil ribbon is suspended between the poles of a permanent magnet. As the ribbon diaphragm moves, it generates a small electrical signal, which is strengthened by a small step-up transformer before amplification (Figure 3-19). The advantage of the ribbon mike is the warm, rich, gentle quality of the sound it produces.

FIGURE 3–19. The ribbon transducer.

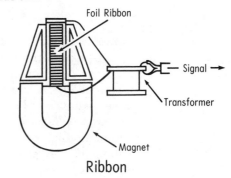

Ribbon

The ribbon microphone has two basic disadvantages. For one, it has always been more expensive than other types due to the additional electronics needed to amplify its low output signal. Although it has come down in price somewhat, it is still relatively expensive at this writing. The second drawback is that this mike is delicate Older model ribbon mikes are very fragile. Blowing into them to see if they are live can break the delicate foil ribbon. (Blowing into, whistling into, or tapping any type of mike is not recommended. If you want to see if the mike is on, just talk into it.) Newer ribbon mikes are much less fragile. So ribbon mikes aren't found in the field very often, probably because historically they have been used in the studio—due to their fragility.

### Crystal Ceramic Transducer

This is the most inexpensive mike available. It's the one you get when you buy an under-$30 monaural tape recorder. It is really suited only for voice or other uncritical recording, and it should generally not be used in video work. In a pinch, however, it can be used for recording background sound with surprisingly good results.

PICK-UP PATTERNS

Besides transducer types, microphones are also referred to by their pick-up patterns, which indicates the direction from which the mike is designed to pick up sound. The common pick-up patterns are:

1. omnidirectional,
2. bidirectional,
3. unidirectional,
4. cardioid, and
5. super cardioid.

### Omnidirectional Pattern

This type of microphone can pick up sound from any direction in a 360-degree pattern (Figure 3-20). A mike with an omnidirectional pattern can be used whenever a number of people have to use the same mike simultaneously, or in any other situation calling for the pick-up of sound from all directions.

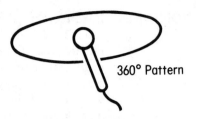

Omnidirectional

FIGURE 3-20. Omnidirectional pick-up pattern.

### Bidirectional Pattern

A microphone with a figure-eight pick-up pattern that picks up sound from two opposing directions is called bidirectional (Figure 3-21). This type of mike is useful in crowded outdoor or indoor interview situations, when sounds coming from other directions are distracting and must be eliminated.

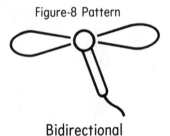

Bidirectional

FIGURE 3-21. Bidirectional pick-up pattern.

### Unidirectional Pattern

The unidirectional microphone, often called a "shotgun" mike, picks up sound from a very narrow, specific direction, while rejecting sound coming from other directions. This type of mike is extremely useful in situations that call for picking up sound from a distance. A shotgun may be used inside or outside for miking moving people when microphones must not appear in the shot. Electro-Voice, Inc. (see Source Index) produces a professional line of shotgun microphones that are especially useful in video production. The CL42S (Figure 3-22) is designed either to be used with a screw-on handle for hand-held operation or to be attached to a stand or boom for following the action. Most video production is done under time constraints, and "miking" moving people can be a problem if the "talent" gets off-mike slightly. Retakes take time. For this reason, this particular shotgun is designed to hold the tonal qualities of the voice even if the talent does get slightly off-mike. This feature is especially important in producing commercial advertising in which the budgets are generally tight and the time extremely limited.

FIGURE 3-22. The Electro-Voice CL42-S shotgun unidirectional microphone. (Photo courtesy of Electro-Voice, Inc.)

## Cardioid Pattern

The cardioid pattern allows sound to be picked up in front of and to the front sides of the mike, while rejecting sound from behind it. The pattern looks like a heart, hence the name "cardioid" (Figure 3-23). The cardioid pattern is helpful when unwanted sound is originating from in front of the person speaking, such as in the television studio situation.

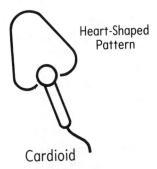

FIGURE 3-23. Cardioid pick-up pattern.

## Super Cardioid

This mike simply uses a more extreme cardioid pattern. To be picked up, the sound must originate from almost directly in front of the microphone (Figure 3-24). Both the cardioid and super cardioid patterns are sometimes referred to as "unidirectional patterns."

FIGURE 3-24. Supercardioid pick-up pattern.

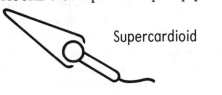

## TYPES OF MICROPHONES

Microphone transducer types and pick-up patterns are "mixed," that is, you might have a condenser cardioid mike, a dynamic omni-directional mike, and so on. The type of microphone you need depends on its intended application.

The appearance of a mike usually does not tell you what type it is or how well it works. For example, the Electro-Voice DS35 (Figure 3-25) is a high-quality dynamic cardioid microphone used extensively by professional entertainers. From its appearance, you cannot differentiate it from other Electro-Voice microphones of different designs. Neither can you tell how it reproduces sound without trying it out. The tone and color of sound that each microphone produces is unique.

FIGURE 3-25. Electro-Voice DS35 dynamic cardioid microphone. "Dynamic" is the transducer type, and "cardioid" is the pick-up pattern. (Photo courtesy of Electro-Voice, Inc.)

The DS35 can be plugged directly into the microphone jack on a videotape recorder for recording narration, music, or both. On one occasion, we had to record narration and music without a mixer, to prepare a rough sound track for demonstration purposes. The audio dubbing button on the VTR made it possible to record audio while watching the video portion of the program. A little experimentation with the DS35 proved that the cardioid pick-up pattern was useful in narrating while sitting near a home stereo speaker. When the music was to be faded up during a pause in narration, the mike was just smoothly tipped toward the speaker. The result was a fade up and then down as the mike was returned to the proper hand-held position for narration. It took a little while to get the timing just right, but, after a short practice period, the quality using this method was surprisingly good.

In choosing a microphone, there are several things to consider besides transducer type and pick-up pattern. They are

1. frequency response,
2. impedance, and
3. line balance.

## Frequency Response

Inasmuch as a good ¾-inch videotape recorder can record and play back a frequency range of about 50 to 15,000 Hz, it makes sense to spend a little more money on a microphone that handles 20 to 20,000 Hz. Although a mike with a frequency response range of 70 to 12,000 Hz is adequate, you must recognize that such a mike is not using the full frequency response range of the VTR. So the best possible combination obliges you to match the capabilities of the microphone to the capabilities of the VTR.

## Impedance

Matching is also extremely important in the case of impedance. *Impedance* is the resistance of the electronic device to the electrical voltage or to the signal that it generates; this resistance is measured in ohms, the symbol for which looks like a horseshoe ($\Omega$). Low impedance (lo-Z or low-Z) is 50 to 250 ohms; high impedance (hi-Z or high-Z) is 10,000 ohms and up. "Line level impedance," a term heard often, is 600 ohms.

All audio-related electronic devices have either input impedances, output impedances, or both. For instance, a microphone has an output impedance, which has to match the VTR input impedance. Most VTRs have low-impedance inputs for microphones, because low-impedance mikes work well with the long cables that are frequently necessary in video work. High-impedance mikes do not. Impedance-matching transformers are available to match high-impedance mikes with low-impedance inputs and to match low-impedance mikes with high-impedance inputs. They are inexpensive, but it's still best to match the microphone with the input rather than to use a matching transformer.

## Balanced and Unbalanced Lines

The difference between balanced and unbalanced audio lines, which are encountered often in video work, is at first confusing for beginning videographers.

First of all, there is a physical difference between the two: A balanced line has three leads and terminals, whereas an unbalanced line has only two. The balanced line has three leads because, while two are connected to the signal circuit conductors between the microphone and recorder, the third is connected to a metal shield, which is wound around the two conductors carrying the signal. The metal shield, which may be wire-mesh or foil, protects the signal-carrying conductors against interference from stray RF and from any other electrical sources by passing the interference directly to ground. In other words, the metal shield is a ground. The balanced line is especially helpful (and almost essential) in populated areas with a lot of interference from CB'ers, radio stations, television stations, radar, and other sources, which may show up as noise or interference in the audio portion of your video recording. Since the balanced audio line has three leads, it should always have an XLR or Cannon plug attached to the end of it.

The unbalanced line has only two leads. Both are signal circuit conductors between the microphone and the recorder. Since they have no shield to protect them from interference, any interference that is present can show up in the audio portion of the recording. Balanced audio is therefore always preferable to unbalanced. Unfortunately, most ½-inch and ¾-inch video equipment doesn't use XLR or Cannon plugs for audio inputs.

To convert microphones with balanced lines for use with unbalanced inputs, solder the shield to the neutral conductor of the signal-carrying circuit, and then connect both to the cold or ground side of the two-lead plug that fits into the jack of the deck. The hot lead is connected to the center of the plug, which is almost always a phone, Phono (RCA), or mini—all of which have only two terminals. Once a balanced line is converted to an unbalanced line, it is no longer balanced.

An unbalanced line cannot be converted to a balanced line without using three-lead shielded cable. If any simple three-to-two-lead adaptor is used anywhere in a balanced line, it usually changes the entire balanced line to an unbalanced line, thus sacrificing all the benefits of the balanced line. But using a transformer at the video deck's audio input between the balanced line and the unbalanced mike input retains the benefits of the balanced line. (This trick works if the secondary winding of the transformer going to the unbalanced audio input is impedance-matched to the audio input. The audio input impedance is usually printed in the VTR's operation manual.) Such transformers are available through commercial audio equipment vendors, or they may be assembled by anyone with a little skill in electronics.

## HANDLING MICROPHONES

How is a mike to be used? This is the primary question in choosing a mike. Some mikes are sensitive to handling and make a lot of noise if you move them around in your hand while recording. Other mikes are not meant to be hand-held at all. They are meant to be used on stands or supported in a rubber cradle—called a *shock-mount*—on booms. Sometimes the appearance of a microphone makes its intended use evident, but usually it does not. The best way to find out is to read the operating instructions. Also make sure you have an alternate so that, if the first choice doesn't work the way you think it should, you're not stuck without a microphone. If available, the built-in mike on the camera is usually a good alternate. One thing to remember about using a different mike from the one on the camera is that, when you plug a mike into the VTR, the built-in mike is usually automatically disconnected. So don't plan on using both simultaneously. If you're planning to do a lot of voice work, be sure to use a *pop-filter*, which is usually made of wire mesh and which fits over the mike to cut down on hisses and pops in voice recording. Outside, use a *wind screen*, which is usually made of foam rubber and which fits over the mike to cut down on wind noise.

## OTHER MICROPHONE EQUIPMENT

Two other items of microphone equipment seem to be in a category all their own: (1) wireless microphones and (2) parabolic dishes.

### Wireless Mikes

Wireless mikes are normally used when stringing long microphone cables would be difficult, impossible, or visible in the camera shot—and lip sync is essential. The wireless mike is really a small FM transmitter (Figure 3-26). The signal it transmits is sent to a small receiver, which amplifies it for recording on the videotape. Some older wireless mikes were sensitive to many types of through-the-air interference, such as electrical discharges, radar, radio transmissions, and random electromagnetic emissions from electrical tools, to name only a few. Even with later models, it's a good idea to closely monitor any recording. To be fair, there are some good wireless microphones, which can operate on more than one frequency and which are much less vulnerable to such interference.

FIGURE 3-26. A wireless mike is a small FM transmitter. (Photo courtesy of Edcor)

The Edcor Company (see Source Index) produces an ECOM series of wireless mikes that are used extensively in video production. Especially resistant to external noise and electrical disturbance, they are designed for use indoors or outside (Figure 3-27).

### Parabolic Dishes

The parabolic dish, or sound dish as it is sometimes called, gets its name from its shape (Figure 3-28). When used with an omnidirectional mike, it picks up sound from a relatively distant source, by aiming the dish directly at the source. Dishes seem to work best for recording the sound "presence" of outside sporting events, such as the contact sounds of football players on a field or the response of an audience to an event. They are not generally designed to be selective at a distance, although very expensive special-purpose units are quite selective.

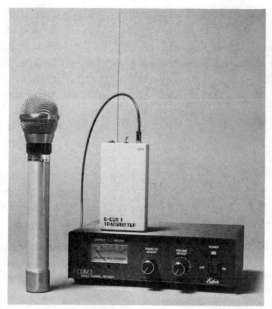

FIGURE 3–27. A wireless receiver and microphone in the Ecom series. (Photo courtesy of Edcor)

FIGURE 3–28. A parabolic dish for recording ambient sound or sound "presence."

Of the basic types of recording systems, one that is often used consists of only the camera and built-in mike. The advantages to this system are that it is light and easy to use and that it requires only one individual to run.

### BUILT-IN MIKES

The quality of the built-in mike varies, but most work surprisingly well within about 15 feet of the camera. Some of the newer built-in mikes are mounted on a short antenna-like boom, which can be extended to a point just above the camera lens, but out of the shot. (Be careful! Sometimes the shadow of the boom ends up in close-up shots.) Some cameras have detachable mikes, which can be hand-held if desired, but many haven't come that far yet.

Built-in mikes, do, however, pose a couple of difficulties: First, the camera has to be aimed in the direction of the sound in order to record it best. This can sometimes be a problem. For instance, if a mariachi band is playing in one area and people are dancing to the music in another, you may have to choose between the dancers and the music. Distance is also a factor. Recording from beyond 20 feet works okay for presence, but forget recording a monolog or a verbal ex-

change between two people. The mike is just not that selective.

### AGC/ALC

Many inexpensive video recording decks come with AGC (automatic gain control) or ALC (automatic level control), as it is variously called. With AGC/ALC, the deck electronically adjusts the strength of the incoming audio signal to a preset level. This feature frees camera operators from having to make audio level adjustments while they're shooting. If a sound is too loud, for example, the AGC cuts it down. This capability works fine, but, if a sound is interrupted temporarily, the AGC "reaches" for whatever else there is to amplify. The result is called *swelling*—a sudden increase in background noise. Depending on the circumstances, this swelling may or may not be distracting. Perhaps you can see how a manual override switch and a VU meter built into all decks would enable a second person to monitor sound levels. Such a modification would really be a positive development for audio.

### MULTIPLE MIKES

In many situations, the problems with the built-in mike can be overcome by using several mikes and a mixer. In a typical set-up, the mikes are connected to the mixer, and the mixer is connected to the VTR from AUX (high-level output) on the mixer to Line IN on the VTR. The level of each mike is adjusted for the best mix using the mixer's VU meter, if it has one.

To adjust the level, you simply turn the knob, or move the slide control, until the needle dances back and forth near the red zone on the meter. It can occasionally jump into the red zone without causing distortion. Then adjust the master control on the mixer to the proper recording level for the VTR.

If the mixer has no VU meter, use the one on the VTR for the proper level of each mike. If there is no VU meter on the VTR, there may be some other type of audio level indicator. If not, you have to record and play back the audio several times to make sure that the levels are right. Pencil marks or pieces of masking tape on the mixer work as reference marks to remind you how far the mixer controls should be moved for best recording.

The advantages of a mixer are numerous. Sound coming from any direction can be mixed with any other sound. In the situation with the mariachi band, the sound from the band could be recorded on one mike, while the people dancing to the music could be recorded on another. Unfortunately, if the video deck has no AGC override, the same "swelling" effect can occur, even with a mixer. Sometimes, by using the Line IN jack on the deck rather than the Mike IN or Audio IN, you can bypass the AGC circuit. If you cannot, then you should use a *gated-compressor mixer,* which is a relatively new development that handles swelling better than its predecessors.

## Mike Uses and Placement

When a mike is *hand-held,* depending on its particular characteristics, it may be better to talk across it rather than directly into it, to avoid hisses and pops. Tapping, fingering, or handling the microphone while recording ordinarily results in thumping and bumping in the audio. Hold the microphone firmly, and don't move your hand around on it. When interviewing someone with a hand-held mike, alternate the mike between yourself and the other person so that the distance from both your mouths to the microphone is about equal. If the other person speaks much softer or much louder than you do, hold it a little closer or a little

farther away accordingly. Thus you prevent the soft-spoken person from being lost and the loud person from "booming" in comparison to you.

Microphones are used *on stands* when they do not have to be hidden and when performers need their hands free, such as in recording sessions or musical performances. Recording a small musical group, for example, may require a number of stand microphones for the singers, drums, cymbals, keyboard instruments, and so on. The intended use and placement of the mikes determine which type—diaphragm type and pick-up pattern are needed. Let's say we want to record a kick drum. What do we do? We know that we want to record it and as little else as possible so that we have control over its volume relative to the other instruments. So place the mike close to the drum. We also know that the sound of the drum is extremely loud. So a dynamic mike transducer is probably best.

But what happens if all we have is omnidirectional condenser mikes? In that case, put the drums in another room and do the best you can. Here again, trying things out is the best solution. If there is no way to isolate the drums, it might be best to move the omnis back and record areas of the band rather than specific instruments. With this solution, you have less control over the mix, but at least you will have a recording. Sometimes you can hook directly into the band's PA mixer. If so, the problems are solved if all the band's instruments are being amplified through the PA. Whatever isn't has to be miked separately. As you can see, bands are fun to do and offer a lot of opportunities for experience.

When recording a group discussion, mikes may be placed *on table stands.* If you aim the mikes at the collar bone of the group members and place them at a 45-degree angle to them, you have fewer problems with hisses and pops. If the mike stand doesn't have some kind of felt, foam, or rubber separating it from the table, you can count on picking up sound and vibrations from the table top.

A microphone can also be *hung from the ceiling* in a fixed position, if the speakers don't have to move very far from it in the course of their presentation. If the speakers have to move, and if the microphone must be kept out of the shot, attach the mike to a pole or boom to follow the action.

Many times mikes about the size of a small shotgun shell are *worn around the neck*. Called *lavaliers*, these mikes are used extensively in television studio work. Also, very small microphones, called *lapel mikes*, are clipped to the lapel or collar. Very often on talk shows, double lapels, or two lapel mikes in one clip-on unit, are used in case one fails.

### Mike Maintenance

No matter how the mike is used, everyone should observe some common-sense maintenance procedures:

1. Don't drop or throw a microphone on the floor. Even the rugged dynamic mike won't function with a broken diaphragm.
2. Do not tap, slap, or snap a microphone, nor blow into it, to find out if it's live—just talk. Doing anything else can cause diaphragm damage.
3. Keep the mike clean and free of dust and dirt. Keep it wrapped or packaged when it's not in use. Dust, dirt, food, and soft drinks can interfere with the proper functioning of the diaphragm.
4. Check a condenser mike's batteries or external power supply before using it. Store batteries separately from the mike, and date them so that you have some idea of how old they are. If the battery is run down or leaks inside the mike, you'll have problems.

Although not strictly a maintenance procedure, avoid microphone feedback, which occurs when a microphone is placed too close to its own speaker. The sound from the speaker enters the microphone, is amplified, sent back to the speaker, enters the mike again, and quickly follows this loop until a roar of noise is created. The sound "feeds" upon itself (Figure 3-30). Feedback occurs a lot when using a monitor to watch what is being recorded on the tape. If you are listening to the sound through the monitor, which is within about 10 feet of the mike, you'll probably get feedback, and it will be recorded on the tape. To break the feedback loop, just turn down the volume knob on the amplifier—in this case, the monitor/receiver volume—or move the mike farther away from the speaker—in this case, the speaker in the monitor.

## OTHER AUDIO SOURCES

Other common audio sources include:

1. television receivers,
2. home stereo sets,
3. tape recorders,
4. PA systems, and
5. audiovisual (AV) equipment.

### Television Receivers

How you go about recording directly off-the-air (both audio and video)—a very common practice—depends on what kind of "tube" you use. In video work, you encounter three types of "tubes":

1. *Monitors* have neither tuners (channel selectors) nor audio systems (amplifiers and speakers). They are set up only to "monitor" the television picture. They do, however, have external connectors somewhere on them, for hooking up other monitors or test equipment, and sometimes for access to the audio signal.
2. *Receivers* are what we buy for home use. Generally, they have no external connectors for audio and video, but they do have a place to connect VHF and UHF antenna leads, as well as in some cases a headphone or speaker jack. Some newer receivers come with an F connector to which an antenna or closed-circuit cable may be attached.
3. A *monitor/receiver* has the best of both: external connectors for audio and video, as well as VHF, UHF, or F antenna connections.

If you want to record and play back audio and video from a home receiver, with only VHF and UHF antenna connections, you need a VTR with a built-in or external tuner, along with a built-in or external RF unit. Connect the cable from the RF unit, which has a small impedance-matching transformer attached to it, to the VHF antenna connections on the back of the set.

FIGURE 3-29. Feedback loop.

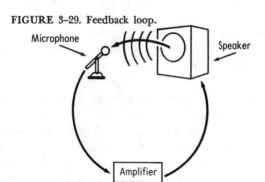

Attach your antenna cable to the built-in or external tuner. When the video deck is put in record mode, you can record both video and audio on the tape.

If the receiver has a headphone or speaker jack, and if you want only the audio portion of the broadcast, just connect it to Audio IN or Line IN on the video deck. Be aware of the strength of the signal, which may be too high (that is, too many decibels) for Mike or Audio IN. To test the levels coming from any audio source, turn the volume control on the source all the way down, make the hookup(s), and then make a test recording while turning the volume control slowly up until the level is right. Usually the signal level coming from any jack labeled "Headphone," "Speaker," or "Line OUT" is going to be high. So it doesn't make sense to connect it to the Mike IN jack on the VTR, since Mike IN accepts the signal generated by the transducer in the mike—a very low signal.

The monitor/receiver has separate external connectors for audio and video. The audio OUT and video OUT connectors are connected to the audio IN and video IN connectors on the VTR. If all you want is the audio portion, don't hook up the video. (For an in-depth description on these hookups, see Chapter 2, "The INs and OUTs of Video Hookups.")

### Home Stereo Sets

If your VTR has two audio channels, you can record in stereo from the home stereo set. Surprisingly enough, the video deck's audio tracks can be played back through a stereo amp with excellent results. If your VTR has only one audio track, you have to connect the channels of the stereo amp to a Y cord, and then connect the Y cord to the videotape recorder. Most VTRs offer an audio dubbing feature, which lets you record audio without changing the video track (Figure 3-30). When the audio dub control is on, all previously recorded audio is erased, and the new audio is recorded. So, for example, if you make a mistake while watching the video and reading narration, simply rewind the videotape, and read it again. Three-quarter-inch video decks with two audio tracks usually have the audio dubbing feature on track one.

Very often cuts or partial cuts of stereo music, instead of entire music pieces, are recorded on videotape to add impact. These

FIGURE 3–30. The audio dub button makes it possible to record audio without changing the prerecorded video track.

cuts can be recorded directly from a turntable using an active mixer. The active mixer amplifies the low-level signal generated by the phono cartridge enough for it to be recorded through the Line IN jack on the VTR. Since turntables are usually connected to amplifiers of some sort, the music may also be recorded from the amp without using a mixer. If the amp has a Pre-amp OUT jack, that's the ideal place to feed the signal from. If not, you may have to rig something up to get the signal from the speaker connections.

The *voice over* method is applicable whenever lip sync is either unimportant or too difficult to do easily. Voice-over can be accomplished two ways. If your video deck has two audio tracks, you may wish to lay the music down on one track of the video deck. Then you can go back to record narration on the other track, while watching the video playback and listening to the music on headphones. If your video deck has only one audio track, then you have to use a mixer. One channel of the mixer is devoted to music, and the other to the microphone. The music and narration have to be recorded simultaneously. If you make a mistake in the reading, or fade the music at the wrong time, you have to do the whole thing over again. This second method takes a little practice, but you can do a good job after a few test runs.

### Tape Recorders

If your stereo tape recorder can record on one track while playing back on another, you can record the music on one track and then listen to the playback of the music while reading the narration on the other track. Then both tracks can be transferred to the video deck using a Y cord or, better yet, a mixer.

More often than not, however, the available tape recorder has only one track (monaural), or, if it is stereo, it cannot play back on one track while recording on the other. In such a case, you have an alternative. Find a quiet place (maybe late at night in your own living room) and play music on your stereo while reading into the microphone of the tape recorder. You can fade the music down with the volume control on the stereo. Actually this method can also be used to record music and voice directly onto the videotape. Of course, if a plane flies by or a garbage truck pulls up in the alley, the recording has to be done over again.

## PA Systems

If you record a lot of footage of bands, you should know a little more about how to use the PA system as another audio source. First of all, the band members probably know a lot more about how you should hook into their system than you do. They are also likely to know the idiosyncracies of their equipment (there are always some), and how to side-step potential problems.

Usually the hookup is at the mixer. Since all the band's instruments and voices are necessary for the performance, often the only hookup necessary is from the Aux OUT, Line OUT, or Master OUT on the mixer. If, for some reason, some of the instruments or voices are not amplified through the band's PA system, they have to be miked separately. In other words, the line from the band's mixer is run into one channel of a second mixed and then into the VTR. Anything not amplified through the band's PA system is run into the second channel of the second mixer, then into the VTR, and so on. Since band mixers are usually fairly elaborate and flexible, the need for separate miking is really not very likely, but in the event of a malfunction in the band's system or some other untoward event, it may come about. What is more likely is that the band's mix doesn't seem right on the video tape—not enough bass or maybe an instrument doesn't seem loud enough. If there is time, make a few test recordings so that the playback sounds right.

## Audiovisual (AV) Equipment

Several other pieces of audiovisual equipment get involved in the audio-in-video area:

1. motion picture projectors,
2. filmstrip projectors, and
3. slide-tape projectors.

*Motion Picture Projectors.* Motion picture projectors—8 mm, Super-8, and 16 mm—are sometimes the source of both audio and video information. Sometimes the image is projected, while the audio and film images are transferred to video simultaneously. (The various ways to go about this transfer are fully described in Chapter 7, "Putting Your Slides and Film on Videotape.") With motion picture film, you have to use the projector unless you have some kind of sophisticated film editing device with a sound reader. Basically, when transferring sound from a motion picture, you're stuck with the projector sound system. Since most motion picture projectors play back sound of limited fidelity—especially if the film is old or damaged—the audio transfer is not always of high quality.

Whether you want just the audio portion or the audio and visual portion of the film in the transfer, the procedure is the same. Somewhere on the projector is one of the following jacks: Speaker OUT or just Speaker, Headsets or Earphones, Line OUT or Line, or Audio OUT or Audio. Since all these signals are most probably amplified, remember to turn down the volume level on the projector and the audio record level on the VTR. Then, when you've connected the projector jack to the VTR's Line IN or Audio IN, put the VTR in record/pause, and turn on the projector. While you watch the audio record level meter on the VTR, slightly increase the volume on the projector and the record level on the VTR. When the audio record level meter begins to dance near the red zone, the level is high enough. Record a short segment on the videotape and play it back to make sure everything sounds right. Usually, if the volume on the projector and the record level on the VTR do not have to be turned up more than half way, the recording will sound good.

*Filmstrip Projectors.* Filmstrip projectors fall into two categories: Some play back sound from a record, and others play back from an audio casette. In both cases the procedure for transferring the sound track is the same as for motion picture projectors.

*Slide-Tape Program Projectors.* Slide-tape projectors are almost the same as film-strip projectors, except that slides are used instead of filmstrips. In the case of either, the sound medium—whether record or tape—is separate from the visual medium—filmstrip or slide. This separation makes the transfer of audio to video a lot easier, because you don't necessarily have to use the projector to play back the audio track. If the audio track is on a filmstrip-projector record, it can be played back on a turntable for transfer to video. If it's a cassette, it can be played back on a cassette player. Since the turntable or cassette player may be of higher quality than the playback electronics in the projector, the quality of sound in the transfer may be vastly improved.

**MIXERS**

Whatever type of microphone and accessories you use, you occasionally have to record with more than one microphone or from more than one source. Such situations call for a *mixer,* which combines two or more signals into one or more signals (Figure 3-31). There are two types of mixers: passive and active.

FIGURE 3–31. A mixer is used to combine two or more signals into one or more signals.

Mixer

Signal 1 — In → [ ⊙⊙⊙⊙ ⊙ ⫶ ] — Out → Signal 4
Signal 2 — In →
Signal 3 — In → — Out → Signal 5

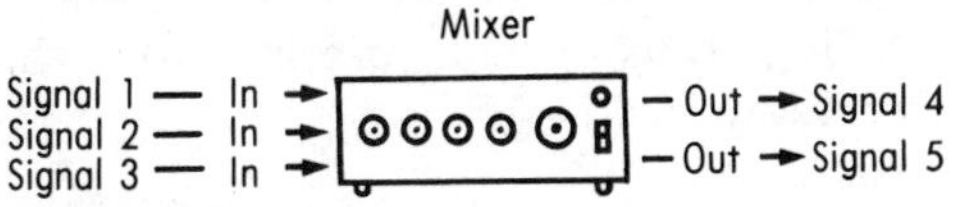

### PASSIVE MIXER

The passive mixer is just a junction box with hookups and ports for several microphones or other inputs. It acts simply as a volume control to adjust the levels of the signals sent through it. Being "passive," it doesn't act on the signal in any way. In other words, it doesn't have any built-in electronics to strengthen or to condition the signal. So some signal loss always occurs in a passive mixer. Passive mixers are just fine for limited applications, and they are very inexpensive.

### ACTIVE MIXERS

Active mixers "act on" the signal. Although they can be small and inexpensive, the most inexpensive ones simply compensate for any signal loss by amplifying the signal to a preset level. The most expensive ones are incredibly complex and capable of a great deal of sound "sweetening." Besides controlling levels, they offer equalization controls for boosting or cutting various frequencies to obtain the precise tonal qualities desired. They may also feature compressors, limiters, expanders, reverb, or echo.

Usually all you need is a small transistorized active mixer, which typically has four to six switchable inputs. The inputs may be switched from mike level to line level, or from mike level to phono level. In other words, the mixer can accept weak signals like those from microphones and phono-cartridges, as well as strong signals like those from the pre-amp or amplifier section of stereos and motion picture projectors.

### MIXER POWER

Small active mixers may be AC, DC, or switchable between AC and DC. The best choice, switchable, is also the most expensive. The DC battery-operated type is the best for field use, since access to AC power is often a problem in the field.

**EDITING AUDIO TAPE**

The only way to get precise and accurate timing in an auto track is to edit the audio tape. Audio editing consists of physically cutting the audio tape and then adding or subtracting sections of it to get what you desire. Since the editing is done with an audio tape recorder, the type of recorder you use has a great effect on the ease with which the editing is accomplished. The recorder has to handle 1/4-inch tape and have several playback speeds. Also, a tape recorder without a tape counter is of no use in editing; it's essential to know where you are on the tape. Unfortunately, the ones that are the easiest to work with are also the most expensive.

Editing starts with rewinding the audio tape and setting the tape counter on the recorder to zero. Then put the tape recorder in play and start listening to the tape. At any point where an addition on deletion is to be made, note the counter number on a piece of paper. This notation makes it easy to find the approximate edit points later. Then rewind the tape to the first number you've noted. This becomes the first edit point.

Let's say, for the sake of an easy edit, that there was a two-second pause. You started to say something, mispronounced a word, left a pause, and said it again correctly. So all you're interested in doing is pulling out the phrase with the mispronounced word. You can do so with just about any average-to-good tape recorder. You just have to locate a point on the tape in the pause preceding the mistake and in the pause after the mistake, and physically remove the section of tape in between from the recording. Here's how you do it. Since the play head plays back the audio information, you must: (1) locate the play head on the tape recorder, (2) stop the tape in the pause mode, (3) mark the tape at the play head, and (4) make the actual cut.

1. How do you locate the play head? Well, you have to look at the tape recorder's heads. Sometimes there's a plastic or metal plate over the head assembly, held in place by one or two screws. Remove the screws so you can take off the plate for a closer look at the heads. With the plate removed, you'll see one, two, or three heads.

How many heads do you see? No matter how many heads you see, the play head is always the one farthest to the right. From left to right, the order is erase, record, and play. If you like mnemonic devices, try "ERP"—erase, record, play! Or perhaps you prefer something a little more genteel: Always remember to make the *right* decision. If only one, all three are in one assembly. If so, you should probably consider using another tape recorder since tape recorders with this type of head assembly usually aren't very high in quality. If you see two, the erase is on the left, and record and play are on the right. If there are three, each head is separate: Erase is on the left, record is in the middle, and play is on the right.

2. Now play the tape until you hear the pause just before the mistake you made.

Stop the tape on this pause. If the tape recorder has a pause control on it, use it to stop the tape in the pause between the sentence with the mistake and the prior sentence.

3. Using a grease marker, mark the tape at the play head. Always mark the tape on the side facing away from the head. You can do so in two ways: Some people prefer to mark the tape while it is still resting against the play head (Figure 3-32). Others prefer to mark the tape by grabbing it at the spot between the thumb and first finger, pulling the tape away from the head, and placing it on something flat. Then they mark the tape where their fingers were rather than pressing the grease pencil against the tape and play head. People who use their fingers sometimes skip the grease pencil all together. They just place the tape on the editing block and cut it where their fingers were holding it, rather than marking it at all. This method works for all but the most precise edits, which have to be marked.

FIGURE 3–32a. Locate and mark the edit point at the play head.

FIGURE 3–32b. Cut the tape at a 45 degree angle using an editing block.

FIGURE 3–32c. Butt the ends of the edited recording tape together on the editing block and tape them with about 1 inch of special editing adhesive tape.

4. Once the first edit point is located, the tape has to be cut. This is done using an editing block and a razor blade. The editing block holds the tape in position and has a groove for the razor blade to follow for a precise 45-degree cut (Figure 3-32b). Then put the tape recorder in play mode again. Depending on the motor arrangement of the tape recorder, you may have to pull the cut end of the tape slowly past the tape recorder's heads to find the next edit point. When located, it has to be cut exactly like the first edit point.

Remove the piece of tape with the two cut ends and put it aside. The ends of the tape on the recorder are then butted together on the editing block and taped with about one inch of adhesive editing tape (Figure 3-32c). Make sure the editing tape is parallel to the edges of the recording tape and does not overlap the edges. If it does, trim it off.

Now rewind the tape a few inches and listen to the edit. There should be no audible pops or physical tape bounce at the edit. If there is, you did something wrong, and you'll have to redo the edit—probably just a better job of butting the ends together or taping. If unwanted audio is still at the edit—maybe you cut off too much of the following tape and cut into the next sen-

tence—you have to make another edit. But if you're reasonably careful, this sort of error won't happen again.

If possible, use a tape recorder that records at 15 ips (inches per second), for two reasons. First, since the tape is moving past the heads faster, the quality is improved. Second, the editing is made easier. A 15-ips tape has physically more space between words and phrases than a tape recorded at a lower speed. Consequently, finding the edit point and cutting the tape are much easier.

Also, if possible, use a tape recorder with a pause/play feature, which enables you to stop the tape in play mode. The tape doesn't move but the machine is in play mode. So you can manually move the tape back and forth past the play head until the exact edit point is located by listening to the slowed down sound coming through the speakers or headphones (Figure 3-33). Since most tape recorders do not have this feature, searching for an edit point is hit and miss. You have to rewind the tape, play, stop; rewind, play, stop; and so on ad nauseum. Even then, if you're doing fine editing, you won't be 100-percent sure if you have found the precise point. On a more encouraging note, most editing does not have to be so exact.

FIGURE 3-33. A tape recorder with a pause/play feature makes it easier to locate edit points by listening to the slowed-down sound from speakers or headphones, while manually moving the tape back and forth past the play head.

FIGURE 3–34. Music libraries are usually available in both record album and reel-to-reel tape formats. (Photo courtesy of Soper Sound Music Library)

## MUSIC AND MUSIC LIBRARIES

Editing narration is one thing. Editing music is another. First of all, most music is protected by copyright so it's illegal to use someone else's. But you can buy the right to use music or other types of sound effects from music libraries, which are usually offered on records and reel-to-reel tapes (Figure 3-34). Charges and agreements vary. Sometimes there is a charge "per needle-drop"—each time the cartridge's needle is brought into contact with the record album, you are charged a fee. This can quickly become very expensive. Frequently, a charge is fixed either for the entire production or for unlimited use over a fixed period, usually a year. The problem with most record libraries is that much of the music in them seems to be overly uniform and often terribly uninspiring. With a "concerted" search, however, you can usually locate a library that's right for your needs.

The Soper Sound Music Library is particularly good. Unlike many other libraries, which are produced outside of the United States and have a disconcertingly foreign flavor, the Soper Library consists of contemporary American music produced entirely in this country. And it is varied enough in style and in the length of cuts to work well in all types of video productions from full-length programs to television commercials. The best part, as far as the video producer is concerned, is that the entire library is available for one-time purchase with unlimited use. No needle drops, royalty fees, or paper work to deal with. The music library is by far, the fastest and most inexpensive way to obtain music.

In the event that no music library works for your production, or works for only part of it, you have to hire musicians to create original music for you. Sometimes aspiring musicians or musical groups let you record their music in return for exposure, a small fee, or both. The advantage to this option is that they can help you with style decisions, timing, and recording. The disadvantage is that sometimes, if they haven't had a lot of experience, it takes an enormous amount of time to get musical selections recorded, and, even then, the quality may be marginal. Doing a good job of music timing, mixing, editing, and dubbing takes sophisticated equipment and experience. You can, however, get surprisingly good results using the techniques discussed earlier.

To synchronize the audio track on a tape recorder to slides or filmstrips for transfer to videotape, you need a stereo or four-track tape recorder with separate record and play controls on each track. (Synchronization is discussed fully in Chapter 7, "Putting Your Slides and Film on Videotape.") One track is used for music, narration, or both. The other track is used to encode an advance signal for slides or filmstrips. A dissolve unit, slide programmer, or any other control device can be used to "read" the encoded advance signal, and to run the projection devices so that sound and visuals are in sync.

This is the usual procedure, which is done to save time in the transfer to video. With this approach, you can do much of the work involved in inexpensive television ads or PSAs before going to the television studio. If video camera moves are to be done on certain slides in the visual sequence to be transferred, it's best to transfer the entire visual sequence first and then insert edit the moves. This approach saves everyone a lot of money.

On the other hand, if audio and video are recorded separately, and if you don't use some sort of synchronizing device to keep the audio and video tracks in step with each other, your timing will be off. Several different methods are used to conform the audio track to the video track or vice versa, that is, to conform the video track to the audio track.

## CONFORMING AUDIO AND VIDEO

Let's start with conforming the audio track to the video track. Suppose the video track starts out as animation on Super-8 film. Once the film is shot, all the scenes are transferred to video using the rear-screen method (discussed in Chapter 7), and editing is done on a video editing system. (The reason for editing on videotape is clear to anyone who does much editing with Super-8. Handling Super-8 film is difficult due to its size, and edits almost always "flash" as they pass through the film gate of the projector.)

Once the film is transferred and edited on videotape, the big problem is getting the narration and sound effects timed exactly to the visuals. First transfer part of a SMPTE film leader to the videotape just before the film sequence. (A SMPTE film leader is the reverse number sequence, you see just before a film begins: "5 . . . 4 . . . 3 . . . 2 . . . Beginning!") Use the SMPTE film leader as a starting point from which to time your narration and effects, using a stop watch. For example, a scene starts with a little toy car pulling up to a stop sign. Roll the videotape, and start your stop watch at ". . . 2 . . ." on the SMPTE leader. The car pulls up to the sign in about five seconds. So you know that the sound of an auto pulling to a halt has to be five seconds into the audio track to match the video.

This approach is very time-consuming. When we once had to conform the audio to the video for a thirty-second spot, it took about six hours. The sound effects were recorded on one track of an audio tape and precisely edited, the narrator recorded the narration on another track as he watched the video and listened to the pre-recorded sound effects. By using a second audio track, the narration could be redone several times without affecting the completed sound effects track. Then effects and narration were combined onto one track and transferred to video. Usually audio and video do not have to be conformed so "tightly." But if a lot of effects are used and timing is crucial, believe it or not, this is the only inexpensive way to do it.

Conforming video to audio is done by first recording the audio track on videotape. Then the video sequences are selected and recorded using a video editing system. Fortunately, most video editing systems have built-in digital timers and pre-roll devices that make very accurate timing a breeze. However, many video ¾-inch helical scan systems guarantee accuracy of only plus or minus four video frames. So the video edit may take place as much as one-seventh of a second from where it should—a discrepancy that can sometimes be troublesome. Again, the question is how accurate does everything have to be?

A bigger problem than the timing, when conforming video to audio, is a lack of enough appropriate video for a given audio sequence. For instance, if the audio is a long passage of flowing, melodic, classical music, and the only video available is a series of quick cuts, it may be impossible to do a good job of conforming the two. If the pre-planning was done correctly, this shouldn't happen.

Practically speaking, the audio equipment associated with a single-camera video production system doesn't have to be very expensive to offer the flexibility necessary for most audio work. Much of the basic equipment needed is usually part of the home stereo system. A basic set-up consists of an amplifier, speakers, turntable, cassette deck, open reel tape recorder (with the features already mentioned), a small mixer, and several microphones. A graphic equalizer is also very nice to have, but not necessary.

In Figure 3-35 the amplifier and mixer are the keys to the audio system. The audio OUT of the playback VTR is run to two of the four inputs on the mixer, whose inputs are switchable. Two of them switch between mike and line, and two between mike and phono. Channels one and two of the video playback deck are hooked to two of the four mixer inputs switched to line. Since the mixer can be switched to stereo or mono output, other inputs, such as mikes, can be hooked into it if only one audio track on the VTR has audio on it. The mixer itself is hooked to the auxiliary IN on the amplifier.

Good amps have two special features that make them especially useful. Besides inputs for the turntable, turner, and mixer (Aux IN), they have inputs and outputs for two tape units. In this case, one of the tape units can be an audio cassette recorder, and the other the editing VTR. The other important feature is the amp's internal switching capability for dubbing and monitoring. The dubbing switch lets you record from an audio cassette deck to a video editing deck, or from a video editing deck to an audio cassette deck. It also allows you to record from any other inputs to the audio cassette deck or video editing deck—such as from phono to the audio cassette or from phono to the video editing deck. This capability, by eliminating the need to patch one piece of equipment to another, is a real time saver. It also saves money that would otherwise have to be spent on a larger mixer. The monitor switch on the amp makes it possible to listen to what is being recorded or to listen to something else while the recording is being done. Very nice for killing time while doing certain types of dubs.

Both the audio cassette recorder and the turntable should have what is called *variable pitch control* or *variable speed adjustment*. This useful feature enables you to slightly change the speed of the playback on both. If, for example, an audio track is being recorded "over" (in sync) with a pre-recorded video track, and the audio is "getting slightly ahead" of the video, you can, using the variable pitch control, slow the audio down to match the video. This is especially helpful when the audio track was "matched" to the video track on another audio recorder. Very often, audio recorders run at slightly different speeds from one another. So it helps

FIGURE 3–35. A practical audio system.

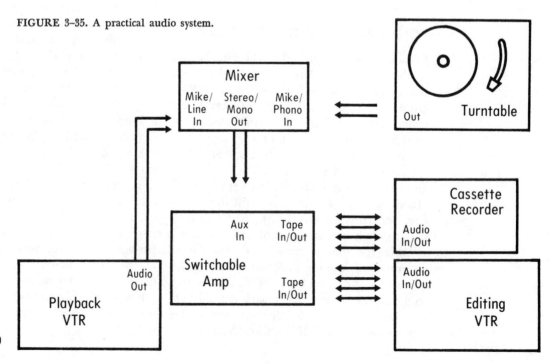

to be able to slightly compensate for these speed differences, by speeding up or slowing down playback speed. The only problem is that speeding up or slowing down the audio track very much perceptibly changes its tone.

The equalizer is normally patched between the play and record decks in an audio system. If the audio from a pre-recorded video cassette, or from some other source, has an undesirable tonal "flavor"—is too "bassy," too "tinny," or sibilant—the equalizer can be used to accentuate or to cut certain bands of frequencies until just the right tone is produced.

## SUMMARY

The mastery of audio in video production depends, to some extent, on the nature of the equipment available. It's somewhat frustrating to attempt producing a flawless, complex audio track without the necessary basic equipment. But a willingness to try things out is probably even more important than the equipment. Many times, you can do a more-than-adequate job with just the built-in mike, or with the built-in mike, a second mike, and a small battery-operated mixer.

The key is to get as much experience as possible with the equipment available. Then, when you're sure that the problems are really due to equipment deficiencies and not just a lack of experience, start thinking about more equipment.

Audio is a very interesting and rewarding part of video production. A little enthusiasm and inventiveness in audio production add depth, dimension, and effervescence to your entire video presentation.

# 4
# 4
# 4
# 4
# 4
# 4
# 4 LIGHTING

Of the objections raised to the appearance of the electronic image, the "harsh" or austere look of video seems to draw the greatest criticism. Many people mistakenly believe that "harshness" is an inescapable reality of video production, and that, to avoid it, the only alternative is to produce in the film medium. This belief not only demonstrates a specious kind of reasoning, but it is also a prime example of "medium bigotry."

Video happens to be faster to produce than film. So it tends to be used in situations where producers have to "get something on tape," particularly in ENG production. These situations normally don't permit enough time to pay proper attention to lighting, and so lighting takes a back seat to expedience. The apparent harshness of video is therefore caused by poor lighting rather than by some vague inherent flaw of the medium. Shot under expedient circumstances, film would suffer as much as tape does.

This is not to say, however that video can be made to look exactly like film. If necessary, with good equipment and careful lighting, a "film look" can be approximated. But since both media are generated differently, they will never look exactly the same. Newer video cameras, which can handle a greater range of contrast and lower light levels, are making it increasingly easier to capture nuances of lighting thought to be the exclusive domain of film. Film, however, still has many advantages, and will continue to be a very viable medium of production for years to come.

## LIGHT MEASUREMENT

The most vital concern in lighting for video is providing the correct amount of light for the equipment to function properly. The amount of light necessary to get a well-defined image with properly rendered colors is technically referred to as *base light*. Base light can also be considered to be the total amount of light from all sources falling on the important areas of a scene, measured in footcandles on the scale of a footcandle meter (Figure 4-1). The minimum number of footcandles necessary for a given camera to produce a good electronic image is usually printed in the operating instructions of the owner's manual. To determine whether you have the specified base light, aim the footcandle meter at the primary light source, and take a reading from the subject's position (Figure 4-2).

FIGURE 4–1. A footcandle meter for measuring the amount of light present.

FIGURE 4–2. To take a reading, the footcandle meter is aimed at the primary light source from the subject's position.

In video, as in film, the correct "exposure" to light is very important. While the correct exposure of film is determined by a photo-chemical process, in video it is determined electronically. "Overexposure," or recording at too high a video level, causes grave electronic problems and, ultimately, damage to the camera's tubes. "Underexposure," or recording at a video level slightly less than 100 percent does not cause significant problems but looks muddy. The best procedure is therefore to record at the proper level.

The correct "exposure" in video can be accomplished in several ways. The best and most accurate way is to use a *waveform monitor,* which continuously displays information about the electronic signal coming from the camera. Part of this information is the level of the signal, which must be kept nearly 100-percent (represented by a certain line on the waveform monitor's screen). If too much light is present, the signal level is too high and the camera lens has to be adjusted to a smaller opening so that less light strikes the tube. If too little light is present, the level of the signal is too low, and the iris has to be opened so that more light strikes the camera's tube until the correct level is reached. This procedure is analogous to setting the f-stop to maintain the correct exposure in film.

While using a waveform monitor is the most accurate way to insure that the correct amount of light is getting to the video system's electronics, there are other ways. Most less expensive portable single-camera systems have either automatic iris controls, video gain controls, or both. Without getting into a technical description, the easiest way to describe these controls is to say that they automatically compensate for differences in lighting conditions. They are not as accurate as using a waveform monitor, and they can be fooled by unusual lighting conditions such as excessive back light, but they are adequate for most purposes.

## INSUFFICIENT LIGHT

Usually the problem in video is insufficient light. Although, the newer, more expensive single-camera systems are able in many cases to record a "clean" video signal in available light, the less expensive equipment, though improving all the time, needs more light. Within the "less-expensive" category, black-and-white video equipment generally requires fewer footcandles of light than color equipment, because the black-and-white video signal does not have a "chroma" component and therefore displays less noise at lower light levels. Also there are no filters, mirrors, or prisms between the lens and the pickup tube to cut down the transmitted light as there are in color cameras. Although individual pieces of equipment vary, black-and-white probably needs at least 10 to 100 footcandles, and color equipment a minimum of 75 to 300 footcandles. Also, newer equipment of all types usually requires less light than older equipment.

The design of the camera is such that a specific minimum level of light is necessary to reproduce color and detail well. So if you do not have enough light for a satisfactory image, a number of difficulties arise. First, the image becomes very "grainy," that is, its resolution is relatively poor. This condition, known as excessive "noise," comes about because the amplifiers in the camera are trying to boost a weak signal coming from the pick-up tubes. The inherent noise in the amplifiers' design is also boosted, resulting in poor picture quality. For much the same reason, colors lack crispness and clarity, and they appear "muddy"—some colors more than others. In low light, the video image also lacks "depth" and appears very "flat." Light differences account for what we perceive as depth and dimension. If not much light is available, there is little room for light differences, and hence very little depth and dimension. In addition to a degraded image, the video camera's lens has to be operated with the iris opened to maximum aperture, to allow as much light into the camera as possible. This condition causes a marked decrease in depth of field, making it more difficult to keep the camera in focus while following action. In a dark enough room, we have similar problems with our eyes. But video cameras are not nearly as sensitive as our eyes, and so they need much more light to do the same things, but even less efficiently.

## EXCESSIVE LIGHT

Excessive light can also be a problem. If too much light is present, the camera's iris has to be "stopped down" to one of its smallest openings, which results in maximum depth of field. In other words, everything from a few feet in front of the camera to infinity is in crisp focus. This effect is great if there is nothing distracting in the background, but there often is. In fact, crisp focus to infinity is also great for doing camera moves and for following action, but it contributes to the feeling of "harshness" that many people object to in the video image. To "drop focus" on the background, you have to use neutral-density filters over the lens. Neutral-density filters do not affect color balance, but they do cut down on the amount of light allowed into the camera. If such filters are not available, telephoto lenses can be used to create "limited" depth of field. Many newer portable cameras are equipped with built-in neutral-density filters, which can be dialed into place with color-correction filters. Some cameras, such as the JVC 1900, have extra "blank" positions on the filter wheel for installing neutral density, color, or special effects filters of your choice.

Reflections and specular light, which are side effects of excessive light, are also exceedingly troublesome in some circumstances. The glare from windows, from the chrome of passing cars, or from other reflective surfaces can cause the camera's automatic iris control to compensate for the sudden rise in light level by suddenly darkening the entire image. This effect can be very irksome if it happens right in the middle of getting some award-winning footage.

If the sudden rise in level is not enough to cause the iris to fluctuate significantly, it most likely causes "ghosting"—or "smearing," "lag," "afterimage," or "comet-tailing," as it is variously called. Whatever you call it, it is characterized by bright ghosts or paths appearing in the wake of moving people or objects. It can also occur as something passes through the scene reflecting light brightly, or by simply moving the camera across such an object that is standing still in the scene. This problem is especially prevalent with single-tube and Vidicon cameras, but even happens occasionally with the more expensive cameras.

## EXCESSIVE CONTRAST

Contrast, which is the presence of low and high light levels in the same scene, also presents problems. The human eye can handle a greater range of contrast than any other medium yet devised. In this context, "handling" is intended to mean being able to perceive detail in very bright and very dark areas of the same scene at the same time. In video, you can "handle" only a relatively narrow range. In other words, the brightest and the darkest parts of a scene cannot be too far apart in brightness value, or you have to sacrifice detail in one part or the other. In video the best equipment can reproduce a contrast range of about 20:1. In other words, the brightest area of a scene should not be more than twenty times brighter than the darkest, or roughly four f-stops from bright to dark. Most of the less-expensive video cameras aren't even able to handle four f-stops.

Basically, three types of contrast can cause problems:

1. *Subject contrast* is contrast that is part of or within the subject, such as a woman wearing a bleached-white blouse and a black skirt.
2. *Subject-to-subject contrast* is contrast between subjects such as an actor standing in the shade in dark clothing speaking to another actor standing in the sun in a light-colored summer suit. The subjects don't have to be people; they can be objects as well.
3. *Subject-to-nonsubject contrast* is the brightness difference between the subject and anything else, such as a light yellow car against a black backdrop.

If any of these types of contrast has excessive ranges, the video image either "burns out" in the bright areas or "blacks out" in the dark areas. "Burn-out" causes the most problems: If the proper video level is exceeded in all or any part of a scene, the camera's tube can be damaged, or, at the very least, the video image has a totally burned-out area with no detail.

The optimum contrast range is found in scenes with no more than 60 percent white reflectance and no less than 3 percent black reflectance. Notice that the ratio of 60 percent to 3 percent is 20:1. Whites that reflect no more than 60 percent of the light striking them look more like gray, and blacks reflecting more than 3 percent of the light striking them don't look totally black. But since they are the values best reproduced by the video medium, they are called "television white" and "television black." If there is one thing you should remember about contrast, it's to tell people not to wear anything white or black or their equivalents—especially if there is no easy way to control the light they will be working in, and if inexpensive video gear will be used.

## COLOR BALANCE

Besides having the right amount of light and a reasonable contrast range, you also need light of the correct "color temperature" or "color balance." Color temperature is a measure of the proportional amounts, or balance, of the primary colors—red, green, and blue—in the light source. It is measured in Kelvin degrees.

There is nothing mysterious about color temperature. You can best understand it by closely examining the "color" of light in certain conditions. Outside light tends to be blue during the day, and orange or reddish at sunrise and sundown. Inside light from incandescent bulbs tends toward brownish orange. From fluorescent fixtures, light tends to be green. If you examine different types of light very closely, it's easy to see what color it really is.

Because white light seems to be different colors under different conditions, people in the video business had to decide which "white" would be considered white. Since light with a color temperature rating of 3,200 degrees Kelvin (written 3,200 K) renders flesh tones most flatteringly, it was chosen as a standard for television. Other

colors are divided into "warm" and "cold" categories. Warm colors include any colors of fire and earth-like red, orange, yellow, brown, beige, and the like. Warm colors may not be technically correct, but they tend to flatter flesh tones. Cold colors—green, purple, blue, and so on—appear cold, unappealing, or alien as flesh tones.

Thankfully, most portable color video cameras can be adjusted for color temperature differences in two ways: by color-correction filters and by white balance.

The built-in color-correction filters provide a rough adjustment for prevailing lighting conditions. Some cameras have Kelvin degree readings from low to high. Others simply have filters for "Outdoors," "Indoors," "Cloudy," and so on. "Indoors" would equate to 3,200 K, "Outdoors" to approximately 5,500 K, and so on. These adjustments, however, are all approximate.

Once they are set, the fine tuning comes with the adjustment of the white balance. Adjusting the white balance tells the camera's electronics what "white" is. Once the camera knows what white is, it can figure out what "color" all other colors should be. This very useful adjustment enables you to get "balanced" color under widely varying lighting conditions. In this respect video has it all over film, since in film, different filters or film types must be used every time a different lighting condition is encountered. In video, you just dial in the appropriate filter, set the white balance, and shoot.

## STUDIO LIGHTING

Studio lighting differs dramatically from location lighting. Basically, lighting in the studio is much more controlled, and it can be manipulated much more easily than on location, because the studio normally contains a number of lighting units with specialized applications and accessories.

### LIGHTING GRID

Most of these specialized units are clamped onto a lighting grid, which is a criss-cross arrangement of pipes fastened to the ceiling. Each lighting unit can be moved around on the lighting grid to attain the desired lighting angle or effect.

### WIRING RUN

A "wiring run" parallel to the lighting grid has numbered outlets for each of the lighting units (Figure 4-3).

### PATCH PANEL

In theory, each numbered outlet on the wiring run corresponds to a number on a patch panel or breaker box, so that the lighting unit at the outlet can be turned on or off as desired (Figure 4-4). The larger the patch panel or breaker box, the better. Large panels or breaker boxes make it possible to plug in a greater number of units at one

FIGURE 4–3. The wiring run has numbered outlets for connecting lighting units to power.

FIGURE 4–4. The patch panel has numbers corresponding to the wiring run so that selected outlets on the wiring run can be turned off or on as desired.

time. They also let you run more than just a few lights at a time, and they don't necessitate your having to repatch the power supply everytime you move a light to a different position on the grid.

## FADER PANEL

With a patch panel you can attach a fader panel to the lighting grid, allowing selected lights to be faded for rehearsal or any other reason (Figure 4-5). Some fader panels are very large and have a great number of fader controls.

FIGURE 4–5. Fader panel.

## LIGHTING UNITS AND ACCESSORIES

For work in the studio, there are a number of commonly used lighting units designed to meet specific lighting needs. The four most common types are: the fresnel, the scoop, the cyc light, and the ellipsoidal spot.

## FRESNEL

The fresnel is probably the most widely used of all these devices (Figure 4-6). Inside it has a movable reflector, along with a glass fresnel lens that closes over the front of the unit (Figure 4-7). The knob on the

FIGURE 4–6. Fresnel lighting unit on a grid.

FIGURE 4–7. Inside a fresnel lighting unit.

outside of the fresnel, which is connected to the reflector inside, can be adjusted to throw a wide or a narrow beam of light (Figure 4-8).

FIGURE 4–8. Adjusting the beam spread of a fresnel lighting unit.

## SCOOP

The scoop, so-called because of its shape, is used as a floodlight to provide softer light to a wider area (Figure 4-9). Some scoops can be partially focused, but the beam width is not as "tight" as that of the fresnel.

FIGURE 4-9. A scoop.

## CYC LIGHTS

Cyc lights, short for cyclorama lights, are used to illuminate the cyclorama or background (Figure 4-10).

FIGURE 4–10. A cyc-lite.

## ELLIPSOIDAL SPOT

Ellipsoidal spotlights are often used to cast patterns on the cyclorama during dramatic presentations (Figure 4-11).

FIGURE 4–11. An ellipsoidal spot is frequently used to cast patterns on the background.

## ACCESSORIES

All the lighting units mentioned so far may be used with any one or a combination of the following accessories:

### Lamps

All modern lighting units use quartz iodine or tungsten halogen lamps, also called "quartz" lamps, which burn at a very high temperature (Figure 4-12). These lamps use a special type of incandescent bulb that is designed to put out a lot of light for a long period of time with consistent color balance.

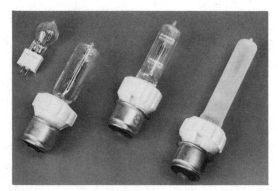

FIGURE 4–12. Tungsten-halogen lamps for lighting units.

## Barndoors

Fresnel units, as well as some others, accept detachable metal flaps called "barndoors" (Figure 4-13). Barndoors, which are a permanent part of some lighting units, may be mounted on the front of lighting units to prevent light from falling where it is not desired. Light leaks around barndoors may be blocked with aluminum foil if they are distracting.

FIGURE 4–13. Barndoors.

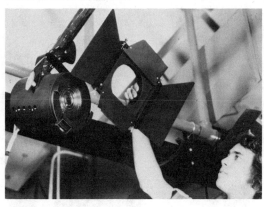

## Snoots

A "snoot" is sometimes put on the front of a fresnel so that the fresnel can throw a very "tight" spot of light (Figure 4-14).

FIGURE 4–14. A fresnel with a snoot on the front of it.

## Scrims

Scoops, fresnels, and other lighting units have holders on the front of them for scrims, diffusers, and gels. Scrims are used to cut down or to "attenuate" light in all or part of the area illuminated by a given lighting unit. Scrims, often made of metal screening material, may cover the entire beam of the light or only part of it, such as the lower half (Figure 4-15). If you want more attenuation, place additional layers of scrim material over the first. Scrims are especially helpful when the lighting system is not equipped with a fader panel. Without a fader, the lights are either full on or full off. With scrims, selected lights can be made less bright than others.

FIGURE 4–15. A scoop with a wire screen across the bottom half.

## Diffusers

Diffusers are theoretically used to diffuse light rather than to attenuate it (Figure 4-16). While diffusers like the one shown do soften light without cutting down its intensity to a great degree, anything placed in

FIGURE 4–16. A scoop with a spun glass diffuser.

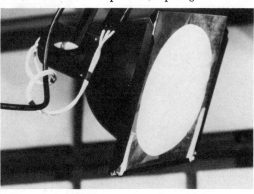

front of a light beam cuts its intensity to some degree. Large diffusers, such as silk stretched on a frame, are used in the studio or on location to diffuse light over large areas.

### Gels

Heat-resistant colored gels may be placed in front of lighting units to produce dramatic color effects. If the lighting unit does not have a gel holder, the gel material can simply be attached to the unit in front of the light beam with metal clamps or paper clips. But if the gel is close to the quartz lamp, be careful to watch the gel. It may, over a period of minutes, expand, bubble, or bend,

and touch the quartz lamp. This will at the very least, destroy the quartz lamp. It could start a gel "melt down" with the melted gel getting into the lighting fixture causing smoke and damage, and making it difficult to clean up the fixture.

### Patterns

Ellipsoidal spots are used to cast a great variety of patterns on the background or cyclorama. The shapes of the patterns are controlled by the designs stamped in a thin metal disc, which is placed in a slot near the condensing lens. A catalog of some of the patterns is available, free of charge, from The Great American Market (*see* Source Index).

FIGURE 4–17. Various pattern shapes available for projection on a background. (All designs Copyright by The Great American Market)

341 LEAF PATTERN    351 SAPPLINGS    337 NEBULA    353 FLAME

334 CAROUSEL    336 BALLOONS    335 CLOWN    344 G-CLEF

340 SEASON'S GREETINGS    339 BELLS    350 CHAMPAGNE    343 SKULL

338 INTERMISSION    345 VERTICAL BREAKUP    342 ARROW    352 COBWEB

346 FLASH!    347 BAM!    348 POW!    349 SIZZLE!

### Cookies

Cookies, made of wood or other materials, are also used to cast shadows (Figure 4-18). Since these patterns are used at a slight distance from the lighting unit, the pattern cast on the background or cyclorama is not as distinct or resolute as patterns cast by the focused light from ellipsoidal spots.

FIGURE 4–18. A cookie pattern made of wood.

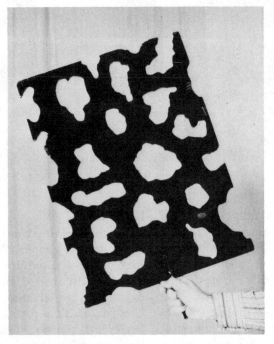

### Pantographs

Sometimes lighting units attached to the lighting grid are too high for the effect desired. When low-angle light is needed, lighting units may be lowered closer to the floor on flexible extenders called "pantographs," or placed on stands on the floor of the studio (Figure 4-19).

FIGURE 4–19. For low-angle light, lighting units may be placed on flexible extenders called pantographs or on floor stands.

### STUDIO LIGHTING TECHNIQUES

In the studio, lighting units are typically used in fairly standard ways to light a scene. This is not to say that there is some kind of hard and fast formula for lighting a scene, since there are probably as many exceptions to basic lighting rules as there are rules themselves. Each lighting unit, depending on its design, is likely to be used as:

1. key light,
2. fill light,
3. back light,
4. background light.

### Key Light

A key light—and there may have to be more than one to light large areas—is usually positioned in front of, higher than, and to one side of what is to be lighted (Figure 4-20).

FIGURE 4–20. A technician adjusts the key light.

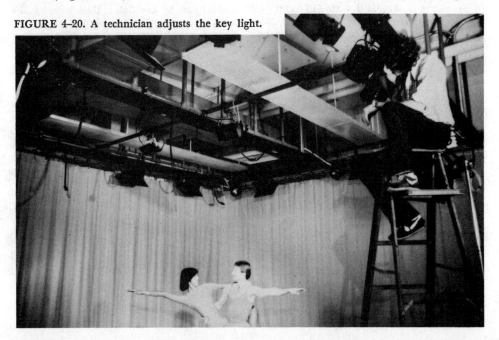

FIGURE 4–21. Key lights determine where shadows fall, creating the texture of the scene.

Since key lighting is usually focused or specular light, fresnel lighting units are most often used as key lights. The fresnel throws focused light creating dark shadows, which gives the impression of texture, depth, and dimension.

Key lights should be the brightest source of light falling on a scene. They are the most important lights since they determine where shadows will fall, thus setting the mood of the scene. Used alone, key lights produce a "contrasty" effect and dark shadows. Since dark shadows should usually be thrown in only one direction, key lights are usually placed on one side or the other of what is being lighted (Figure 4-21).

## Fill Light

Fill lights are frequently placed above and closer to the camera than key lights, but they may be placed anywhere that fill light is needed. In general, they lower the overall contrast range of the scene (Figure 4-22). Used alone, they produce a flat effect with fairly low contrast. Combined with other lighting units, they lower the contrast or fill in the shadows cast by the key lights or by other light sources.

Fill light is usually provided by scoops or by other "broad" light sources. Since light coming from scoops is soft and diffused, it does not cause deep shadows, and so it does not compete with the key light in the crea-

FIGURE 4–22. Fill lights "fill" shadows cast by key lights, thus lowering the overall contrast range of the scene and increasing detail in shadow areas.

FIGURE 4–23. Back light.

tion of texture, depth, and dimension. It just helps to reduce the contrast range of the scene to a point more easily handled by television equipment. It "fills" the dark shadow areas caused by the key. Since the fill light is frequently kept close to the camera, the soft shadows caused by the fill light are thrown to the rear of the subject, out of sight of the camera. So, although some fill shadows may be present, they usually aren't seen in the video image.

### Back Light
Back light is illumination from the rear of the subject (Figure 4-23). This light is used to produce highlights on hair, shoulders, or the top edges of subjects, giving the im-

pression of roundness and separating the subject from the background. For normal purposes, back light must be positioned high and behind the subject so that the camera lens doesn't pick up lens flare from the back light during a take. Sometimes lens flare is desirable, sometimes not. Expensive cameras handle lens flare much better than inexpensive cameras, which tend to comet tail or lag a great deal. Prolonged direct exposure to bright light can permanently damage the pick-up tubes in many video cameras.

### Background Light
Background or "set" light is used to illuminate the set or background (Figure 4-24). It brightens the background and controls

FIGURE 4–24. Background light.

shadows cast on the background by other lights. Background light is usually kept less intense than light on the foreground, so that it doesn't draw the viewer's attention away from the subject in the foreground.

### Four-Point Lighting
This sort of illumination, very simply, consists of a combination of the previous four types of lighting.

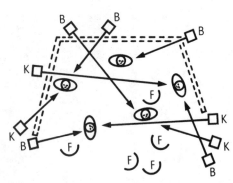

FIGURE 4–25. A lighting diagram of frequently used lighting arrangements cuts down set-up time.

## CONTROLLING LIGHT

With all the control offered by studio lighting, a number of things can be done in the studio that are very difficult, if not impossible, to do on location. For instance, to accommodate movement and action on the studio set, you may have to light several areas similarly with key, fill, back and background lights in each area. In that case, once the lighting has been arranged for a given studio set-up, make a lighting diagram to keep on file (Figure 4-25). The next time that same studio set-up is used, arranging the lights will take much less time.

As another example, a fresnel projecting a tight pool of light can be used in dramatic monologues or for other creative lighting purposes (Figure 4-26). Creating such an effect without the total control of the lighting conditions in the area would be very difficult indeed.

Along the same lines, controlling contrast in the studio is much easier than elsewhere. Take our example of subject contrast, the woman wearing a white blouse and a black skirt. In the studio the contrast range between the blouse and the skirt could be lessened by scrimming down the light falling on the blouse, and by lifting the intensity of the light falling on the skirt. Actually, she could just make things simple and change blouses, if another were available, but our solution shows what can be done. Or refer again to our example of subject-to-subject contrast, the actor standing in the shade in subdued clothing speaking to another actor standing in the sunlight in a light suit. If this scene took place in the studio, you would just keep the two simulated "outdoor" lighting conditions close enough together in

FIGURE 4–26. The studio offers tight control of lighting techniques.

brightness to avoid problems in the contrast range. The same holds for the light-colored car against a dark backdrop.

Sometimes it is a mistake to over-react to contrast differences. Often, the lighting differences work out rather well. If the darker areas go completely black in a scene, perhaps the scene is better for it or maybe it better fits the mood intended by the script. On the other hand, if the image suffers in quality due to the scene's excessive contrast range, then there's too much contrast in the scene.

## STUDIO LIGHTING PROBLEMS AND SOLUTIONS

Although lighting effects and contrast are much more easily handled in the studio than elsewhere, even the studio is not without its problems.

Once in a while the lamp in a lighting unit burns out. Because they burn so hot, lamps that have just burned out must be removed from the lighting unit with heavy gloves or with specially designed tongs (Figure 4-27). The alternative is to wait until the lamp cools down before removing it, but this is usually not really an alternative, because the lighting unit is needed.

FIGURE 4-27. Removing a lamp from a lighting unit with tongs.

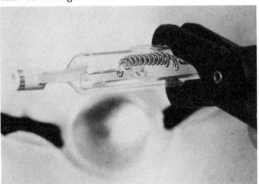

When putting in the new lamp, do not bring its bare surface in contact with your hand, since oil and dirt from your fingers can contaminate the lamp's surface and shorten its life. Avoid this problem by using the paper supplied with the lamp by the manufacturer. If you unintentionally touch the lamp's surface, wipe it thoroughly with alcohol and a clean cloth. Be sure also to double-check the lamp's wattage against the wattage that the unit is designed to handle: Do not use a lamp of greater wattage than

that listed on the unit (Figure 4-28). If you do, you risk heat build-up that can damage the lamp, the unit, and possibly even start a fire. Whenever changing lamps, check the lamp sockets, connections, and wiring for arcing, melting, discoloration, or any type of bad connection. It's not a bad idea to do this every few weeks.

FIGURE 4-28. Do not use a lamp of greater wattage than the rating of the lighting unit.

Along with the equipment, be aware of the effect of lighting on the performers. Some performers are bothered by the intensity of television lighting, especially if they are standing in intense light while everyone else is behind the cameras in semi-darkness. Usually if the house lights are turned on, the performers do not perceive the studio lights to be as bright. If the show is not live, fade the lights down during rest periods or rehearsals and then bring them up during takes. This practice makes it easier on the performers, saves energy, and increases lamp life.

Sometimes shiny objects or parts of objects that cannot be removed from the scene reflect light too intensely, causing comet tails or burned-out areas in the image. If so, cut down on the reflected light by using dulling spray. Use the nondrying type (Figure 4-29).

FIGURE 4-29. Dulling spray.

One of the most common problems on television is reflection from glasses. In this case, either position the light differently, move the subject slightly to one side or the other, or tip the glasses slightly forward with the bows resting higher up on the ear.

When using less expensive single-camera systems in the studio, caution performers **not** to wear anything white. Expensive cameras can usually handle white, but the less expensive ones may have problems with it.

## INDOOR LOCATION LIGHTING

How involved you get with location lighting seems to depend on the nature of your production. ENG (electronic news gathering) people usually have very little time to arrange adequate lighting since getting something on tape in time to make the news schedule takes precedence over everything else. Considering the time constraints they work under, the quality of their work is impressive. Commercials and full-length productions usually enjoy more flexibility in scheduling, so more time can be spent on lighting aesthetics.

### SCOUTING THE LOCATION

If time permits, pre-planning for a location shoot should begin with scouting the location. A few minutes on location tell you a lot about the prevailing conditions and about the type of accessories you will need to do a good job of lighting. You find out what sources of light are available, how much space you have to work in, and how much power is accessible. If working inside, are the light conditions mixed? If so, is there a predominant source of light? These questions are important to answer before planning the shoot.

### AVAILABLE POWER

Since most indoor locations do not have enough light, you have to figure out whether there is enough power available for portable lighting units. Most newer homes have 20-amp circuits for house lighting. Commercial buildings may or may not have circuits with more capacity. So if nothing else is being run on the circuit, you can plug about 2,000 watts of equipment into one household circuit—or, say, two 650-watt spots and maybe one broader source of light for fill, like a Lowel Softlite. Just remember that the lamp

wattage shouldn't exceed 2,000 watts. The reason for this is that some lighting units like the Lowel Softlite take two lamps. The lamps can be 500 or 750 watts each. Obviously, if the higher-wattage lamps were used in the Softlite, only one additional spot could be used for the total power not to exceed 2,000 watts.

Since it's always difficult to figure out whether the lighting units you plug in are on one circuit or several, and whether something else is running on the same circuit, you have to either trace the circuits, or just "try it and see."

The first method, tracing the circuits, is time-consuming. The easiest way to do it is to go to the service entry box and turn off all the 20-amp circuits but one. Don't bother turning off heavy-duty circuits like 30 amps and up because they usually have only one "load" or appliance on them, such as an electric range or dryer. The household wall outlets usually don't tie in with those circuits at all. Next, to find out which outlets are connected to the circuit you haven't turned off, take a small lamp and plug it into each outlet in the house. When the lamp lights, the outlet is on the circuit with power to it. You can find out if anything else is being run from the same circuit by trying light switches, and listening for running motors like the refrigerator. If anything else is on the circuit, it should be either turned off or figured in when deciding how much wattage the circuit can handle.

The second approach, "try it and see," takes much less time. When you're getting ready to shoot, you just plug everything in, turn it on, and see if the circuit breaker or fuse pops. This is not the safest thing to do and it is not recommended. Unfortunately, it's what most people do. If the service entry is old and takes fuses instead of circuit breakers, it's a good idea to have several extras around during the production in case one pops. Also, if you decide to just plug things in, it's a good idea to use extension cords to reach outlets in different parts of the house. With any luck, you'll plug into several different circuits and thus diminish the possibility of overloading one circuit. Spreading out the load is especially necessary when shooting in older houses, which may have circuits with a capacity of only 15 amps rather than 20.

## MIXED LIGHTING CONDITIONS

For indoor location lighting, what has to be done depends a great deal on the existing lighting conditions. Sometimes there is one type of light, sometimes others. Sometimes the conditions are mixed with light coming from fluorescent fixtures, windows, and unbalanced incandescent lights. Depending on the effect desired and on the time available to create the effect, location lighting may be a very simple task or relatively complex. If you don't have much time, and if there is one predominant source of lighting, and if the level of that source is good enough to record a clean signal, don't complicate the situation by trying to set up additional lighting.

Usually the predominant type of lighting is not of sufficient level. Even more frequently, you find a predominant source of light of one type, several less dominant types of another, and some window light—and all of them combined are not enough to record a good image. In such cases, if colors are to be accurate and if the image is to be of good resolution, you have to use location lighting equipment.

In mixed lighting conditions, the color or "color balance" varies from one source to another. For instance, unbalanced incandescent bulbs may have a Kelvin rating on the "warm" side, maybe around 2,500 K. They don't throw the balance off very much. Flesh tones take on a kind of tan, healthy look. But if the incandescents are also of low wattage, the tan, healthy look may begin to look brownish. The image color depends on the camera's ability to handle low light and to white balance in low light. Putting a couple of photo floods into existing lamps may be all you need. Since photo flood bulbs have a higher wattage rating than normal light bulbs, they throw more light, and they are color balanced so they put out the right color light (Figure 4-30).

FIGURE 4-30. Photoflood bulbs.

Since photo floods have high wattage ratings, usually starting at about 250 watts, you have to be careful not to overpower the fixture or singe anything nearby. You can use small clamp-on fixtures, which can be purchased in a hardware store or lumber yard and which are built to withstand higher wattages. Floods can be clamped to stands or doors and directed at specific areas. Sometimes they are all that is necessary (Figure 4-31).

FIGURE 4-31. A photoflood in a metal clamp-on fixture being used to light a relatively small area.

In other situations, when the camera's filter and white balance controls are not able to compensate for the color imbalance in the light sources, one type of light may have to be excluded and perhaps another added. For example, if you are trying to make a recording in a room illuminated mainly by fluorescent lights, but with a great deal of daylight coming in through large windows, you might find it difficult to get away from a "cold" look. Fluorescents tend toward green and daylight tends toward blue. Under these conditions, you might be wise to turn off the fluorescents, move the subject closer to the windows, use the outside filter, and white balance the camera in light coming from outside. If this solution doesn't work, maybe the opposite approach would. Pull the shades and try to adjust the camera for fluorescent light. If this doesn't work well enough, maybe "area lighting" will.

Area lighting is used as a fast substitute for more complex lighting arrangements. Basically it consists of setting up one or two 650- to 1,000-watt spots at about 45-degree angles from the subject and close enough to the subject to dominate the existing light. In the lighted area, the color balance and level of the light are adequate to get an image. In other areas, such as behind the subject, the color balance is not correct, and the light in most circumstances falls off in brightness. This approach may work well enough since the background should, in most cases, be less intensely illuminated than the foreground.

All the methods for location lighting indoors mentioned to this point have been fast ways of solving commonly encountered problems with a minimum of equipment. Yet since every situation varies, and since your approach depends to a large extent on how well the camera handles light, precise instructions for solving every lighting problem are impossible to give. When working with unknown quantities like existing light, there are a lot of exceptions to even the most basic lighting rules. So the best thing to do is to try several approaches and to work with the one that results in the desired effect. Generally, under mixed lighting conditions, it's usually best to adjust the filter and white balance controls for the predominant source of light, but try several different filters, because a filter other than the one recommended may give the best results.

## PORTABLE LIGHTING EQUIPMENT AND TECHNIQUES

If you have time, and if you seek the best possible quality and wish to leave nothing to chance, you can use portable lighting equipment and accessories to establish more control over indoor existing light conditions. With a wealth of portable lighting equipment available and an almost unlimited number of ways in which to use it, we will examine only the basic principles, equipment, and accessories. You should then know enough to solve just about any location lighting problem.

All portable lighting equipment is designed to control the quantity, quality, color, and direction of the light it produces.

## Quantity

The quantity of light from a piece of equipment depends on several factors: The first is its wattage: the more wattage, the more light. (It is always safe to use a lamp of lower wattage than the lighting unit is designed to handle, but it is never safe to overpower the unit by using a lamp of greater wattage than recommended.) Second, the transmission efficiency of the equipment depends on the type of reflector used and on whether the light can be focused. A highly polished reflector transmits more light than a dull or matte-surfaced reflector. The light from the two different reflectors also has a different "feel" or quality. The matte-surfaced reflector produces a slightly more diffused light. Some units, like spotlights, have even greater transmission efficiency since they have a condensing lens to focus and to concentrate the light.

## Quality

The *quality* of light, which refers to its "hardness" or "softness," has a great effect on the visual statement created. *Hard* light, also called *specular* light, is composed of focused, direct, parallel rays, which originate from a comparatively small or "point" light source (Figure 4-32). Such light has a hard, crisp quality with deep shadows, and it is often used as key light. *Soft* or diffuse light is produced by units with larger lamps and reflectors. Sometimes the light is "bounced" against the lamp's reflector so that no rays are sent directly to the subject. They are first broken up, scattered, and forced out of the parallel configuration, to produce a "soft"— that is a gentle and diffuse—quality with less intense shadows (Figure 4-33). Such lighting

FIGURE 4-32. A point light source.

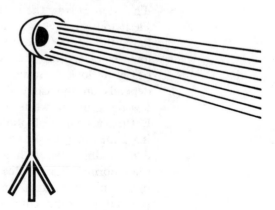

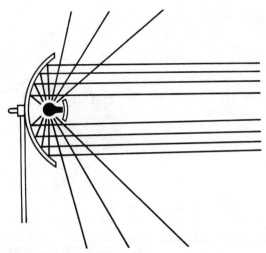

FIGURE 4–33. A diffuse light source.

units, very popular in the studio and on location, are usually used for fill light. If you do not have both types of gear, choose the spots, because diffusing material, scrims, or distance can be used to produce fill with spotlights. Hard light can also be softened or diffused by bouncing it from a light-colored ceiling or a reflector. Just make sure the ceiling or reflector doesn't get too hot. But conversely, it's not usually feasible to produce hard light with units designed primarily for fill.

### Color

The color of light can be controlled, as in the studio, by using gels over light sources. Gels are not very widely used in location work, but they could be. A gel with a pattern, projected on an otherwise bland background, is a quick way to "dress" a location. If you don't have an ellipsoidal spot, use either a cookie or a slide projector. The slide projector should have a wide projection lens to cover more area. A design on a Kodalith negative can serve as the "pattern." The gel can either be sandwiched in the slide mount with the Kodalith negative or taped over the front of the lens. With a number of patterns and gels, this system can provide variety and visual interest to the background without drawing attention away from the subject.

### Direction

In the studio, everything is designed for lighting in a certain direction, but on location such is rarely the case. In fact, the direction of light is sometimes very difficult to control on location, especially in cramped quarters. Accordingly, the direction of light

has to be manipulated in any way possible to make the image look "right."

*Barndoors and flags.* Several accessories help you to do so, the most common of which are barndoors, those adjustable metal flaps that fit onto the front of some types of lighting units. Barndoors are indispensable on location. "Flags," another type of light-control device that are so-called due to their shape, can be mounted on some types of equipment or clamped on stands (Figure 4-34). Some flags are very large, and most are used to block light from falling on parts of a scene or from getting into the camera's lens.

FIGURE 4–34. A small metal flag.

On location, for example, back light becomes a problem since frequently you just can't get the lighting unit high enough so that light from it doesn't shine directly into the camera's lens. To solve such a problem, put barndoors on the unit emitting the back light and a flag just above the camera's lens, out of the shot but providing shade for the lens. Some flags are made of cloth, while others are made of lightweight metal. Some metal flags are coated on one side to serve the dual purpose of flag and reflector.

### Reflectors

Reflectors are also very handy on location, inside or out. Some people think of a reflector as a monstrous square piece of shiny metal or board on a stand. While this type of reflector has very definite applications outdoors, it is rarely used indoors. Indoors, a reflector can be just about anything white. Large pieces of white artboard have a myriad of uses—everything from cue cards to reflectors—and they should be part of the standard location lighting kit. They can be used either to reflect light or to block it like a flag. They can be bent, taped to a wall or ceiling for "bouncing" light, or cut into smaller pieces for reflecting light into small recesses like those on indented patch panels or switchboards. (Of course, this can also be done with pieces of white writing paper, which are also reflectors.) Reflectors are great for providing almost shadow-free fill light for any purpose.

## OTHER HARDWARE

Many handy pieces of accessory hardware are available with better sets of lighting units to make location lighting a lot easier, especially when there is not much floor space:

1. Specially designed clamps can be used to fasten lightweight lighting units to doors, door jambs, or chairs (Figure 4-35).

FIGURE 4–35. A special clamp holding a Lowel Tota-Light light on a chair.

2. Some multi-purpose clamp-stands can be used on doors, walls, or floors (Figure 4-36).

FIGURE 4–36. A clamp-stand supporting a Lowel Tota-Light on a wall bracket.

3. Flexible connector arms can sometimes be used with clamps to mount flags on a wall, to adjust the position of flags attached to lighting units, or to stack flags (Figure 4-37).

FIGURE 4–37. A flexible connector arm holding a flag on a Lowell Omni-Light.

4. The connectors on the lighting units, flags, clamps, and flexible connector arms make the possible combinations almost unlimited (Figure 4-38).

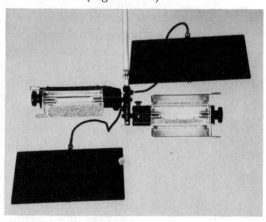

FIGURE 4–38. Combination of Lowel Tota-Lights flexible connector arms, and flags.

5. Another type of handy clamp, called a "gaffer grip," is also very useful to hold lighting equipment when floor space is limited (Figure 4-39).

FIGURE 4–39. A gaffer grip holding a Lowel Tota-Light on a wall bracket.

6. Lighting booms are used to supply light from directly overhead (Figure 4-40). Some booms are fashioned more on the order of a framework so that they can be lighter without sacrificing strength.

FIGURE 4-40. A lighting boom for supplying light from directly overhead.

## BATTERY-OPERATED LIGHTS

If you have very little preparation time and a lot of movement in the shot, battery-operated lights can be used (Figure 4-41).

FIGURE 4-41. A battery-operated Frezzi-Lite head.

The Fiezzi-Lite and battery pack shown in Figures 4-41 and 4-42 are extremely light-weight and versatile (see Source Index). Battery-operated lights are usually used inside, outdoors at night, or in other low-light situations, but they can also be used outside in daylight to lessen the contrast between shadow and highlighted areas. Using them in daylight poses very little color balance problems since the light from the sun is so much brighter. Battery-operated lights are balanced for 3200 K and come with a battery pack that powers them for about 20 to 50 minutes, depending on the wattage of the lamp (Figure 4-42). Several battery-operated lights should be used at once to provide at least key and fill. This arrangement helps to avoid the "harsh" look so often criticized in video lighting. Battery-operated lights should be used only when appropriate, but they are undeniably absolutely essential sometimes.

FIGURE 4-42. A Frezzi battery belt shown with the Frezzi-Lite head. Battery belt powers head for about thirty minutes of shooting time before requiring recharge.

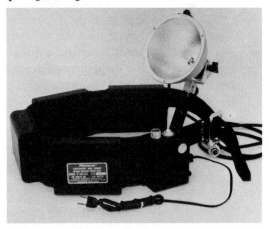

## LOCATION LIGHTING WITH A FLAIR

With the lighting units and accessories covered so far, you should be able to do a good job of lighting in any location situation. Although the lighting arrangements on location are largely a matter of your personal taste regarding the desired effect and of the constraints imposed by time and the location itself, you will probably use four-point lighting or some derivation of it. Yet, as we have pointed out several times in this chapter, lighting does not always follow a simple formula. Four-point lighting is by far the best way to light a subject, but it's not always necessary or even possible. A knowledge of four-point lighting, lighting theory, con-

FIGURE 4-43. Creative lighting arrangement.

trast ratios, color balance, and the rest comes in handy, but relying too heavily on theory and formula can turn out to be more of a hindrance than an asset. To insist on four-point "formula lighting" in a situation calling for more creative lighting or "light-with-a-twist" is not reasonable. Lighting indoors is often a problem-solving experience, and always a fascinating, intriguing process. Of prime importance is what looks best even if an unconventional lighting arrangement is used.

Case in point: On one occasion, our group was called on to light a car showroom for an automobile ad. The showroom was a huge glass box with mixed fluorescent and incandescent lighting, its windows extending from ceiling to floor. The car was vivid red, and the floor of the showroom was a screaming burnt orange. How could we standardize this type of light, separate the car from the floor, and avoid lighting reflections in the car or in the windows? We decided to wait until dark to exclude daylight. We used the fluorescents and incandescents to set up, but turned off the fluorescents during takes. We bounced fill from the ceiling, which thankfully was white, and barndoored the location lighting units so that more light fell on the car than on the floor. This separated the horrible burnt orange from the red of the car. Lowel Tota-lights were used for key and the Lowel Softlight for fill (see Source

Index). We manipulated everything for each shot until reflections from the car and the showroom windows were minimized. Although our lighting arrangement had elements of four-point lighting, it looked more like the surround-the-car-and-turn-everything-on approach (Figure 4-43).

But there was one other problem. We were working with live mountain lions, who frequently tried to duck out of the showroom (Figure 4-44). Even though they liked

FIGURE 4-44. Barry J. Fuller, one of the authors, with a resting mountain lion used in a Mercury-Cougar commercial.

FIGURE 4–45. A pattern projected behind the actor adds depth and dimension to the studio.

being stars, they didn't care for the heat of the lights. So all lighting units had to be placed fairly high off the showroom floor. As it turned out, this was no problem, since we had to place the lights high enough to avoid picking up their reflections in the showroom windows. There was a close call when one of the lion cubs tried to make a break for the door and the trainer had to hurdle extension cords and lighting stands to stop him. This feisty little cub still had his teeth and claws, and none of the lighting crew intended to tackle him. The Lowel Softlight nearly took a fall when a foot got tangled in its cord.

On another occasion we were lighting a marathon three-day production (that's as long as everyone could stand up) for Media Works called: "Single-Camera Production Techniques." We had a hybrid array of lighting equipment—from the newest, most sophisticated lighting gear to the most inefficient and ridiculous. We found a use for

it all. The set was a "bubble cyc" or "infinity cyc," with a wrap-around ceiling and floor background in one long unbroken line. It had been painted white, and when you walked into the room, you couldn't tell how far away the wall was. This was great for fashion shots, but it wouldn't work for video. We repainted it light blue, but the problem with the "infinity look" still persisted. We thought about fastening decorations to the backdrop to give it dimension. But, since it was made of gunnite, a sprayed concrete, there was no easy way to do so. No adhesive tape would hold. Then we had the bright idea (pun intended) of using ellipsoidal spots with patterns and gels to splash colored patterns of light across the background. This broke up the background, gave a feeling of depth and dimension to the room, and, since the gels were bronze, added a warmth and coziness to the set (Figure 4-45).

## OUTDOOR LOCATION LIGHTING

### SCOUTING LOCATIONS

Scouting outside locations is a really good idea since you have even less control over daylight than over indoor lighting. During the scouting, you can figure out where the

sun is going to be and therefore the best time for the shoot. If you plan on shooting more than one location, you may have to shoot them in a predetermined order, depending on where the shadows fall on each location at a particular time of day. If it looks like you may need some type of auxilliary lighting, a source of power has to be located. If none is available, a generator has to be used. All these and other considerations can be worked out during the scouting.

### Color Temperature

The color temperature of daylight is in the 5,000- to 7,000-K range, depending on the type of weather, on the time of year, on the latitude, and or other factors. You have to adjust the camera's filter to the most appropriate outdoor setting and then set the white balance.

### Camera Adjustments

Usually the f-stop is adjusted to its smaller settings, but under some conditions you have to use a neutral-density filter so that the f-stop can be opened to a larger setting. This larger opening makes it possible to drop focus on distracting backgrounds, and in doing so get away from that "from-here-to-infinity-in-focus" look that adds to harshness in video. A telephoto lens also compresses depth of field somewhat if you don't have access to neutral-density filters.

### Camera Angles

Avoid using predominantly eye-level shots, which are so ubiquitous in ENG production. Low-angle, narrow-angle, and wide-angle shots take a great deal of the monotony out of video imagery. Sometimes the possible camera angles depend on the lighting conditions at the location.

## SPECIAL REQUIREMENTS

### Reflectors

On a sunny day, the light coming from the sun (the great key light in the sky), throws dark shadows across the eye sockets, under the chin, and usually on one side of the face of subjects (Figure 4-46). Anything indented or under an overhang also falls in shadow. Close-up shots of anything become a problem since these deep shadows may distort the shape of the subject or, at the very least, obscure detail. For example, showing a hand operating a control may be a problem if the shadow from the hand covers the control. Reflectors are used to side-step these problems by supplying enough fill light to see detail in areas that would otherwise be totally in shadow. In effect, reflectors compress the contrast range by lifting the light level in the shadow areas. (Remember that even the best video equipment cannot handle a very wide contrast range. Outside, looking at a portable monitor tells you just how narrow the range is; differences that your eyes handle easily do not work with the camera.)

Rented reflectors are usually shiny-surfaced on one side and matte-surfaced on the other. Sometimes, if the light from the shiny side of this type of reflector is too harsh, you may be able to "work from the edge" of the reflector. In other words, use the "peripheral area" of the reflected light to provide the fill rather than the "hotter" central area. If this approach doesn't work, tape a piece of

**FIGURE 4–46. A typical reflector.**

white, matte artboard over the shiny surface of the reflector to soften and attenuate the light. Unfortunately, the board cuts down on the amount of light reflected as well as its harshness. Or you can just use the reflectors as they are and rent or build large diffusers for them. Position the reflectors so that the greatest amount of light possible falls on the subject, but place large 1x2 framed pieces of spun glass or parachute material between the reflector and the subject. This softens the light from the reflector without cutting down its efficiency very much. The diffusers can also be used between the sun and the subject to soften the sun's light.

Reflectors don't always have to be shiny or white. On a recent shoot for a McDonald's ad, a large area had to be covered with even light from a reflector at noon and at dusk. The shoot had to be done simply, efficiently,

and quickly, and the reflector had to be designed to enhance the sunset colors. We nailed together an 8x8' framework of 1x2s and stapled two pieces of 4x8' foamcore over the frame. Then we spray-painted one side light gold. The white side was used at noon and the gold side at sunset. It worked perfectly except that toward evening, when a slight breeze came up, we had to use three T-stands, several 2x2 braces, and about ten sandbags to prevent it from taking flight.

## T-Stands and Sandbags

Both T-stands and sandbags are part of the standard equipment for outdoor shooting because they have an incredible number of applications, mostly for holding or clamping things in place. They are used by filmmakers all the time. Take at least a half-dozen T-stands and a dozen sandbags on any outdoor shoot (Figure 4-47).

FIGURE 4–47. A T-stand (held down by a sand-bag) holding a mesh flag for diffusing light.

FIGURE 4–48. An opaque flag for blocking light and shading lenses. Reflectors in the background.

### Flags and Diffusers

Take flags and diffusers too. The flags used outside are generally larger than those used inside due to the usual absence of space restrictions outdoors. Large flags on T-stands, held down by a sandbag or two, are great to shade the camera and operator in hot sunlight. Flags used outside have the same general light-blocking and lens-shading applications as those used inside (Figure 4-48).

### Auxiliary Lighting

*Generators.* Although usually no auxiliary lighting equipment has to be used on location outdoors, when it is needed, power has to come either from an available source or from a generator. The generator has to be the type that runs quietly, and it has to be operated as far away from the action as possible to avoid being picked up by microphones. (Usually this is not a problem if a highly directional microphone like a shotgun is used.)

Lighting used outside should be balanced for daylight, usually by placing a dichroic filter in front of the lighting source. The dichroic filter simply adds a certain amount of blue to the light from the incandescent lighting units, thus matching the color of light from the equipment with the color of daylight.

*HMIs.* Specially designed lighting units called HMIs produce light by means of an electric arc. Since the color temperature of these units matches daylight, dichroic filters do not have to be used. The advantage of these units is their tremendous light output and their efficiency. They can be run on a common household circuit. The light they produce is very smooth and even across the diameter of the beam, and the flood control built into them works exceptionally well from spot to flood throughout the entire range. (Other spotlights either have very little range or reach a point in the range of their spot-to-flood adjustment where their light is very irregular and mottled.)

The only problems with HMIs are their cost and weight. Even the rental is high. But if you want something that does the job well and you can afford to pay for it, HMIs are the best things around. (Just remember that it takes two strong people to move HMIs around.) HMIs may seem a little out of line with the type of production you have in

96

mind. Maybe you'll never use them, but you should know what's available just in case an application for them comes up.

*Color-Correcting Gel.* As useful in outdoor location lighting as in indoor lighting is color-correcting gel material, which comes in sheets or rolls. When taped over windows, for example, this material converts daylight to 3,200 K, which balances it with incandescent light. The converse is also possible: Another type of gel converts incandescent light to daylight color temperature. The outside-to-inside conversion takes place by pulling a little blue out of the light, and the inside-to-outside conversion by adding a little blue. Once I found myself in a jam because I had to make a few exposures under incandescent light and had only daylight-type reversal (slide) film. I happened to have a light blue piece of gel with me, so I taped it over the lens and made the exposure. It turned out fine. Maybe it was luck.

**SUMMARY** Lighting is more than just aiming a lighting unit. Most of what is written in this chapter is about aiming—that is, about the tools. Much more can be said about lighting, but not without trying to deal with concepts that are better learned through experience. Your success with lighting depends perhaps most on two things: learning to see what you're looking at, and knowing when to use and when to break the rules. Learning to see what you're looking at sounds like a contradiction in terms. We all see what we're looking at, correct? Well, in video lighting you must be able to see light in terms of the video medium. In other words, when you look through the camera's black-and-white viewfinder, you may see a great image, but you must also be able to "see" the color, the contrast, and the resolution. You must know what to do to the lighting if the image doesn't look great. What you decide to do involves you and the tools. You've read about the tools. Now it's up to you.

# 5 5 5 5 5 5 5 SHOOTING

If one dictum applies to shooting, it is, "Plan ahead." Whether you are making home tapies or shooting a story for the six o'clock news, you have to consider many different factors to end up with something to be proud of. Planning ahead not only always helps to create better tapes, but it also makes the overall effort more enjoyable.

Planning also lowers the likelihood of a foul-up due to one or both of two factors: "people" and chance.

You need people, working together to make quality productions.

Shooting with the single-camera system implies that everything is done by one individual. In actuality, rare is the individual who has the ability to conceptualize, write, plan, coordinate, shoot, and edit a complete program. The home tapie producer and the in-company video communicator often find themselves running ragged when they try to accomplish everything alone. The margin for error is also greater, especially when dealing with a tight deadline. So any serious attempt at production requires the talents of a number of people, depending on how much the production budget can bear and on what the finished program will be used for. For example, one individual can easily handle shooting and editing a wedding or family function. On the other hand, the production of a network documentary requires the talents of dozens of people. In both cases, the single-camera shooting approach is used, but the documentary incorporates far more research, planning, and expense.

The other element common to all levels of production is chance. Not everything always follows the anticipated direction. "If it can go wrong, it will . . ." is an unfortunate reality of the production process. The only way to minimize problems is to *plan ahead!*

**PRE-PLANNING**

Efficient pre-production planning insures a smooth operation, cuts down on wasted time, and keeps production budgets under control. Shooting single-camera style particularly demands that you be prepared for a variety of situations: lighting, sound, power availability, and talent requirements. Whether on location or in the studio, you must take all these variables into consideration to minimize any "surprises" during production.

One of the most significant steps in pre-planning is to define the purpose of the project: Who is the intended audience? What will the videotape be used for? Your ability to answer these and other questions makes for a successful presentation.

The next step, a crucial one, is to choose between two entirely different approaches in transforming an idea into a production: the scripted method and the unscripted method. In many instances the choice is made for you. Sometimes you have only enough time to grab your equipment and head for the shooting site. But sometimes the idea you want to develop into a television production calls for one method or the other—or both! Let's start with the scripted approach.

**SCRIPTED APPROACH**

If all involved in a production are to perform at their best, the script they are to follow must be clear and concise. Scripting is largely a matter of practice and experience. Basically, there are two types of scripts. In one, the production begins totally from the mind of the writer who translates ideas to paper. In the second, the writer acts as a reporter of events, selects certain events over others, and creates a narrative from what is going on. Many agree that the writing for prose is quite different from verbiage used as part of a visual presentation on a videotape. The organization of the information, the pacing (or speed) at which it is presented, and the visuals involved in telling the story must follow meaningfully from place to place.

Before you start writing, find out who your intended audience is. Determine their prior knowledge of the subject material, their background, their educational level, and any other information that gives you direction in communicating the message to your audience.

In either case, the scripted approach begins with an outline to give your idea some structure. Most outlines begin with an introduction of some sort and end with a conclusion or summary. Between the introduction and conclusion is the content of the production, that is, what you want to say. Once the outline has been completed, a full script can be developed using the outline as a guide.

A script for television is usually divided into two columns—the video column on the left half of the page and the audio on the right side. (Some prefer the reverse—video on the right, audio on the left.) Use separate sheets to describe the characters, wardrobe, location, props, sets, artwork, and other details. The video column should include:

1. basic camera directions alongside the appropriate audio, and
2. a description of key camera shots, artwork, and other essential information.

In the audio column, you should identify:

1. the sources of all spoken words along with the respective narrative,
2. other audio sources, such as music and sound effects, and
3. directions for talent, such as how lines are to be delivered or what action is happening (on or off camera).

When describing these elements, make sure to separate them from the narrative using parentheses around the direction (Figure 5-1). You can avoid confusion by keeping the layout of your script consistent. Use upper- and lower-case letters and double spacing for all spoken lines. Use all capital letters and single spacing for directions within parentheses.

### UNSCRIPTED APPROACH

While the scripted approach requires writing and planning before shooting, the unscripted approach requires writing and planning after shooting. You will run into many situations that call for an unscripted approach. For example, documenting events—including everything from weddings and birthdays to news coverage and live television—is probably the largest category. The key to obtaining any

kind of documentary footage is to make certain you are prepared for the event factually and technically.

To prepare factually, even though a script is generally not followed, you should accumulate enough background material so that specific areas of interest can be given adequate coverage. You must also determine how you will cover the event. In documentary work, an on-camera narrator usually gives a running commentary about the events taking place, but you may choose not to include the narrator (or interviewer) in the frame of view. Another approach is to simply document the event, letting the pictures and sound tell the story. Since our single-camera approach involves videotape, you can use pre-recorded events as material for eventual inclusion in a scripted program.

From a technical standpoint, you must have full confidence in your equipment, because you usually have only one chance to get it right. Shooting an event requires that you think ahead about such basics as when the event takes place, where it takes place, why it is taking place, who the key figures of interest are, and what will be happening. The answers to all these questions give you clues as to the equipment and accessories you will need to cover the event. You may find, for instance, that existing lighting is all that is available. Are you allowed, or is it wise to bring portable lighting equipment? If not, you will need a very sensitive camera that produces good-quality pictures in low-light situations.

### COMBINATION SCRIPTED/ UNSCRIPTED APPROACH

Many live programs use a combined scripted/ unscripted approach. TV news is a prime example: Live and/or pre-recorded events are brought to us by on-camera talent (newscasters). The significance of such an approach lies in the way you plan for and script a program. The overall program format is first conceived, then scripted. Certain things are planned to happen at certain times. The other elements, the unscripted parts, still require pre-planning just as the overall program does, but they do not require a "tight" script due to the nature of the event. The scripted portion can also be designed to fit around the time frame of the unscripted portion.

**FIGURE 5-1.** Example of a script from a video production. All instructions should be as complete as possible.

Page____of____

Date_____

PRODUCTION:  <u>Single Camera Production Techniques</u>

| <u>VIDEO</u> | <u>AUDIO</u> |
|---|---|
| Scene 7a:  WIDE SHOT OF TALENT SETTING UP A WHITE CARD ON THE EASEL (card has an outline of a 3 x 4 ratio on it). | (off camera narrator; mix-in with sound from video footage) |
| | Scene 7a:  "A few basic rules apply when preparing graphic materials for video. We have already mentioned that it is important to remember the TV aspect ratio when shooting slides or film for use on video. |
| AS TALENT FINISHES SETTING UP, CAMERA DOES A SLOW ZOOM AND FILLS FRAME WITH THE WHITE CARD.  (shot should time-out to end at..."for television.") | The aspect ratio for the video format is three units high by four units wide. Both slides and film are a little wider than this 3 x 4 ratio, so the slides of the projected image will be cut off more than at the top and bottom.  This is why the main action or focus of attention must be kept towards the center of the frame when shooting for television." |
| Scene 7b:  cut to: TRANSITION OPENS SHOT BY CAMERA ZOOMING-OUT FROM WHITE AREA ON SET; PULLING OUT TO A MEDIUM SHOT OF TALENT SETTING UP A CAMERA CARD ON THE EASEL.  TALENT WALKS TOWARD THE CAMERA.  (time-out action to ..."keep detail etc.")  CUT TO FULL FRAME OF VISUAL, WHICH HAS ONE LINE OF LETTERING. | Scene 7b:  (continued from 7a) "The same basic rules apply for any other artwork, titles, or visual aids. Camera card sizes should fit the 3 x 4 ratio.  Six x 8, 11 x 14, 15 x 20, and so on, are good sizes to work with. |

## STORYBOARDS

If a picture is worth a thousand words, storyboards are worth millions. They not only help you illustrate your ideas, but they also offer the serious producer a high degree of creative control over a project. Used as a reference point to the script and shooting instructions, the "boards" permit only minimal misinterpretation.

Clear and concise images are especially important to your storyboards. The general approach is to use drawings, photographs, illustrations, and/or graphic materials to depict scene-by-scene what you want the viewer to see.

Narrative and instructions for audio usually accompany the storyboards (Figure 5-2). The trick in developing a full script with storyboards is to think in many dimensions at once. You must think of the visuals, narrative, sound effects, music, and many other details. You have the opportunity to define and to illustrate whatever elements you wish to appear in the final product. The key is to pick out the most important visual element from each scene and depict it in your storyboards. If you are not a good artist, you can at least draw stick figures to define character position. Depending on your budget, you can hire artists to help you with your storyboards. When "real" locations are involved in your script, go out to the proposed locations and take photographs to illustrate scenery, backgrounds, or other important visual elements. Your goal should be to offer the people involved in the production a definite visual direction to follow.

## ANIMATICS

An animatic takes the development of storyboards a step further. Shoot the finished storyboards as you would the actual scenes. Camera movements such as pans, tilts, and zooms offer the added dimension of movement. When edited to accompany a prerecorded sound track, the finished animatic is an excellent way to present your ideas, as well as to explore important elements of the proposed production, such as pairing music and narration. Once you and your client (or employer) are satisfied with the animatic, you can complete the remaining phases of the pre-planning process.

## SCOUTING LOCATIONS

In many cases, either traveling to a location is not feasible or practical, or an important event must be covered as it happens. But whenever possible, scout all locations before production begins. Showing up in advance of an event gives you important foreknowledge of lighting and sound situations, the availability of power, and many other physical conditions that may influence your production. Being totally prepared for anything is the key. Since beginners are not generally aware of what to expect, take your portable VTR and camera along on a scouting trip, record appropriate shots, and carefully examine the results. Or, you might go out and shoot a local sporting event to gain experience in obtaining video footage "as it happens." The experience you gain in shooting events as they happen goes a long way in helping you to determine what to look for when scouting locations.

If your production takes you into a public place, you should ascertain the busiest hours —what time of day is best to shoot? Your production may call for a busy crowd scene or, on the other hand, as few people around as possible.

In all cases, it is best to obtain permission in writing before using any location, public or private, especially when producing a program for profit. A location release avoids any legal problems.

## EQUIPMENT

Once you complete scouting your location(s), you need to list all the required equipment— video, video-related, audio, lighting, communications, and miscellaneous items. Precisely what and how much to take varies with the demands of the production. Assembling your list by category not only helps you to keep a running inventory of what equipment is involved, but it also avoids overlooking any items. For example, under "video," you might include:

1. camera,
2. VTR,
3. special filters and/or lenses,
4. white card,
5. chip chart and registration chart,
6. tripod(s),
7. dollies, etc.
8. videotape,

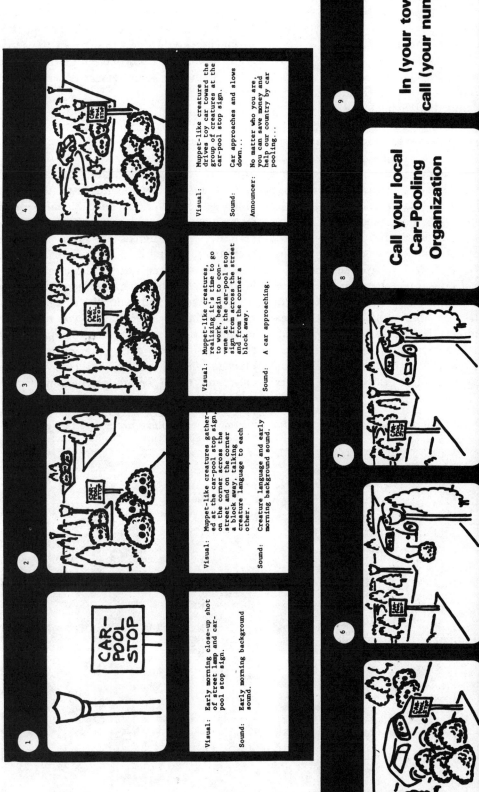

**①**

**Visual:** Early morning close-up shot of street lamp and car-pool stop sign.

**Sound:** Early morning background sound.

**②**

**Visual:** Muppet-like creatures gathered at the car-pool stop sign on the corner across the street and on the corner a block away, talking creature language to each other.

**Sound:** Creature language and early morning background sound.

**③**

**Visual:** Muppet-like creatures, realizing it's time to go to work, begin to convene at the car-pool stop sign from across the street and from the corner a block away.

**Sound:** A car approaching.

**④**

**Visual:** Muppet-like creature drives toy car toward the group of creatures at the car-pool stop sign.

**Sound:** Car approaches and slows down...

**Announcer:** No matter who you are, you can save money and help our country by car pooling...

**⑤**

**Visual:** Muppet-like creature stops car and other creatures jump in.

**Sound:** Car stopping.

**⑥**

**Visual:** Car makes turn and starts away, but a little creature chases car. The driver stops to let him in.

**Sound:** (Little creature) Wait for me! Wait for me!

**⑦**

**Visual:** Car pulls away.

**Sound:** Car pulling away.

**Announcer:** So pool it!

**⑧**

Call your local Car-Pooling Organization

**Visual:** Lettering.

**Announcer:** Call your local car-pooling organization!

**⑨**

In (your town), call (your number)!

**Visual:** Lettering.

**Announcer:** In (your town), Call (your number)!

FIGURE 5-2 Storyboards are used to illustrate your ideas and are used as a reference point to the script and shooting instructions.

9. empty reels,
10. power cables,
11. monitors,
12. varying lengths of cables,
13. extension cords,
14. adaptors,
15. carts, and/or tables.

And what do you use to carry all this around? The right kind of equipment-carrying cart is essential to mobility and ease of transport. Of the carts we've worked with, the line produced by Lee-Ray Industries (see Source Index) is by far the best engineered. The battery holder is free-swinging so that the battery always remains upright. They are the lightest carts made, which is really a factor on long shoots and when loading and unloading. They have a number of unique options including waterproof dust covers, a heavy-duty AC strip that is switched for controlling lights and other equipment when running off AC, an attachment for holding tripods, and a full list of other features. Complete descriptive data are available free from Lee-Ray Industries (Figure 5-3).

Do the same for lighting and audio. Miscellaneous equipment can include every-thing from special props, sets and make-up to gaffer's tape, director's slate, chairs, tables, food and drink, wardrobe, felt-tip markers, ladders, and dulling spray.

As you can see, the equipment list can (and should) be very detailed. The goal is to make everything on the day of the shoot go as smoothly as possible. Forgetting a necessary item can be extremely expensive and embarrassing.

## COMMUNICATIONS

How do you, the crew, and the talent on-camera intend to communicate during a video session? Various hand signals, called *cues*, may be used to communicate nonverbally. These signals are given by either the camera operator or by a floor manager who stands to one side of the camera lens. Since the single-camera style of shooting usually involves only you (the camera operator) and the on-camera talent, you may have to alter the basic cues to suit your particular shooting situation. Either you or your floor manager should go over any cues with the crew and talent before production begins.

FIGURE 5–3a. Equipment cart for portable video equipment.

FIGURE 5–3b. When on location, you'll need to remember everything to make the shoot go smoothly. (Photo courtesy Lee-Ray Industries, Inc.)

At this point, you may be wondering how the camera operator and/or floor manager know which cues to give the talent. Usually, the camera operator, floor manager, and director wear telephone-type head sets, which are part of an *intercom* (intercommunication system), that allows voice communication among all parties on the system. Many systems utilize the circuitry built into the camera and camera control unit. Others use small transmitters and pocket receivers, which pick up signals sent by the transmitting source, but these are limited in that they have no talk-back capability (Figure 5-4). When crew members and/or talent are working at some distance from the camera, you may also need other types of communication tools, such as walkie-talkies, CB radios, and megaphones.

FIGURE 5–4a. The camera operator communicates with the rest of the crew through the headset/intercom. (Photos courtesy KPHO TV5, Phoenix)

FIGURE 5–4b. The director and engineer also use headset-intercoms to communicate with each other, as well as with the camera operator.

Prompting devices are visual aids used to help the performer(s) read lines of copy during the actual taping session. Two devices are used: cue cards and the teleprompter. Both depend on good eye contact between talent and the camera lens.

### Cue Cards

Generally, cue cards are just large cardboard sheets with hand-lettered copy. The copy should be clearly printed and large enough for the talent to read easily. The cards are held by a crew member as close to the lens as possible (Figure 5-5).

FIGURE 5–5. Cue cards are the easiest method of helping the talent with their lines. (Photo courtesy KPHO TV5, Phoenix)

### Teleprompter

The better of the two types of prompting devices, the teleprompter contains copy that is typed or hand-lettered on a roll of paper. which is mounted on motorized rollers with variable speed control. A black-and-white video camera picks up the copy as it passes by, and it feeds the signal to a monitor mounted on (or above) the lens of the active production camera. A mirror is used to project the information from the monitor onto a glass plate positioned directly over the camera lens. The production camera does not "see" the image of the copy on the glass because it's too close to the lens to come into focus. This arrangement allows for maximum eye contact. Variations of this system use computer keyboards and storage devices, which are used to "type in" and to directly display the copy on the monitor (Figure 5-6).

FIGURE 5–6a. A teleprompter offers maximum eye contact between talent and camera. It is actually a TV monitor in front of the camera, with the image reflecting off a piece of glass. (Photo courtesy KPHO TV5, Phoenix)

FIGURE 5–6b. The monitor is fed by a small black-and-white camera that picks up the copy from a scroll of paper. A motor is used to speed up or to slow down the rate at which the scroll advances, allowing the teleprompter operator to "read along" with the on-camera talent. (Photo courtesy KPHO TV5, Phoenix)

Almost every television production needs "talent," that is, the on-camera performer(s) who communicate a message to the TV camera.

To hire the best person(s) for your program, hold numerous interviews so you have a wide range of people to choose from. Don't hire the first person you interview unless he or she fits the bill. Take note as to whether the prospect has a good one-to-one working relationship with you in the interview. If so, more than likely he or she will have a good rapport with the audience.

Since you will probably interview union and nonunion performers, remember that one group is not better than the other; there is talent in both. But be aware of talent union regulations.

When you have picked your talent, make sure also that they all sign releases. A release permits you to use the talent's name, voice, and performance in your production and to use them without paying further compensation then whatever was agreed on when the talent was hired.

On the day of shooting have your talent wear simple plain colors. Avoid contrasting colors, like a white blouse and black skirt, as well as shiny, studded, or sequin accessories, which catch the light and glare on the TV screen. Also avoid bold, multi-patterned clothing unless it is required for a humorous effect, since they tend to be eye-boggling on the screen.

Instruct your talent to move slowly and to give little indications if they plan on standing up (if seated) or moving to another area. If they plan on standing up, for example, perhaps they can place their hands on the chair arm or shift their weight forward. Verbal indications of a move to another area can be, "As I go over to the table . . .". By these simple indications, the camera won't lose the talent if they rapidly stand up or quickly move to another area of the set. Before shooting, have rehearsals (if possible) so your talent can become accustomed to the set or location, to their lines, and to each other. If they are familiarized there will be fewer mistakes.

Some sound advice to talent is to "Know your lines!" The worst thing the talent can do is to appear at the studio set or location site unprepared. If time is wasted for them to learn their lines, you can be sure that they didn't make points with the director and that they might not be called again for work in the future.

## DELEGATING RESPONSIBILITIES

For a smooth production, responsibilities have to be delegated to various crew members. Each member should be assigned a certain job. By doing so, you can take care of all necessary details and avoid duplication of efforts. In a typical production, six basic positions may be assigned:

1. producer,
2. director,
3. cameraperson,
4. video engineer,
5. audio engineer, and
6. floor manager.

### Producer
The producer not only originates the program from an idea, but also draws up a production budget to include talent, crew salary, additional set costs, copyright and release fees, and other expenses. The budget is actually an estimated cost of the production that helps the producer to determine whether the idea is economically feasible to produce.

### Director
The producer then appoints a director, and they discuss the staging, lighting, audio, talent, and tone for the program. The director, knowing the producer's idea and objectives for the program:

1. assigns positions to qualified staff members, and
2. plans and explains the set design, lighting, audio and video requirements, camera angles, and staging to the appropriate people.

On the day of production, the director is in command and gives the cues to the cameraperson, floor manager, audio engineer, and video tape operator. The director's performance affects everyone in the studio. If he or she is well prepared and performs the duties in a professional manner, the shoot will be successful.

## Cameraperson

The cameraperson operates the camera, studies the shot list, and practices the shots for the program given by the director. In a small crew, the cameraperson also sets up the proper lighting and arranges props by the director's floor plan. During the actual production, the cameraperson's responsibilities are also framing shots, leaving enough head and nose room, filling the picture, following the director's cues and the like. At times the cameraperson may double as floor manager to cue the talent.

## Video Engineer

The video engineer's major function is to make sure all video equipment, including the camera and VTR, are in perfect working condition. This person also works with the lighting director for proper set lighting and adjusts the camera and video levels.

## Audio Engineer

The audio engineer selects the right microphone for the shoot and tests the talent's voice level through the microphones. During the program, the audio engineer maintains a zero-dB audio level and reacts to the director's audio cues. He or she is also in charge of getting any desired sound effects if needed.

## Floor Manager

The floor manager is in charge of the production in the studio or on location. The manager not only delivers the time cues, talent cues, and all other instructions sent through the headset by the director, but also makes sure the props are placed on the set according to the director's plan.

## PRODUCTION SCHEDULE

To finish your program by deadline, set up a production schedule. When as a producer you think of an idea and start it rolling, you should also set the production on a schedule, which includes the script and storyboard deadlines, scouting location dates, talent interviews, the shooting dates, and editing time. Schedules should always be flexible, that is, you should allow time for error or uncontrollable factors, such as weather changes.

On the day of production, have a shooting schedule as well. If you are shooting on a number of days, log the scenes to be shot each day. Give yourself enough time to compensate for equipment malfunctions, problems with props and sets, and other delays. When the shoot is finished, the editing begins. If you successfully logged every shot taken (good and bad) and commented as to which is the best, you won't waste precious time deciding which shots to edit into the program. By setting up and following a production schedule, you will achieve the results you want in an orderly fashion instead of haphazardly.

## SHOOTING TECHNIQUES

By using different camera angles, basic camera movements, and transitions, you can develop a distinctive shooting style for your programs.

videotape log sheet of all your shots so that, when you edit, you know where the various shots are located on the tape and which shots you want to use.

### SHOOTING OUT OF SEQUENCE

If you are shooting at different locations for various points in your program, you don't want to be running back and forth and setting up your camera equipment from one location to another. So to utilize your time wisely, you will probably find yourself shooting scenes out of sequence. Simply shoot all your scenes designed for one location and then move on to the next. Keep a

### MATCHING ACTION

Also keep track of the character's position and movement so you can match action. *Matching action* is the technique of changing camera angles without breaking the continuity of motion from scene to scene. For example, you might be shooting a scene where a male narrator ends a shot opening the door and leaving. You must make sure you know which hand opened the door,

**FIGURE 5–7a.** The talent's nose is too close to the left side of the image area.

**FIGURE 5–7b.** The talent is positioned with enough space between the talent's nose and the edge of the screen.

**FIGURE 5–8a.** Too much head room.

**FIGURE 5–8b.** Good framing with the talent's eyes about a third from the top of the frame.

which foot stepped out first, and so on. In your next shot (from the outside of the door), have your talent walk through the same motions as in the previous scene. From there you can edit from when his hand opens the door or his foot steps outside. The position of your camera and the way you choose to compose the subject matter in the frame also affect the finished product.

## FRAMING

In every production certain framing principles help you achieve an appropriate picture. When the camera "sees" an object or talent, your duty is to make sure the framing is correct. The space you create in front of, above, and around your subject is critical in achieving a well-framed and composed image. Here are some tips:

1. To achieve a symmetrically balanced picture, place the object or the talent with eye contact to the audience near the center of the screen, especially in close-ups. Placing the object or talent too far off-center may cause some of the important information to be cut off due to misaligned receivers at home.
2. If your talent is looking in a certain direction, you should position the camera slightly off-center to give proper "nose room." By not doing so, you bring the talent's nose too close to the edge of the screen, thus creating an annoying picture (Figure 5-7).
3. "Head room," which is the space between a talent's head and the top of the screen, is equally important. To achieve adequate head room, place the eyes one-third of the way down from the top of the screen.
4. Don't frame your talent by the natural cut-off lines on the body—the neck, waist, hands, or knees. Instead make your cut-off lines above or below the natural lines. For example, for a more appealing picture, cut off not at the neck, but just a little below the shoulders (Figure 5-8).
5. Framing asymmetrically can be effective when you have prominent horizontal and vertical lines. For example, when framing a view of a city, place the skyscraper slightly to the left of the screen instead of screen-center. Or when you have a small child and a tall man, compensate for this noticeable difference by having

the child sit on a stool or the man stoop down to the child.

6. If you frame talent in a scene with an object like a tall plant in the background, make sure the plant doesn't look like it's growing out of the talent's head. To correct this sort of situation, simply move your camera to one side.

7. When following lateral motion, "lead" the person or object in motion with your camera, don't follow it (Figure 5-9).

FIGURE 5–9. When you "lead" a moving person or object with your camera, you should allow for enough space in front of the subject.

## CAMERA ANGLES

A good camera angle can add psychological effects to a scene. The basic camera angles are (Figure 5-10):

1. eye level,
2. high angle,
3. low angle, and
4. extreme overhead.

### Eye Level

In the most common camera angle, the eye-level shot, the talent's eyes should be located one-third from the top of the screen. If the camera moves in for a tighter shot, crop the head to keep the eyes one-third from the top. Don't drop the talent's eyes to the center of the screen.

### High Angle

A high-angle shot, which looks down on the subject, can make a person appear smaller and weaker. For example, a high-angle shot can show a child being scolded by mother. To achieve this angle, the camera must be located on a raised platform or other stable apparatus.

### Low Angle

A low-angle shot looks up on the subject. From this angle, a person looks larger than life and domineering. In the scene with the mother and child, the mother would be shot from the low angle showing her scolding the child. To achieve this shot, the camera has to be low to the ground or the talent on a raised platform.

FIGURE 5–10. Different camera angles.

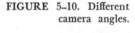

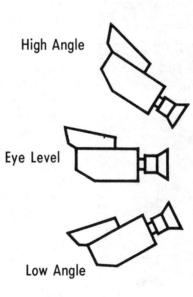

In this angle, the camera is directly above the talent shooting downward. This angle can be seen in a college football game at half-time when the marching band spells out a message.

## CAMERA SHOTS

These camera angles can portray your subject in a number of ways when combined with varied distances from your subject (Figure 5-11):

1. The *long shot* (LS) or *establishing shot* encompasses a large area of the scene and establishes where the action is taking place.

FIGURE 5-11a. An example of a long shot.

2. The *medium* shot (MS) focuses on one or two persons, showing just their heads, shoulders, and upper torsos. The background becomes secondary.

FIGURE 5-11b. A medium shot.

3. A *close-up shot* (CU) zeros in on one person or object. It's used to show facial expression or a certain detail in a demonstration or on an object. The close-up shot is used most often in television.

FIGURE 5-11c. A close-up.

4. For dramatic effect or to show very tiny detail, the *extreme close-up* (ECU) is used—for example, eyes filled with tears or the street number on a house.

FIGURE 5-11d. An extreme close-up.

## BASIC CAMERA MOVEMENTS

Camera movements add variety to your footage, especially when shooting stationary subject matter. There are several basic camera movements (Figure 5-12):

1. A *pan* is a horizontal move to the left or right that is often used to follow action. (Remember that a movement to the "right" or "left" is from the camera's point of view.)

FIGURE 5-12a. A *pan* is a horizontal camera movement from right to left and vice-versa.

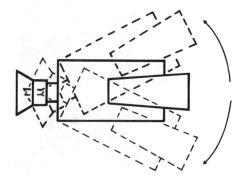

2. A *tilt* is a vertical move up or down. It is used to follow vertical action, such as a parachuter floating downward, or to show a skyscraper.

FIGURE 5–12b. A *tilt* is a vertical camera movement.

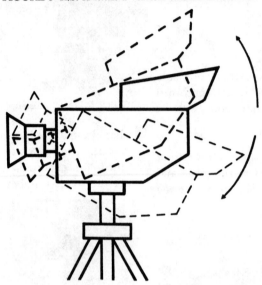

3. A *dolly* is a camera movement toward or away from an object or person. If you "dolly in," you move the camera toward the object; "dolly out" moves the camera away from the object.

FIGURE 5–12c. *Dollying* the camera involves moving the camera towards or away from the subject.

4. A *zoom* is a camera lens movement. When "zooming in" to a narrow angle of view, the scene appears closer on the screen. "Zooming out" to a wide-angle view moves the scene farther away.

FIGURE 5–12d. A *zoom* is a lens movement.

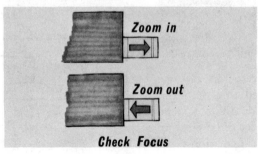

5. To *truck* the camera means physically moving the camera in a left or right lateral movement. This camera movement is utilized when you want to move the camera from stage right to stage left or vice versa, or to move alongside the direction of the action.

FIGURE 5–12e. A *truck* is a camera movement from left to right or vice-versa.

6. To *pedestal up* or *pedestal down* is to raise or lower the camera and mount.
7. *Follow-through-focus* refers to your ability to keep your subject in focus while you zoom in or out. First zoom in as tight as you can, focus your picture, then zoom out.
8. A *crane* or *boom movement* is similar to a pedestal movement (up and down) except the range of movement is greater.

Cranes, specialized dollies, body pods, special mounts, and other such sophisticated camera-mounting equipment can offer operators more possibilities in covering their subject matter. These pieces of equipment are quite expensive, but they can be leased or rented for short periods of time.

## CAMERA MOUNTS

Nothing contributes more to smooth and steady camera work than a rigid, high-quality tripod, along with a heavy-duty pan head. The *tripod* in its basic form is a three-legged unit to which the camera and camera head are attached. To achieve different camera heights on the tripod, you regulate the leg shafts. A portable tripod has three shafts, one inside the other on all three legs. By pulling the shafts out and tightening the rings, you can mount the camera at various heights (Figure 5-13).

FIGURE 5-13. Setting up a tripod (above). The camera height is changed by raising or lowering the legs (left).

Some types of tripods are designed for use with fluid heads. Made of wood or metal, these tripods have a concave top that fits the base of the head, as well as adjustable legs to accommodate uneven terrain. They vary in height from standard to "baby," the latter of which is used for extreme low-angle shooting (Figure 5-14).

The advantage of fluid heads is that they enable you to move the camera without the jerky movements that you get without these heads. The fluid in the heads eliminates the friction of conventional tripods. Thus you can pan, tilt, or perform any camera moves with the camera lens in telephoto position without very apparent aberrations in movement. To avoid such jumpy moves, it's necessary to use a fluid head. Fluid heads are also mandatory for slow camera moves across graphic title information or in any other shots that must be slow, smooth, and continuous. Friction heads, however, tend to "stutter" or "pause/jump" in such applications. The best tripods and fluid heads are made by Universal Fluid Heads (*see* Source Index).

Two features of Universal Fluid Heads that are particularly helpful in video work are trademarked Hydralok and Autoslip. Hydralok is a positive locking feature that assures safe locking of the camera head in any tilt position without "creeping." This is very useful in holding angle shots and in not overbalancing the tripod and dumping the camera. Autoslip makes it possible to break away from the pre-set friction adjustment of a given pan shot to change angles quickly or to follow faster action. The fluid head adjusts itself for the change in speed automatically without loosening any knobs. A good fluid head and tripod are essential for professional-looking camera moves.

FIGURE 5-14a. (below) Tripods designed to be used with fluid heads often vary in height from standard to baby.

FIGURE 5-14b. A fluid head with unique trademarked Hydrolok and Autoslip features. (Photos courtesy of Universal Fluid Heads)

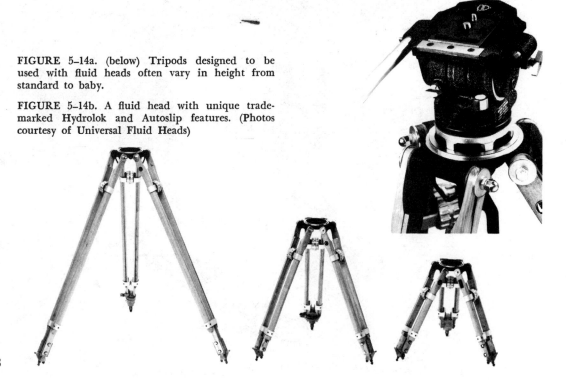

FIGURE 5–15a. A dolly base attaches to a tripod and allows for dolly and truck movements.

FIGURE 5–15b. Cable guards prevent the dolly's wheels from running over cables.

For further movement, the tripod can be equipped with a three-caster dolly base, which allows dolly and truck movements. To achieve a stationary position, lock the wheels on the dolly. Cable guards, an important feature of a dolly, prevent the dolly's wheels from running over the cables from the camera. If the dolly does not have cable guards, the problem can be partially solved by fastening the camera's cable(s) to the bottom of one tripod leg just above the wheel. The cable is stiff enough to keep it out of the way of the wheel as the dolly is moved (Figure 5-15).

You should consider the many other types of camera mounts used for location shooting, where studio tripods and other heavy equipment are impractical. Collapsible monopods, which are simply one leg of a three-legged tripod, can be adjusted to accommodate low-angle and eye-level shooting (Figure 5-16).

When hand-holding the camera, brace yourself against a wall, tree, post, or car—anything that offers added support. If nothing is available, stand with your feet apart, holding the elbows against the body. Since relaxed muscles are easier to control than tense, rigid muscles, relax, hold your breath for short takes, and swivel at the hips when following the action.

FIGURE 5–16. A monopod can be used for quick camera support on location.

The way you choose to go from one scene to another is a transition. These transitions become the connecting thread as you develop your action. You may want also to pre-plan how your audio will change from scene-to-scene. You may want to fade out the audio as one scene changes and fade in the new audio as the new scene comes up. Common transitions are:

1. cut,
2. blackout,
3. swish pan,
4. fade-to-black,
5. defocus/refocus, and
6. black surface.

### Cut

The most common transition is a *cut,* which is a sudden change in camera angle or viewpoint to another. Remember to match the action, to plan your points of view, and to develop a rhythm. Add variety and keep pace with what is happening. Also maintain screen direction. For example, your talent walks toward a door from right to left. You decide to cut (later in editing) to a close-up of her hand reaching for the door knob. To maintain the direction of action, shoot the hand entering the frame from the right side of the screen, with the door knob on the left.

### Black-Out

In this transition, the talent walks toward the camera lens until the entire picture is "blacked-out" from the lack of light. The next scene starts with the talent walking away from the camera's lens into a new scene.

### Swish Pan

A swish pan is used to indicate a change in time or place between scenes. A scene is shot, and the camera is panned so quickly that everything blurs. Then the camera is set up to shoot the next scene. You can cut either directly to the next scene or to a quick pan, stopping on the new subject.

### Fade-to-Black

A fade-to-black is done simply by turning the f-stop ring of the camera lens to its most closed setting. If the scene doesn't go entirely black, put a card or lens cap in front of the lens. The next scene is begun by doing the reverse.

### Defocus/Refocus

A defocus/refocus transition can be used for either passage of time or a change in scene. At the end of one scene, defocus your lens so the image becomes blurred. Start the next scene with the subject out of focus going into focus.

### Black Surface

Another way to portray a change in scene or time is to use a black surface, or a uniformly colored surface, in a scene to zoom in and then cut. For example, you zoom into a white wall, cut to the next scene, start again on a white wall, and then zoom out to include the new scene.

## GETTING OFF TO A GOOD START

After you've lined everything up, and everyone is in place and ready to go, you have to let everyone know that you are ready to videotape—to "roll 'em!" Depending on the size of your crew, you need to develop a sequence of events that signals everyone to expect the beginning of a "take." If *you* are operating the camera, VTR, and audio, it is also up to you to "slate" your scenes and cue talent. When your talent is in place and ready, have them go over their lines so you can set audio levels. Then go through any camera movements required for the scene. When you feel comfortable with the talent and your equipment, notify your talent by saying "stand-by," hold your hand in front of the camera lens with one finger raised (to indicate take one), and then cue your talent by pointing at the talent. The talent should wait a second or two, then deliver the lines. When you get a good take, log which scene and take number(s) were good (Figure 5-17).

In case you have the luxury of hiring crew members, you must develop a set sequence of verbal and silent cues that crew members respond to. For example, let's say you have a directory, a cameraperson, a floor manager, and an engineer (who watches both audio

FIGURE 5–17. When shooting by yourself, you can slate scenes by holding up fingers to indicate take numbers.

FIGURE 5–18. A slate card should indicate at least scene number and take number.

and video levels and operates VTR audio and camera controls). These are the people typically around the set for electronic field production (EFP). The camera is either portable or a studio camera, which is connected to a CCU to allow the engineer to control video levels and set-up. An intercom with headsets is also used so that the director and crew can communicate:

1. When talent, equipment, and crew are ready, the director tests the intercom to verify communication with each crew member.
2. The director then tells the **floor manager,** "Stand by on set."
3. The floor manager relays the director's message loudly enough to alert everyone on the set.
4. The floor manager then "slates" the scene by using a card or director's slate which visually indicates the scene number and take number (Figure 5-18). Sometimes, the director requests that each slate contain other information, such as the production name, camera operator, engineer, and director.

5. The director tells the engineers, "Stand by to record," followed by the engineer's reply, "Rolling in record." These cues are given at least 30 seconds before cueing the talent to provide the necessary amount of recorded video before each take.
6. The director then tells the floor manager and camera operator, "Ready camera, stand by to cue talent."
7. The floor manager responds by raising his or her right hand as a cue to all involved that a take is imminent.
8. The director then instructs the floor director to, "Cue talent" "Action." The floor manager lowers his or her arm, pointing at the talent.
9. The talent delivers the lines and/or the action.

Since this sequence may vary from crew to crew or from director to director, it serves as a reference point only. The main point is that all involved should be organized so that each session follows a set pattern that all can anticipate.

**LENSES** You can change the way your video looks by changing the camera lens to allow the way your camera "sees." Most cameras come with a lens that is an all-purpose design. Many high-priced cameras are sold without lenses to allow you to choose the type of lens you need for your particular shooting situations.

**116**

## FOCAL LENGTH

*Focal length* is the distance from the optical center of a lens to the front surface of the camera's pick-up tube or optical block (in the case of multiple-tube cameras). Lenses with short focal lengths have a wide angle of view—everything looks small. With a long focal length, you see less because there is a narrow angle of view. Focal lengths are usually measured in millimeters. Lenses with fixed focal length have only one specific focal length, whereas a variable focal length, or zoom lens can be changed continuously from wide-angle to narrow-angle and vice-versa.

The focal length of a particular lens bears an important relationship to the size of the pick-up tube(s). Although pick-up tubes come in various sizes, the majority of cameras today use either ⅔-inch or 1-inch tubes. A lens with, say, a 55-millimeter focal length yields two different angles of view when mounted on cameras with ⅔-inch and 1-inch pick-up tubes. The larger pick-up tube "sees" with a wider angle than the ⅔-inch camera. Remember this relationship especially when using extremely wide-angle and narrow-angle lenses. Be sure to match the correct lens to the size of pick-up tubes in your camera.

## f-STOP

The *f-stop* refers to the different iris openings that allow certain amounts of light to fall on the camera pick-up tubes. When the diaphragm or iris of the camera lens is "opened up," it allows more light in; "stopped down," it lets only a small amount

FIGURE 5–19a. The f-stops on your camera lens allow you to vary the amount of light hitting the camera pick-up tubes.

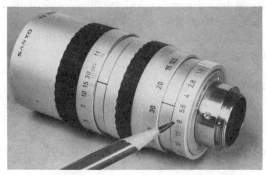

**FIGURE 5–19b.**

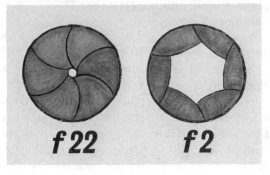

of light in. The opening that allows light to pass through the lens is called an *aperture,* and the different openings are called *f-stops.* Small f-stop numbers, like f-1.4, have relatively large iris openings, which permit greater amounts of light in. Large f-stop numbers, like f-22, have small iris openings and permit less light in.

A *fast lens* (with short focal length or wide-angle lens) allows a lot of light to pass through and can be used in low-light situations. A *slow lens* with long focal length or narrow-angle lens) allows little light to pass through and requires more available light.

Now you see why you can use the f-stop ring to fade into or out of a picture. By stopping down the f-stop to C (closed), you fade out. Doing the reverse, opening up, fades into your next scene. On television you see a fade-out from a program and a fade-in to a commercial, and then back to the program (Figure 5-19).

## DEPTH OF FIELD

*Depth of field* is the area between the camera lens and the object that appears in focus. Three factors determine depth of field:

1. The *focal length of the lens:* A short focal length (wide-angle lens or a zoom lens zoomed-out) offers a great depth of field. A long focal length (long lens or zoom lens zoomed-in) results in a shallow depth of field.
2. *f-stop:* Small f-stop settings allow a lot of light to enter, but they offer a shallow depth of field. Big f-stop settings (small iris openings) offer greater depth of field.
3. *The distance between object and camera:* The farther away a subject is from the camera, the greater the depth of field. A shallow depth of field occurs when the distance between object and camera is close.

A shallow depth of field can be used to your advantage when you want to put special emphasis on a foreground object, thus making your background out of focus. By doing so, you don't have to bother setting up a special background. In this technique, called *selective focus,* you focus on one area or object and have the other areas or objects out of focus. With selective focus you can "move" from one object to another quite

FIGURE 5-20. Selective focus allows you to shift emphasis from one subject to the other.

easily. For example, you can be zoomed-in on a foreground object, and then, by *racking focus* or refocusing on the object behind, you move the emphasis from the foreground to the middleground or background (Figure 5-20).

You need a great depth of field if you are taping a substantial amount of action or need to keep two or more subjects in focus during a take. Stop down your lens (if sufficient light is available), or use a lens with a short focal length.

### WIDE-ANGLE LENS

The wide-angle lens has a great depth of field due to the fact that proportions are distorted, creating an illusion of depth. For example, a small room can look quite large, and a normal hallway can turn into an endless tunnel. Objects near the camera look large and objects a short way from the camera look small. It also makes objects—cars, houses—look longer because parallel lines converge faster with a wide-angle lens. Any of these wide-angle effects can be either advantages or drawbacks, depending on your production needs.

A more clear-cut advantage of a wide-angle lens is that it is a good lens to use when dollying the camera because it makes the camera movement appear smooth and keeps refocusing to a minimum. Keep in mind that, as objects move toward or away from your field of view, their speed appears faster than it actually is. The same applies to their size relationships, depending on how much coverage the lens offers.

A definite disadvantage is *barrel distortion,* which means vertical lines in the background appear somewhat curved, much like the curved sides of a barrel.

### TELEPHOTO LENSES

The telephoto lens has a large focal length, along with a very narrow and shallow depth of field. Objects in its field of view are magnified and appear to be closer than they really are. With a telephoto lens you can make a busy freeway look like a traffic jam simply because the background appears larger than the foreground, thus shortening the distance between the cars. Depth distortion can work against you too. In a baseball game the pitcher, the batter, the catcher, and the umpire look closer than they really are. Thus the distance between the individual players and the umpire looks inaccurate.

Telephoto lenses can be used for selective focus. In a crowded scene, for example, you can select one person and blur out the others, thus focusing on one person's actions. Unlike the wide-angle lens, the telephoto lens reduces an object's speed toward or away from the camera because an object's size changes gradually, thus creating the reduced speed illusion. With a telephoto lens you cannot dolly or truck, because movement is impossible due to its great magnifying qualities. In fact, even a slight movement of the camera registers on the television screen.

### ZOOM LENSES

The zoom lens has a variable focal length. In one continuous move of the lens, you can change from wide angle to telephoto. The very versatile zoom lens can be used to replace individual lenses of various focal lengths. The zoom *range* is the widest angle or zoomed-out position to the narrowest angle or telephoto position, and it is expressed as a ratio of the largest focal length

**118**

to the shortest focal length. For example, a lens whose longest focal length is 120 mm and whose shortest is 12 mm would have a zoom ratio of 10:1. In other words, the field of coverage at the telephoto position is one-tenth the coverage of the wide-angle position (Figure 5-22).

FIGURE 5-21. A servo zoom lens on an ENG camera. (Photo courtesy KPHO TV5, Phoenix)

When utilizing the zoom lens, you must execute the movements smoothly. Since you have the ability to move from wide-angle to telephoto, your camera movements must be as smooth as possible since any vibration or shakey movement registers on the monitor and/or videotape. Practicing camera movements is the only way to achieve professional results. The basic, manually controlled zoom lens has variable f-stops, a zoom ring (which allows you to change focal length), and a focusing ring, usually at the front of the lens. To achieve smooth zooms, however, higher-priced electromechanical zoom lenses are the ultimate way to go. Servo zoom controls are available for studio, ENG, and EFP cameras. The servo controls are tied to a complex motor system which drives the zoom mechanism in the lens. Focusing is still done manually, but it is easy to pre-

FIGURE 5-22.

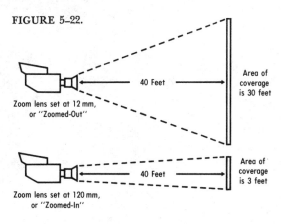

Zoom lens set at 12 mm, or "Zoomed-Out"

40 Feet — Area of coverage is 30 feet

Zoom lens set at 120 mm, or "Zoomed-In"

40 Feet — Area of coverage is 3 feet

12 To 120 Zoom Range

focus or zoom in to your subject, focus, then zoom out. These types of zoom lenses are usually accompanied by automatic iris control devices which automatically set the f-stops. This *auto-iris* can usually be switched over to manual operation.

## CLOSE-UP LENSES

Close-up lenses are used when you want to focus on an object only inches away from the camera lens. Doing so is difficult with most lenses since they focus only one to three feet away from the subject. To reduce the focusing distance, you can use three methods:

1. *Diopters* mounted on the front of a camera lens turn it into a closeup lens. They come in graduations of +1, +2, +3, and so on: the higher the number, the closer you get, and the larger your object becomes.
2. *Extension tubes* are extra lens barrel lengths that are placed between the lens and the camera lens mount. The extenders change the lens focal length and raise the lowest f-stop.
3. *Macro lenses* have extreme magnifying qualities. They can magnify a penny to fill the screen, which means that it can focus down to a couple of inches from the object.

Find out the diameter of the front element of your lens so that you can obtain the close-up lenses of the proper diameter that fit. For example, if you have a lens with a 52-mm diameter front element, you need close-up lenses that fit the 52-mm size.

## MOUNTS AND ADAPTORS

A *lens mount* is the assembly on the front of the video camera where the lens is attached. The most common mount in both film and video is the C-mount. Any camera with this assembly can house a C-mount lens. C-mount assemblies are used in the majority of lower- and medium-priced cameras, but the higher-priced cameras usually have their own specific design for mounting lenses. Many of these cameras, in fact, are sold without lenses so you can select a specific lens to fit your particular application (Figure 5-23).

FIGURE 5–23a. C-mount assembly with lens in place.

FIGURE 5–23b. With lens removed.

Adaptors can be used to match the mounting assembly of one lens to the mounting assembly of a different camera. For example, lenses used on a 35-mm still camera can be adapted to the C-mount format of a video camera by using the proper adaptor. But the f-stops on a 35-mm camera lens or on a non-C-mount lens may not correspond to the normal settings on a C-mount lens, so you must compensate for the difference.

## FILTERS

A *filter* is a piece of glass or plastic that fits on the front of the lens to regulate the intensity and/or color of light entering the lens. Filters can exclude, transmit, absorb, and exaggerate all or parts of the visible spectrum. Filters are rated by their *transmission ability*, which refers to how much light (expressed as a percentage) passes through the filter (Figure 5-24).

1. A commonly used filter is the *neutral-density filter*, which cuts down on the amount of light hitting the pick-up tubes without changing the scene's natural colors.
2. A *fog filter*, which can be used to create a misty haze appearance in a scene, can vary in density from heavy fog to a light fog depending on your situation.
3. *Polarizing filters* let you penetrate through haze. Colors become richer, skies become "bluer," and surface reflections are eliminated.

FIGURE 5–24a. The center spot filter diffuses the subject (except at the center).

FIGURE 5–24b. The fog filter creates a misty haze in a scene.

FIGURE 5–24c. The star filter creates starburst patterns. The star filter can be used to cut down on harsh reflections, but be careful to avoid burn-in and subsequent damage to your camera's pick-up tubes.

**120**

4. A *center-spot* filter can single out a center object, keeping it crisp and clear while diffusing the background. It can also be used to create "dreamy" backgrounds.
5. Color can be added to a part of a scene with a *color-grade filter.* You can change the colors of the sky, reduce glare, and make a day scene into night.
6. *Fluorescent light filters* eliminate the blue/green effect caused by shooting under fluorescent lights, while protecting natural skin tones.
7. The *star filter* creates a starburst pattern in highlighted areas.

When using filters on a color camera to change and/or to exaggerate the colors in a scene, white balance the camera before adding the filter. Doing so gives you the true effect of the filter. You may also find that some filters cut down too much of the overall light hitting the pick-up tubes. In this case, you may need to get a filter with a higher percentage of transmission.

Colored filters used with a black-and-white video camera yield the following results:

1. Yellow filters increase your contrast slightly and darken skies.
2. Red filters give you strong contrast and a surrealistic effect.
3. Green filters lighten up green subjects and make skies darker.
4. Blue filters lighten blue tones and bring out atmospheric haze.
5. Red and green filters together darken skies and foliage.

## SPECIAL APPLICATIONS

The video camera can be adapted to many optical devices that are commonly used in industry, education, and medicine. Two such devices are microscopes and endoscopes. Most manufacturers of microscopes and endoscopes have optional adapters for use with video cameras, usually with C-mounts. Check with the manufacturers to see what is available (Figure 5-25).

For a sharp picture through a *microscope,* one must reduce vibration from movement. The microscope is mounted on a rigid structure with a light trap between the microscope and camera. The mountings are usually composed of a natural or synthetic rubber for further vibration reduction. If the microscope and the camera are locked together mechanically, a sudden movement is transmitted uniformly throughout the whole system (camera, microscope, and specimen). So any slight movement does not show on the screen. This technique is useful if the equipment cannot be large or heavy due to its being moved frequently.

An *endoscope* is an optical instrument coupled to the camera to view and to examine the interior body cavity or inaccessible small objects. A wide-angle lens with a very short focal length is fitted to the end

FIGURE 5-25. Video camera mounted on a microscope.

of a slender repeater-type telescope. An endoscope's best feature is its outstanding perspective of objects without distortion.

## SUMMARY

Every successful production requires pre-planning. For creative purposes, the various types of camera movements, framing techniques, camera mounts, and different types of lenses all serve to create various effects. Utilizing all these tools helps you develop a distinctive shooting style and to bring a professional approach to your productions.

# 6
# 6
# 6
# 6
# 6
# 6
# 6 EDITING

Editing is one of the most creative aspects of video production. The responsibility of the editor is to select the shots that tell the story best. Editors contribute so much to the finished product, that directors often involve them in the early phases of a production, so that they establish good communications with everyone involved and maintain a good understanding of the script and program format. With this input, the editor is best able to take on the task of determining the order and length of each sequence as well as setting the pace and continuity of the finished videotape. When you are doing everything—producing, writing, directing, shooting, and audio—don't downplay the role of editing. The bulk of what the editor does is technical and creative in nature, and you need a basic understanding of the editing process. The single-camera style of shooting depends especially heavily on videotape editing equipment. Although you can assemble a program using only one VTR, you soon find out that this approach is not realistic. Inasmuch as editing basically consists of playing back pre-recorded scenes on one VTR while recording select scenes on a second one, thus building a logical sequence of events, the single-camera style of shooting out-of-sequence footage necessitates the use of a post-production facility.

Like any skill, the most important factor in editing is practice. The serious editor spends a great deal of time developing a "feel" for how a sequence should flow together. One of the easiest ways to develop your editorial skills is to go out and shoot some footage of an interesting event. Get as many different views of the event as you can. When you feel that you have enough to work with, come back to the studio and try editing the footage to one of your favorite pieces of music. As you build the sequence, experiment a little—try different ways of editing the video to the audio track.

In case you're not interested in operating VTRs and related equipment, you can always hire the services of a post-production studio whose editor will follow your instructions. Be well prepared to communicate your desires. Since most post-production studios charge hourly fees, your efficiency will show up on the "bottom line." Planning and communicating your needs saves dollars.

## AN ORGANIZED APPROACH

In addition to learning how the editing equipment operates and functions, take on an organized attitude about the editing process. Either keep the editor involved in the entire production process, or, if you're going to do your own editing, keep the editing in mind during all prior stages of production. Although a producer may bring in an editor at the very end, after everything has been shot, the editor actually has to become familiar with the script (if there is one) and work with the producer to determine key elements such as the intended audience, the sound track, and the pace. The editor also needs to know any other aspects of the intended product that will help in filling the producer's needs. This relationship works both ways: while the editor should learn to listen and communicate with the producer, the producer may find that an experienced editor can offer suggestions that can benefit the finished program.

The next step is to familiarize yourself with all the video footage to be edited. Has it been slated? Has anyone taken the time to indicate which takes are "good"? Did the camera operator get extra close-ups, cutaways, and so on? If no notes were taken, or worse yet, if the reels are not marked, you'll have to start by viewing all the footage, making notes and marking each reel (or cassette). If you ever have to go through such an experience, you know that the pre-planning failed to include the editing phase.

As an editor, you must also organize your equipment in a practical and workable fashion. Editing can take many hours of concentrated work. The layout of your facility should be designed for efficient, comfortable operation. All the controls should be accessible, at a good working height. The editing equipment should also be situated in a room conducive to a creative process. Also helpful is an environment that is out of the mainstream of traffic, that lets you control room lighting, and that offers adequate monitoring of the video and audio aspects of the production (Figure 6-1).

FIGURE 6–1. The editing room should be comfortable and conducive to the creative process. (Photo courtesy KPHO TV5, Phoenix)

**USING ONE RECORDER**

Assuming that you're interested in how an editing system works, let's look at what you can do with one VTR, then build up to the capabilities of more complex systems. You can use only one VTR to build a meaningful message. Planning becomes very critical, especially if the VTR has no built-in editing capabilities. Your approach can go either of two ways. The first way is to plan your program so that you can shoot the entire program in one "take." The second approach is to shoot your first scene, set up and shoot the second scene, and so on, until the program is complete. The problem with this method is that the nonediting VTR is not capable of giving you an invisible cut to each scene. So you will probably have a great deal of picture break-up as you start and stop the VTR (to record each successive scene). One way to ease these abrupt visual changes is to use the scene transition techniques described in the last chapter. Also, the amount of picture interruption or "break-up" varies from recorder to recorder.

**124**

## EDITING VTRs

Certain types of VTRs have been designed to allow for assembling scenes in sequence electronically, instead of splicing sections of tape together (as in motion picture editing). They also permit the insertion of new video and/or audio information into existing videotape footage. These editing VTRs open up a great deal of flexibility for the single-camera/VTR user. They not only offer clean edits with little or no picture break-up, but they also offer, for example, the possibility of recording a narration track, music, and visuals all separately.

Keeping the pulse of the editing VTR is the servo control system.

### Servo Control

A servo control system reads its own output and regulates the output of the system, somewhat like an automatic cruise control on an automobile. Once you set the speed at which you want the car to run, the cruise control compares the setting to the actual speed of the car and either increases or decreases the amount of fuel necessary to maintain that speed. A servo control does much the same for a VTR:

1. *Capstan servo* refers to the regulation of the rotation speed of the capstan, as it pulls the tape through the VTR past the heads.
2. *Head drum servo* applies to the speed at which the heads rotate.
3. The *reel servo system* is used to stabilize playback and record. Two separate motors drive the videotape feed and take-up reels. A reel servo constantly adjusts the relative speed of one reel to the other. Remember that the rotating speed of the reels constantly changes as the circumferences of the tape on the reels change. The reel servo minimizes possible tape stretch and/or variations in tape tension, thus offering

additional stability. This feature is especially useful when anticipating heavy use of the VTR.

How does the servo system work? Remember that each frame of video is comprised of two fields, which are completed in one-thirtieth of a second. So each frame has sixty vertical sync pulses every second. The control track head records these vertical sync pulses and uses them as a reference point in regulating constant head drum speed (in the case of head drum servo) and capstan rotation speed (capstan servo). Many updated VTRs utilizing vertical lock for head drum servo control also use the horizontal sync pulses as a point of reference. The resulting "H-locked" VTR offers very stable playback and recording capabilities (Figure 6-2).

Now you may be wondering what all this has to do with editing. All the scanning and synchronizing signals that make up the video signal are very important to the editing

FIGURE 6–2.

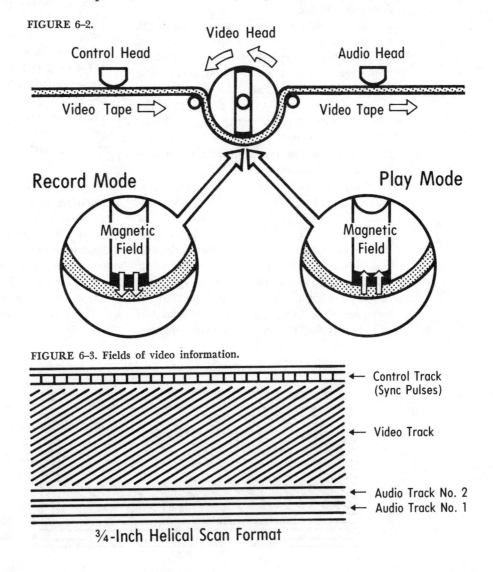

FIGURE 6–3. Fields of video information.

¾-Inch Helical Scan Format

process (Figure 6-3). To achieve clean edits, with no picture break-up, the editing VTR must have some way of recording new information (at the edit point), without the loss of synchronization between old (pre-recorded) and new (incoming video) information. Most helical scan editing VTRs use servo control systems to accomplish "clean" edits and to offer a greater degree of stability during playback and record modes. Similarly, servo controls are incorporated into professional playback-only and nonediting VTRs.

Two basic modes are incorporated into an editing VTR:

1. *The assemble mode:* Assemble edits allow you to add scenes onto a blank and/or bulk erased videotape in consecutive fashion.
2. *The insert mode:* Insert edits allow you to record new video and/or audio information over pre-recorded footage.

## Assemble Mode

In the assemble edit mode, an editing VTR records everything—video, control track, and audio. When you want to assemble, or add new information at a particular point in a pre-recorded piece of tape, the editing VTR has to go from play to record without the loss of synchronization at the edit point. In single-camera/single (editing VTR) system, the user has to use the camera as the source of new video information. With the editing VTR to start reading the incoming synchroni-back (long enough to maintain stable playback), and at the point where you want new information to come in, you hit the record button to start recording the new information. The edit button then signals the editing VTR to start reading the incoming syncronization pulses. The capstan and/or head drum locks up to the incoming sync, so that at the edit point the record mechanism engages

with no loss of sync. The result is a clean edit with no picture roll, no break-up.

## Insert Editing

The same principle applies. Suppose you have on-camera talent giving a lecture on a recorded segment of tape. After the taping session, you wish to insert edit graphics, art cards, and/or close-ups of the talent pointing to some visual aid used in the lecture. Here's what you would do:

1. With the editing VTR in the video-only insert edit mode, compose the necessary shot, perhaps an opening graphic or title card.
2. View the pre-recorded tape to determine the "in point" and the "out point" of the insert edit.
3. Rewind the tape beyond the in point.
4. Then put the VTR into play, to allow the capstan and/or head drum servo to lock up to the incoming signal from the video.
5. When the in point is reached, hit the record or insert-in button (depending on VTR make). The VTR begins to erase the pre-recorded video, but it does not erase the existing control track or audio signals.
6. Press the edit-out button to stop the process, and the new video information switches back to the pre-recorded video.

This explanation of the overall process of assemble and insert editing is, of course, very basic. Like almost any technology, the level of sophistication of the editing VTR is directly proportional to its cost. Half-inch videocassette recorder/editors represent the low end of the spectrum, while 1-inch and 2-inch open-reel VTRs offer the state-of-the-art in accuracy, quality, and flexibility (Figure 6-4).

FIGURE 6–4a. ¾-inch helical scan assemble edit.

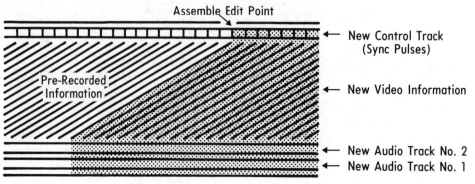

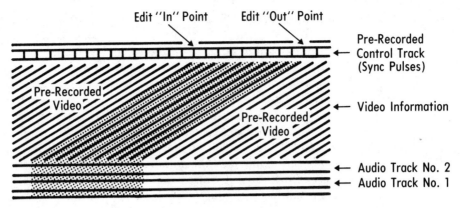

FIGURE 6–4b. Video and/or audio-only insert editing.

## WRONG FIELD EDITS

Many edits made on inexpensive VTRs flash, break-up, or "flag" during playback. Since these picture disturbances are described with many different terms, let's just examine them from the standpoint of their causes. The first cause of picture disturbance stems from the editing VTR's lack of vertical interval switching capability. If the editing VTR starts recording new information with no regard to the vertical interval of the pre-recorded signal, there will be a great deal of picture break-up (at the edit point) upon playback. The second major cause arises from the edit point's occurring on the wrong field.

A vertical interval switch at the edit point insures that the edit happens during the time it takes for the vertical blanking pulses to cut off the scanning beam (in a picture monitor or pick-up tube) as it travels from the bottom to the top of the picture after each field of scanning. The scanning pulses (fields) and synchronization pulses (control track) are, of course, recorded on the videotape. When the VTR plays back pre-recorded information, an edit should logically occur at the correct field to achieve a "glitch-free" edit.

Recall that the scanning of each frame of video starts with the odd field (field one) at the top left of the camera pick-up tube(s) and ends at bottom center. Next, the even field (field two) starts scanning after the vertical interval (vertical blanking) at top center and ends at bottom right (refer to Figure 1-8). The correct sequence is fields 1-2, 1-2, etc. If an edit occurs at the wrong field, changing the sequence to fields 1-2, 1-2, 2-1, for example, a momentary disturbance in the picture occurs during playback. Since many VTRs are not capable of recognizing one frame from the other, a servo system was designed to eliminate wrong field edits.

A framing servo, a highly desired option in an editing VTR, is basically an additional circuit in the VTR that can tell the difference between the last line of a field and the last line of a frame. The framing servo delays an edit until the last line of a complete frame occurs in both incoming video and pre-recorded video. Similarly, the edit-out point of an insert edit also occurs at the end of a complete frame. By starting and ending each edit during the vertical interval, the next retrace is always in the right place, so no "flagging" or other picture disturbance occurs.

## AN EDITING SYSTEM

The basic editing system is comprised of an editing VTR, which is used to assemble a complete program, and other sources of video, such as a camera and/or other VTRs. With this system, the editor has a combination of assemble and insert edits, not to mention a great deal of flexibility in accomplishing the task.

Since the single-camera style of shooting requires the use of editing equipment and facilities, both shooting and editing take on equal weight in the overall process of video production. Although shooting single-camera style fundamentally requires only a camera and VTR, the use to which the finished product will be put should dictate how elaborate the hardware needs to be for editing as well as for shooting.

## DETERMINING YOUR NEEDS

Let two things guide your decisions when you're buying and/or using editing facilities:

The first is budget. Portable VTRs, players, editors, related support equipment, and facilities can add up to a sizable investment. A basic ¾-inch editing system can easily cost from $10,000 to $30,000. Broadcast-quality systems can climb into the hundreds-of-thousands. Obviously, if you want to invest in an editing and single-camera/VTR system, you'll need finances.

The second area to consider is the type of programs you'll be generating. If the bulk of what you'll be editing has very limited distribution—anything from weddings and birthdays to corporate training tapes and local cable TV programs—then ½-inch and ¾-inch systems will probably suffice. If your programs are to be used commercially, however, you're better off going with the best you can get, that is, 1-inch and 2-inch broadcast-quality systems. The video producer breaking into the field often finds that renting facilities and hiring out talent is a viable alternative to the outright purchase of equipment. Many producers, directors, writers, and technicians often elect to rent editing facilities and either do the editing themselves or hire an edit operator. In either case, you need to establish an organized approach to the overall editing process.

## SUPPORT EQUIPMENT

When it comes to designing an editing system, there are seemingly endless possibilities. Just as cameras and VTRs vary in cost, capability, and quality, support equipment also ranges from basic additions to sky-high limits. Such options include:

1. edit control systems,
2. audio and video sources,
3. monitoring equipment, and
4. signal-processing equipment, mixing capabilities, and duplication facilities.

## EDIT CONTROL SYSTEMS

Edit controllers allow the operator to make precise and, if necessary, repeated edits. The technology built into available systems is reflected both in cost and in accuracy. As a general rule, select an edit controller in proportion to the investment in the editing VTRs. Unless you are doing a great deal of editing, it is simply not cost-effective to purchase an edit controller costing several times the total price of the VTRs used. For example, it is ludicrous to use a computerized edit controller costing tens of thousands of dollars with ½-inch VTRs designed for home use. The money spent on the edit controller could be better spent upgrading the VTRs. On the other hand, try to anticipate future additions to the editing system. Many controllers contain microprocessors that can be expanded at a later time, when more equipment is added. The initial cost in this case may exceed the cost of the VTRs (½-inch and ¾-inch), but the purchase leaves you open to future expansion to 1- or 2-inch VTRs and to eventual control over other peripherals such as audio tape recorders and video mixers/special effects generators.

Two basic types of electronic editing systems are in use today: control track and time code editors.

### Control Track Editors

Control track editors operate by counting video frames according to the control track pulses on the videotape. Generally control track systems use two VTRs, one for playback and one to record. The control track editor, connected to both VTRs, offers remote control of both machines (Figure 6-5).

The basic sequence in control track editing is to find the beginning of a desired scene by playing back the pre-recorded video on the playback (slave) machine.

1. Depending on the manufacturers of the VTRs and of the control track editor, you may be able to search for the scene by manipulating the playback speed in both forward and reverse. Some control track editors allow you to speed up or to slow down the playback of both VTRs (in forward and reverse) from still frame to five or more times normal playback speed with recognizable picture. Once you find the beginning of the desired scene, on the playback VTR, "park" the VTR in still frame. Then you find the in point on

FIGURE 6–5. ¾-inch control track editing VTRs. (Photo courtesy KPHO TV5, Phoenix)

the editing VTR, and "park" the VTR in still frame.

2. Then select the mode of editing—assemble, video and audio insert, video-only insert, or audio-only insert.

3. Push a preview button and the edit controller backs up both VTRs about five or more seconds and stops. The edit controller does so by counting control track pulses as each VTR is reversed. The number of pulses depends on the manufacturer or on the type of VTR and control track editor.

4. When both VTRs have stopped, they go into playback mode. When the edit controller senses that both VTRs have reached the predetermined edit point(s), it switches its visual output from the playback signal of the record VTR to that of the playback (slave) VTR. The operator can then preview what the edit will look like.

5. If satisfied with the preview edit, the operator then presses a return to cue button, which signals the control track editor to automatically cue the VTRs. The tapes are then automatically back up as before. If the record button is pushed, the VTRs are commanded to roll in play. At the in point, the edit controller commands the

record VTR to perform the edit, recording the incoming video and/or audio information.

6. If not satisfied with the preview edit, the operator selects new edit points on one or both VTRs and continues as before.

Control track type editors present a few problems. First, they are not always frame accurate. Due to slippage during rewinding and previewing edits, accuracy can slip by plus or minus one to five—or more—frames. (The VTRs have to rewind, or "back up," before a preview or edit sequence to allow enough time for each to get up to speed and for the edit VTR's servo controls to lock up to the incoming control track pulses.) Another drawback is their inherent design around a two-VTR system. More than two VTRs are necessary for many standard effects, such as dissolves and the like. Also, the control track system is limited to helical scan VTRs, a restriction that eliminates 2-inch quadruplex VTRs because the playback speed of the "quad" VTR cannot be varied from normal play speed and retain a recognizable picture.

The most important thing to remember about insert editing is that the entire process depends on an unbroken control track on both the playback and the edit VTRs. Also, both VTRs must have enough pre-recorded information, or *pre-roll,* before the actual edit point. This allows both VTRs to run up to speed, allows the playback VTR to "lock up" its servos, and allows the edit VTR to lock up and compare incoming video to pre-recorded control track pulses. This is why ample time (10 or more seconds) should be recorded before an actual "take" of footage intended for eventual editing. Likewise, the edit VTR also needs a stable, unbroken control track when assemble editing. So record 10 seconds or so of "video black" at the very beginning of the tape. There must be some sort of signal on the tape to start to electronically edit videotape. This signal gives the edit VTR a point to start. Video black can easily be obtained by turning on your video camera, leaving the lens cap on. Record a short segment on your edit VTR if you intend to assemble edit the entire program. This gives the edit (master) VTR something to "lock" onto as all subsequent edits are made. Although assemble editing is faster than insert editing, the finished tape is not as stable as a tape using insert edits on a continuous, pre-recorded "black" signal. This technique of using insert only is referred to as *editing into black.* Some people prefer to record color bars throughout the tape. This works as well as black, but if you intend to "go to black" anywhere in the tape, it's easier to simply record "black" in the first place. For a continuous, uninterrupted signal, record a control track (recorded with "black") on your master tape that is no longer than the anticipated length of the finished program. From there, perform all edits with the VTR in the video and/or audio insert mode only. Never use an assemble edit, because it defeats the purpose of using a continuous control track and, in fact, breaks up the control track.

**Time Code Editors**

The most common time code editors utilize a form of frame coding developed by the Society of Motion Picture and Television Engineers (SMPTE). The system was developed to record an 80-bit digital code on one of the unused audio tracks to identify each individual frame on the videotape. Each frame's code number—broken down into hours, minutes, seconds, and frames—is unique to each frame. For example, the start of a scene might be at time code address number 01:32:57:23. This would be read as 1 hour, 32 minutes, 57 seconds and 23 frames. Although a tape may be much less than an hour long, the time code is often started at number one, two, three, or more hours to help identify a particular reel of tape.

A computer, using the time code as a reference point, controls the edit frame by frame. VTRs (and other sources of video) are electronically tied into the computer, allowing access to mechanical control over edit and other control functions. All commands are then given at a computer keyboard. Computer-controlled, frame coded systems are available in a wide variety of designs, capabilities, and price, as well as many non-standard, or non-SMPTE, frame coding techniques that are also in use. Since including all the systems is far beyond the scope of this book, an understanding of the SMPTE time code system becomes a good basis for comparing other frame coded, computer-assisted edit controllers (Figure 6-6).

First, let's start with some original video footage. The tape must be time coded in order to use it with the computerized edit controller. Time code can be added either before, during, or after the video recording takes place. If before, the time code must be recorded along with some other video signal, similar to control track editing, using video black or another source of video. Then the actual recording is made as an insert edit. If a time code generator is available during taping, time code is recorded at the same time. If such a generator is not available, the footage can be taken back to the post-production facility with time code recorded on an unused audio channel.

At this point, you definitely want to make a copy of the original footage with the time code visible in the picture. To do so, play back the original footage with time code through a time code reader, which has the option of inserting the code numbers somewhere in the picture. The output of the time code reader/display is recorded onto a small format ½- or ¾-inch VTR. This extra step generates a "worktape" which allows you to preview the footage with time code numbers without tying up an entire editing system. It also minimizes the handling of original footage.

Worktapes are then edited on ½-inch and/or ¾-inch VTRs and control track editors. Although control track editors are not frame accurate, they allow the editor to

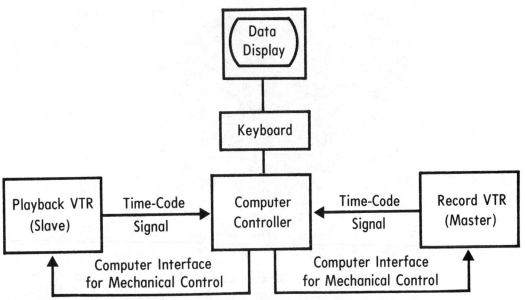

**FIGURE 6–6.** The basic idea behind time-coded, computer-controlled editing is the feedback of time code information on the videotape to the computer controller and the mechanical control of the VTRs by the computer. The operator typically works at a computer console.

assemble good scenes or takes—a rough edit— to get an overall idea of how the finished program will fall into place, as well as for approval. The process of viewing and assembling these tapes with visible time code is called *off-line editing* (Figure 6-7).

*On-line editing* generally refers to using an entire computer-assisted editing system. Since the on-line system is costly to operate and/or to lease time on, the off-line approach makes better economic sense. Once the editor and director are happy with the off-line tape, an edit list is made up, containing a list of all edits with their corresponding time code address numbers. These numbers are then entered into the computer. In turn, the

original tapes' time code numbers are compared to the list entered in the computer. Depending on the manufacturer and design of the system, the computer searches for each time code number and executes all edits automatically (Figure 6-8).

In a basic two-VTR system, tapes are assembled in much the same manner as in control track editing. The big difference is that the edits are absolutely frame accurate, even when edits are rehearsed a number of times. Also, less time is spent in executing the edits because VTR control is taken over by the computer. More time can be spent in creative decision making.

**FIGURE 6–7.** Generating a work tape for off-line editing. With the time code inserted into the video image, a list of time code numbers can be assembled on control track editors, rather than tying up the entire on-line system to make edit decisions.

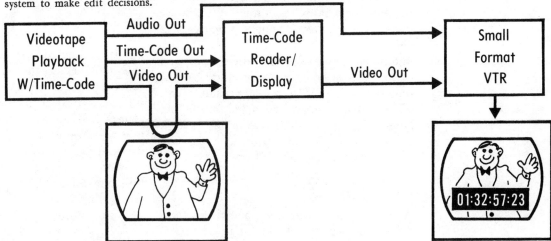

FIGURE 6–8. Computer terminal used in time code editing. (Photo courtesy KPHO TV5, Phoenix)

Once again, remember that the edit VTR needs pre-recorded black video (or some other video signal), along with time code, to allow the VTR to lock up to the pre-recorded control track and to allow the computer to read the time code.

Another feature of the time-code/computer-edit approach is expandability, an area that should influence any purchase decisions when you're looking for a computer-based editing system. Since computer technology is changing at a rapid pace, look for systems that allow for updated circuit changes and that offer expansion possibilities, as more sources of video need to be added on-line.

Computers can be used to control several VTRs, to interface with video and audio mixers, and to control several edit VTRs, as well as to supervise other sources of video such as film chains, electronic graphics, and slide projectors. Naturally, as the computer system grows in capability, so does the cost. As a result, a typical broadcast-quality post-production facility with computer control over several VTRs (using time code), video and audio mixing, and electronic graphics capability can easily reach the million dollar mark. Not to worry though! Single-camera video producers can lease time on a computerized system, time code their tapes, and end up with a high-quality product. On-line time ranges from $250 to $400 per hour, with off-line charges ranging from $25 to $100 per hour. With access to this level of technology, single-camera producers can look forward to a wide range of possibilities.

## AUDIO SOURCES

With so much emphasis on viedo technology and techniques, the audio portion is often almost forgotten or at least taken for granted. Although many sources of audio can be used and/or mixed for use on videotape, most videotape recorders have apparently been designed with limited audio capability. Manufacturers are changing this, however, with the release of ½-inch and ¾-inch VTRs with two channels of audio, capable of recording stereo audio information. Yet if you make a great effort to produce quality video, you should do as much for quality audio. (See Chapter 3, "Audio.")

In computer-controlled time code video editing, the time-code signal is recorded on an unused audio channel. This approach severely limits the audio capabilities of the VTR in most cases, in that only one channel of audio is left. Subsequently, all audio sources have to be monaural. When editing the master videotape, you need a monaural mixer to blend various sources of audio. The mixer's resulting output is then fed to the unused track on the master VTR. Often the pre-recorded audio from the slave VTR is mixed with other audio sources, such as mixing an intro music track (from an audio tape source) with the "wild sound" of a pre-recorded video segment. All the rules about connectors, impedances, and other technical considerations covered in Chapters 2 and 3 apply (Figure 6-9).

The preferred approach of recording time code on a VTR with only two available audio channels is to record the time code on the outermost audio track (usually channel one), and record the audio signal on the innermost audio track (usually channel two). On channel one, which is usually positioned toward the outermost edge of the videotape, frequency response is sometimes affected by the videotape rubbing against mechanical parts in the VTR, such as tape guides or a head drum. Recording the audio signal on the innermost track (channel two), allows for the best possible record and playback quality. Time code is not as vulnerable on channel one, because it is not affected by tonal changes as much as sound reproduction is. The critical element in recording a time code signal on audio one is to make sure that the level of the signal maintains a zero-dB reading on the master VTR's VU meter. A good strong signal is required to allow the time code reading equipment to do its job (Figure 6-2).

Most of the latest 1- and 2-inch VTRs as well as some broadcast-quality versions in

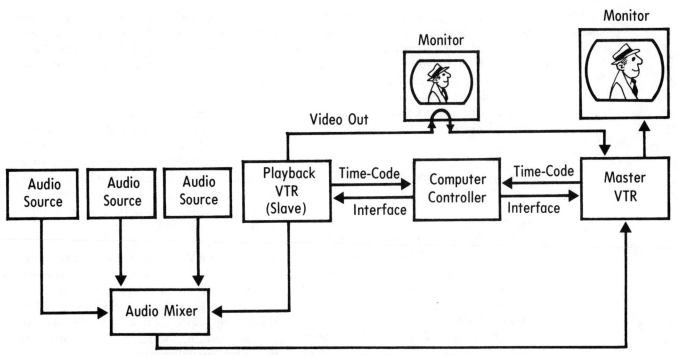

FIGURE 6–9. Mixing several sources of audio. Since many VTRs have only two available tracks of audio, one must be used for time code with the other used for a monaural audio mix-down, possibly from several sources.

the ¾-inch format, have three available channels of audio. This option allows the operator to use the outermost channel for time code and the two innermost channels for recording stereo, bilingual tracks, and/or mixing two separate sources directly on the master videotape.

On occasion, you have to play back multiple tracks of audio with a videotape, to mix down audio for use on a master videotape. To do so, interface a computer with a multi-track audio tape recorder, using one track for time code. With the computer in control of several audio tape recorders, and using the video taped sequences as a visual guide, the audio technician can mix down the tracks of audio, simultaneously recording the final mix onto the VTR.

## VIDEO SOURCES

In the basic single-camera/single-VTR system, your sources of video are limited to one—your video camera. When you're utilizing the basic control track edit controller to assemble a program, you can include not only the camera, but pre-recorded videotape as well. From here, your options once again, become limitless. More VTRs can be added, along with electronic graphics, film chain, and other cameras. Even with this system, however, you have to assemble a finished

tape, scene by scene, using many different sources of video (and audio) to tell the story. This approach is quite limted in that each edit transition is a "straight cut" from one scene to another. The scene transitions described in Chapter 5 were designed with this type of editing in mind.

The next step up is to some sort of system for synchronizing various sources of video to accomplish the special transition effects we are used to seeing in motion pictures—such as dissolves, wipes, and titling. These special effects are easily accomplished with any basic *special effects generator* (SEG) or *switcher,* as it is also commonly referred to. Two or more sources of synchronized video are fed into the SEG, which, in turn, allows you to cut between sources, as well as to perform dissolves, wipes, and many other functions. Time-base correctors and similar video signal-processing equipment, which are used to synchronize videotape sources for use with a switcher, are discussed later. Literally dozens and dozens of switchers are available, and, like everything else, they vary in options and cost. Since a whole chapter could be devoted to SEGs, we will only use them as one of the necessary pieces of support equipment needed to achieve these visual effects.

Beyond technical considerations, familiarize yourself with the many sources of video

**133**

available. The capabilities of each system should be of key interest to the commercial video producer. Being aware of the "state of the art" becomes very important in maintaining a satisfied clientele. The main idea is to consider how various sources of video can be used to achieve your goal: an edited master videotape.

## MONITORING EQUIPMENT

To accurately evaluate pre-recorded videotapes, cameras, videodiscs, and the like, you must be able to make visual judgments of the overall picture fidelity. So various types of monitoring equipment are used to view the output of cameras, VTRs, and other sources of video equipment. Two general categories of television display devices exist: picture monitors and specialized oscilloscopes.

### Picture Monitors

Picture monitors come in three varieties:

1. receivers,
2. monitors, and
3. receiver/monitors.

*Receivers.* We are all familiar with the first—the TV receiver in our homes. Through an antenna and a tuner, the receiver picks up radio frequencies, which are broadcast by a TV station and which carry video and audio signals. A receiver can also be used to view the output of a VTR, if that VTR is equipped with a radio frequency (RF) output. Most consumer VTRs have built-in RF outputs, while most other types require an optional RF unit. For noncritical viewing, a TV receiver is the most economical way to go.

*Monitors.* A monitor, on the other hand, has no tuner and accepts only a video signal, which is fed directly by cable from a camera, VTR, or other video source. Monitors vary a great deal in cost, depending on their intended use and special features. For example, a master color monitor used at a TV station may cost several thousand dollars. On the other hand, a small black-and-white monitor used to view the output of a surveillance camera might cost only a few hundred dollars.

*Receiver/Monitor.* Hybrids of both receivers and monitors, most, if not all, receiver/monitors are adaptations of consumer television sets. This hybrid approach allows manufacturers to take advantage of less expensive, mass-produced picture tubes, chasses, and cabinets. At the same time, however, the units offer many features of professional monitors. Separate video and audio connectors are provided, usually with loop-through capabilities, allowing the option to pass a signal through the monitor to other monitors or video equipment. Many times video and audio processing circuits are added, to offer optimum reproduction.

### Nature of the Video Reproduction Process

*Black-and-white.* The video signal that enters a picture monitor is a steady stream of information containing synchronizing pulses and varying video signals. In a monochrome picture monitor, these signals are converted into varying voltages which cause the intensity of the scanning beam within a TV picture tube to fluctuate. This beam of electrons scans the inner surface of the picture tube exactly in the same way as the pick-up tube(s) in a video camera. The signals stored and retrieved on videotape are reproduced in the same way: Sync pulses, scanning instructions, and audio signals are reproduced by the VTR's heads, recombined by the VTR's circuitry, and then sent on for viewing on a picture monitor (Figure 6-10).

*Color.* In a color picture monitor, the incoming color video signal is recreated in several ways. The inner surface of the screen utilizes three different phosphors which glow in the three primary colors: red, green, and blue. These phosphors are arranged in a mosaic pattern of either three tiny dots or three vertical bars—the RGB groups. This mosaic covers the entire inner surface of the picture tube. Between the screen and the scanning beam of electrons is a shadow mask, a very thin sheet of metal that has tiny perforated dots (or bars) to match up with the red, green, and blue groupings of dots (or bars) on the inner surface of the tube. The function of this shadow mask is to prevent the beam(s) of electrons from spilling onto the wrong dots or bars.

In the case of the dot matrix, three separate electron guns are controlled by their respective RGB signals. Depending on the manufacturer, these RGB signals can be

FIGURE 6–10. Images are reproduced in a number of ways.

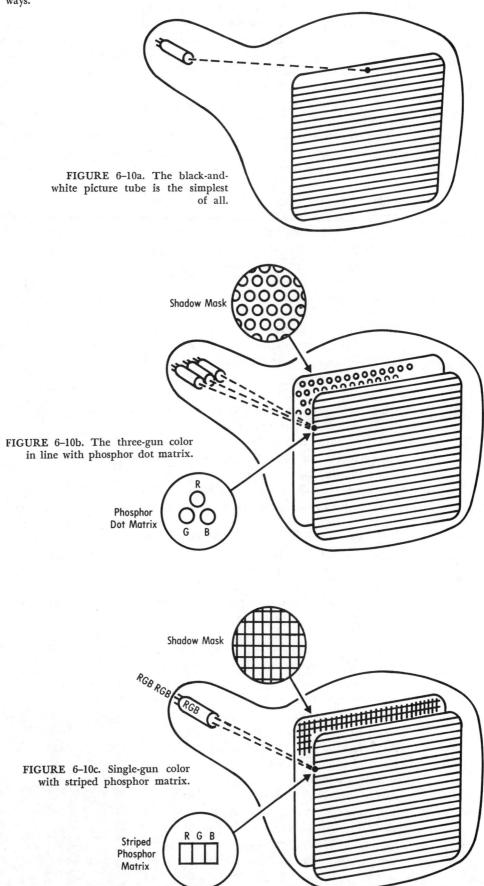

FIGURE 6–10a. The black-and-white picture tube is the simplest of all.

Shadow Mask

FIGURE 6–10b. The three-gun color in line with phosphor dot matrix.

Phosphor Dot Matrix

Shadow Mask

FIGURE 6–10c. Single-gun color with striped phosphor matrix.

Striped Phosphor Matrix

sent directly to the monitor from an RGB video signal such as a color camera encoder. Other monitors accept a normal NTSC signal and derive the RGB signals from the composite input. These three signals sweep across the screen, reproducing the output of a camera, VTR, videodisc, or other source.

As you might imagine, aligning the three guns to allow each beam to hit its respective phosphor requires a great deal of accuracy, or *convergence*. Poor convergence results in color fringing, that is, in the misregistration of the image. Current manufacturing technology is minimizing convergence problems by bonding the three guns together. With the three guns bonded in place at the rear of the picture tube, there is little, if any requirement to realign the scanning beams.

Another approach to eliminating convergence problems is to use a single gun. In this type of picture tube, phosphors are arranged in bars or vertical "stripes," with a red phosphor on the left, green in the middle, and blue on the right. The clusters of RGB bars are scanned by "pulsing" RGB signals out of the single tube. These types of tubes, which offer very good vertical resolution, are found in many consumer TV receivers, as well in many receiver/monitors. Although the picture looks good, it is not an accurate representation of the video signal and is not generally used in critical engineering and test situations. Consequently, engineers often prefer to use color monitors using a three-gun, dot matrix design. This design is capable of displaying higher frequencies, and it also allows the engineer (in most cases) to feed the monitor with separate RGB outputs. The key in selecting the appropriate monitor is to examine the intended use.

*Image Area.* The size of the image area has an effect on reproduction. In general, a small screen (measured diagonally) gives a better image than a large screen, simply because the scan lines on a small screen are closer together than on a large screen. Hence there is always a tradeoff between picture size and picture quality.

The image area size also affects the size of a group viewing. A good rule is to match one viewer with every two inches of picture area (measured diagonally). For example, have no more than six viewers at one 12-inch monitor, ten viewers for a 19-inch monitor, and so on. For very large screen viewing, you may have to use a video projector, which actually projects an image made up of red, green, and blue beams of light. At the low end of the price scale, video projectors are limited in the projector-to-screen distance. At the high end, some projector can throw a 20-foot diagonal image.

## Options

Look for several options when purchasing a monitor or receiver/monitor.

*DC Restoration.* Quite simply, for DC restoration, the monitor produces a blank screen in the absence of a video signal. This option is especially useful when editing, because there is no distracting, bright, screen of "snow" in between searching and assembling segments of video. One-hundred-percent DC restoration is especially desirable when showing videotapes to an audience, because the screen stays dark until the videotape is started.

*Video and Audio Looping.* Looping features refer to the incorporation of input and output connectors, which offer the capability to feed multiple monitors and/or monitor/ receivers. This type of feature allows users to feed a monitor or receiver/monitor with direct video and audio feeds. Look for the switch next to the video OUT connectors, labeled either "75 ohm and Off" or "Hi Z and Term."

*Off-Air Recording Capability.* A monitor/ receiver is especially useful when provided with audio and video outputs for off-air recording of commercial broadcasts, whose signals can be tuned in by the tuner on the front of the receiver/monitor. The outputs can be fed directly to a VTR for recording.

FIGURE 6–11. This receiver/monitor has two provisions for video and audio feeds. When the monitor is last in a system, the terminator switch should be in the 75 ohm position. Also, note that the monitor/receiver has an output for "off-air" signals and eight-pin connectors.

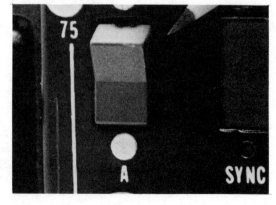

An 8-pin connector is especially desirable when using VTRs manufactured in Japan. With this connector, audio and video can be fed directly to a monitor/receiver. In some cases, the monitor/receiver feeds for off-air broadcast are included. When using 8-pin connectors, make sure that the receiver/ monitor and VTR combination are compatible. If not, a dealer or service shop can easily rewire the individual pins to fit the application (Figure 6-11).

*Viewing Video in Underscanned Position.* At the throwing of a switch, the monitor or monitor/receiver with the underscan feature reduces the total image size of the video signal. By doing so, the image takes up the center portion of the screen. This feature allows the accurate framing of scenes with a video camera.

*Built-In Pulse Cross Display.* The pulse cross function allows users to throw a switch, activating a delay of both horizontal and vertical synchronizing pulses (Figure 6-12). This option is especially useful for the proper adjustment of tape tension, as well as for the viewing at the portion of the scan-

ning that preceded the vertical interval. In all helical scan machines, as the head drum rotates, the scanning of the tape switches back and forth between the record and/or playback heads. The point at which this switchng occurs is called the *head switching* point. When playing back a helical scan videotape, the vertical interval shows the proper head switching point and correct tracking. These two functions vary from one format of VTR to the next. The manufacturer determines where this point should occur, depending on the format, or design of the VTR.

The pulse cross option allows a technician to see where the head switching point is. If the technician sees that the head switching point is in the wrong place, the VTR needs adjustment. With the monitor or monitor/receiver set in the pulse cross display mode, the playback VTR's tape tension is also checked by viewing the amount of skew, or "bend," at the top of the picture. Adjustment of the skew control on the VTR increases or decreases the tension on the tape, allowing you to straighten out the bend at the top of the picture. Proper tension is especially important when editing and/or

FIGURE 6–12. Pulse-cross display showing video playback with skew problem. Head switching point is seen above the vertical interval.

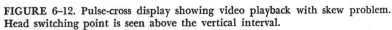
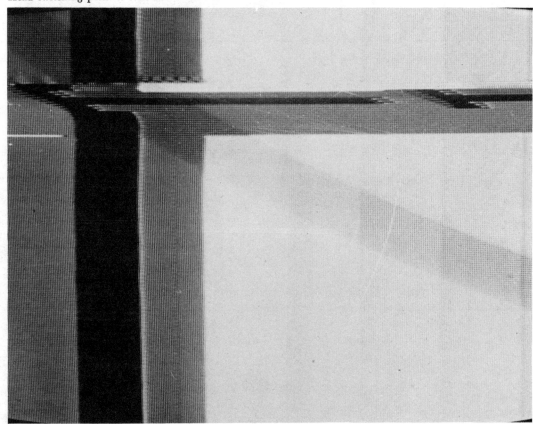

duplicating tapes, since an improper skew is recorded on the copy. If the tape tension cannot be adjusted perfectly, or if the skew keeps drifting out of adjustment, you may need to use a time-base corrector (TBC), discussed later in the chapter.

### Waveform Monitors

One of the most useful tools to the production process is a specialized type of oscilloscope called a waveform monitor, which displays the variations in strength and structure

of a video signal. On the monitor's screen, the strength or brightness of the signal and sync pulses are measured along the vertical axis, and time is measured along the horizontal axis. Initially, the waveform monitor is calibrated so that the video signal fills the waveform scale. This scale is designed so that the darkest areas of the video signal are near the zero line of the scale, with the brightest portion of the signal peaking at 100 percent. Synchronizing pulses appear below the zero line, and should touch −40 units on the scale (Figure 6-13).

FIGURE 6–13. The waveform monitor offers a graphic display of the video signals.

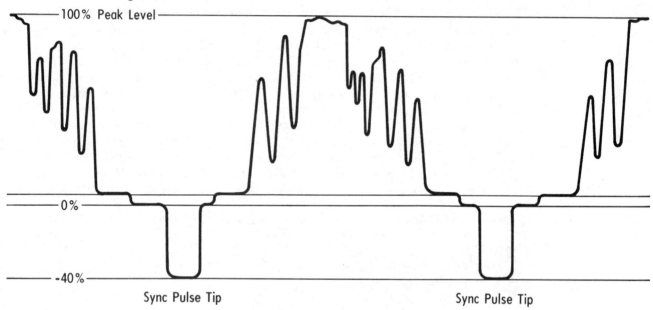

The proper relationships of signal.

Actual device. (Photo courtesy KPHO TV5, Phoenix)

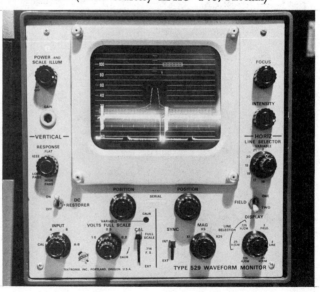

The main objective is to maintain the proper levels to optimize the recording and/or playback of video signals. By adjusting the iris on the camera lens, the amount of light striking the pick-up tube(s) is changed and displayed on the waveform monitor. If the peak level is too low, the iris (f-stop) should be opened up to let in more light. If the peak level goes over 100 percent, the iris should be closed down. Similarly, a waveform monitor can be used to evaluate a pre-recorded signal. If the signal is too high (that is, if it peaks beyond 100 percent) or too low (peaks far below 100 percent), then adjust the signal with signal-processing equipment.

### Monitor Bridges

To save money and to examine the output of several sources of video, a monitor bridge is used. In its basic form, a monitor bridge is a routing switcher that has anywhere from two to ten or more inputs and one output. At the push of a button corresponding to a particular input, you view the signal coming from that input, depending on the application. A routing switcher can send audio signals as well, and it usually costs only a few hundred dollars. Connected to several video sources and monitors, the bridge is a cost-effective tool (Figure 6-14).

### Vectorscopes

Used by engineers and technicians to measure portions of the video signal, a vectorscope is useful for monitoring color video signals. This unit is designed to show the proper relationship between the color reference signal (color burst) and the chroma (color information). The proper set-up and/or color phasing adjustment procedure is done at the camera encoder, which is usually described in the camera operator's manual.

The vectorscope becomes very important when mixing several sources of video through a switcher. Since you are dealing with several different sources of video, the proper color phasing becomes critical when reproducing proper hues. For example, if two sources are mixed during a dissolve, then both sources must be set up with the proper phase relationships to eliminate color shifting during the transition from the first source to the second. Although the vectorscope takes a good deal of technical knowledge to operate and to interpret, you should at least realize why it is used and recognize it when used as a part of an editing system (Figure 6-15.)

FIGURE 6–14. A monitor bridge allows the user to switch between several sources of video to examine their output on a waveform monitor and/or picture monitor.

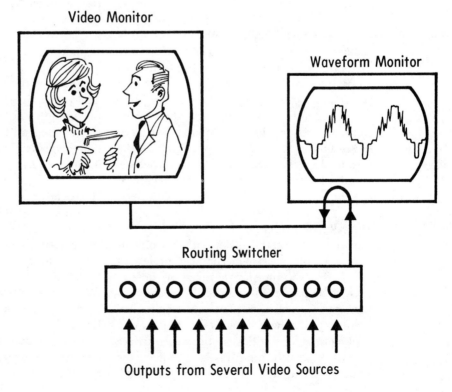

Video Monitor

Waveform Monitor

Routing Switcher

Outputs from Several Video Sources

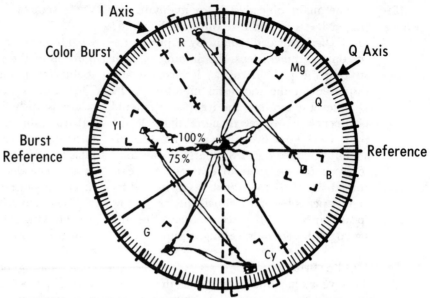

FIGURE 6–15. Vectorscope display of correctly adjusted color bar signals.

## SIGNAL-PROCESSING EQUIPMENT

Many different pieces of the signal-processing equipment available are designed for specific VTRs and uses. Sooner or later, you will probably hear about time-base correctors, frame synchronizers, drop-out compensators, and proc amps. Generally, each device is designed to correct and/or to adjust specific parameters of the video signal played back on a VTR. Since VTRs come in all shapes, sizes, formats, and uses, you must match your VTR to specific types of signal-processing equipment. Beyond this basic consideration, you also have to match the intended use of the played back signal. In other words, don't spend your money on expensive signal-processing gear if you are feeding only one monitor or TV set. On the other hand, if you're duplicating tapes, involved in large closed-circuit applications (or cable television), or broadcasting, you most likely need to send out a stable, jitter-free signal. In the case of the broadcaster, FCC regulations demand that signals meet stringent technical specifications.

### Time-Base Correctors

Due to noise, instability, and other problems caused by the electro-mechanical design of any VTR, various signal-processing devices may be desirable. In addition to mechanical problems (as well as to the electrical circuitry involved), the videotape itself also causes problems. Irregularities in the tape surface and tape stretch can drastically affect the stability and quality of the recorded signal.

As a result, the play-back signals may have signal distortions, noise, poor color reproduction, and especially time-base error, which is basically the difference in horizontal stability between the record and playback signal. For example, if the scanning information varies from one line to the next, the resulting output causes the picture on your TV or monitor to shift, jitter, or skew. In some cases, the particular horizontal sensitivity of your monitor may be the cause, but the playback VTR is usually the major cause. A time-base corrector (TBC) is necessary to restore time-base stability to recorded video signals.

Time-base correctors may be analog or digital.

*Analog TBCs.* In terms of percentages, an analog signal can vary from 0 to 100 percent in strength. As an analogy, if you turn a water faucet on and off, you create an analog flow of water. With the valve shut, there is 0 percent of output; if the water faucet is fully opened, the output is 100 percent. If partially open, the stream is somewhere between 0 and 100 percent. The flow, or output, is variable from 0 to 100 percent. By contrast, in a digital system, a signal is either on or off, with no in-between. The video signal is an analog signal, much like the flow of water from the faucet, because it is a steady stream of varying intensities of luminance and chrominance.

In an analog time-base corrector, the incoming video signal is delayed so that minute deviations in the horizontal and/or color frequency rates are controlled by the rapid switching of the delay electronics. This rapid switching slows down and/or lets the signal pass, depending on the amount of deviation from the standard NTSC horizontal frequency rate of 15.7344 kHz and the NTSC color frequency rate of 3.479545 MHz. The only problem with analog time-base correction is that the delay period is extremely short, that is, the original recording has to be nearly perfect to begin with. So this type of TBC is used with 2-inch quadruplex VTRs, since their time-base stability is very good to begin with.

*Digital TBCs.* In a digital TBC, the incoming analog video signal is changed into a digital signal by an analog-to-digital converter. Indicated simply as "A/D," the conversion is accomplished in three steps:

1. In *sampling*, the A/D converter changes the incoming signal into a large number of samples per second. The rate at which this happens, the *sampling rate,* is designed to happen at either three or four times the NTSC color frequency (depending on the manufacturer).

2. In the *quantitizing phase* of A/D conversion, the strength of the incoming video signal is assigned to predetermined levels of amplitude. Basically, the video signal is broken into specific "blocks" of information that are either "on" or "off," depending on the strength of the signal: obviously, the more blocks, the better the reproduction of the original signal.

3. In most present-day equipment, more than 250 numbers represent dark and light areas of each scan line; low numbers indicate dark areas, while high numbers mean light areas. This on-and-off assignment of each position in the sampled signal is called *coding*. The result is a very long digital number representing the various discrete levels of signal strength in the original analog video signal. Each level is either on or off, depending on the binary code assigned to each bit of information. The binary code consists of a zero or a one, representing on and off respectively.

Since the A/D transformation happens at a constant sampling rate of three or four times 3.579545 (the color frequency), then any fluctuation in time-base error is eliminated when the digitized signal is converted back to analog (D/A). At this point, the signal is easily synchronized with other video equipment, since the TBC can be used as the source of sync pulses. Certain TBCs offer the capability to "gen-lock" to an outside source of sync. In the gen-lock mode, the TBC compares its sampling rate to the vertical, horizontal, and/or color frequencies (or all three frequencies) of the new signal and locks up to that rate (Figure 6-16).

Even though all this sounds quite complicated, the key fact is that a videotape source (pre-recorded signals) can be synchronized and combined with other sources. This capability enables you to mix and blend various sources of video. For the single-camera/VTR user, it opens up tremendous

FIGURE 6–16. Interconnecting a VTR to a time base corrector or other signal processing device is simple. The biggest factor is to match the correct piece of equipment with the type of VTR in use.

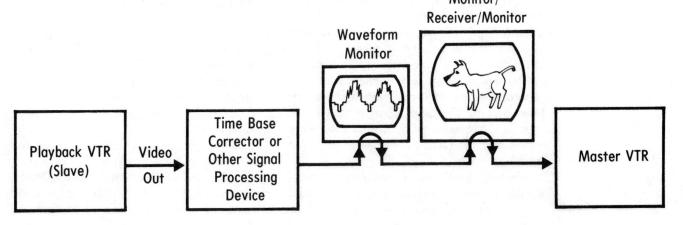

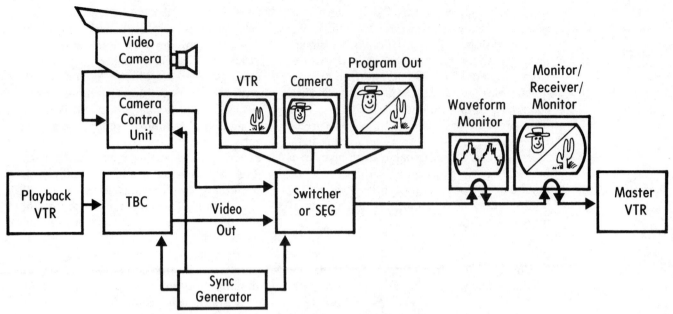

FIGURE 6–17. Mixing video tape source with live camera.

possibilities in the post-production studio (Figure 6-17).

The amount of memory is critical in both the cost and the performance of a **TBC.** Since helical scan recorders have a relatively "jittery" output compared to quadruplex recorders, the range, or *window,* of correction needs to be quite large. This requirement translates into high storage capacity, which was not practical until the advent of digital technology. Some TBCs are capable of only one TV scan line of memory, while others can store a complete frame (525 lines). Due to the increased circuitry and memory capacity, a TBC that stores full frames costs a great deal more. Frame synchronizers can store one whole frame of video and are primarily used by broadcasters where they need to synchronize a "live" remote feed. Generally, frame synchronizers are not intended to be VTR playback signal correctors.

*Direct and Heterodyne Color.* To match the VTR to the correct TBC, you must know whether the VTR records color information as direct color or as heterodyne color. Direct color VTRs record color frequencies directly on the tape, whereas heterodyne VTRs convert color signals to a much lower frequency by combining the color signal with a reference signal generated by the VTR. This second technique is also known as *color-under* recording.

Although TBCs are generally designed to work with one or the other type of VTR, they are sometimes capable of handling both.

All ½-inch and ¾-inch, as well as many 1-inch, VTRs use the heterodyne approach. The color-under method of recording lowers the cost of the VTR by greatly reducing the frequencies that must be recorded on tape.

*Drop-Out Compensation.* Drop-out compensation (DOC), included in some TBCs, is also built into many VTRs. The DOC is a circuit that stores or delays each successive scan line as the video signal is being played back. The purpose is to compensate for any "lost" video as a result of imperfections in the videotape itself. For example, if a small bit of oxide is missing from the tape surface, no signal can be recorded where the "hole" is on the videotape. The DOC, however, can substitute a stored line of information where the hole is.

**Proc Amps**

The proc amp, another common signal-processing device, allows the user to change the hue, video levels, color levels, dark level, and so on. A proc amp is used to change one or more of these elements in the video signal to improve the quality of reproduction. Sometimes, it is used to bring playback up to acceptable levels. Usually built into a TBC, a proc amp can also be purchased as a stand-alone unit.

All signal-processing equipment needs to be used with monitoring equipment to determine input and output signal quality. Making judgments, interpreting the signals, and adjusting these various pieces of equipment

**143**
*Editing*

takes a great deal of technical knowledge. So any of it should be done by a qualified technician or engineer. Each type of equipment is also available in various price and quality ranges, from nonbroadcast to full-broadcast compatibility. Since there are problems inherent in the video recording and playback process, these devices are used to make corrections and/or adjustments. In regard to editing and duplicating videotapes, it is desirable to correct any problems in the playback signal, since the record machine only amplifies the problems. Before investing in any signal-processing device, be certain that the VTRs and other equipment are compatible.

**SUMMARY**

Video sources can be mixed through the use of time-base correctors. Multiple VTRs, cameras, and other sources can be fed to a switcher (SEG), allowing for fades, wipes, dissolves, and titling. Control over the VTRs can be accomplished through the use of time coding and computer assistance, or they can be operated manually. For frame-accurate edits, there is no equal to a computer-assisted system (Figure 6-18).

For the single-camera/VTR user, the use of a multi-VTR/multi-source editing facility offers the ultimate in creative capabilities. Such a system also takes a great deal of financial backing to own and operate. The best alternative for the beginning editor is to learn how to operate "off-line" control track editing equipment and to rent time on the "on-line" system to complete finished productions. As you grow in experience and financial status, you may choose to expand your off-line system to include more equipment.

FIGURE 6-18. An editing system revolving around the single camera/VTR approach. Includes two videotape sources, video camera and electronic graphics.

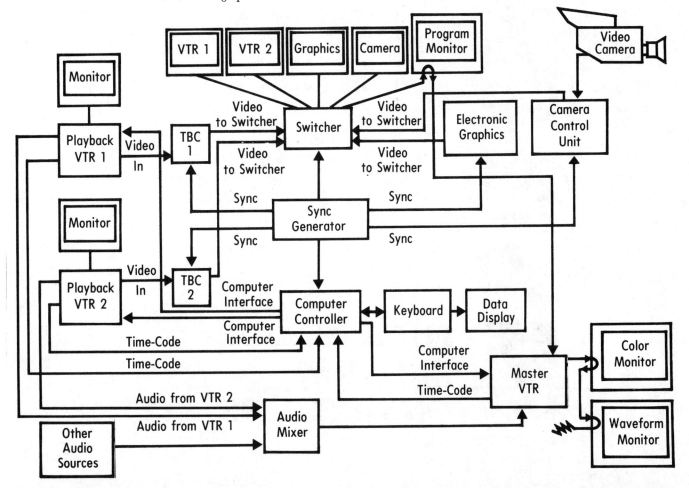

# PUTTING SLIDES AND FILM ON VIDEOTAPE

Incorporating slides, film, and audiovisual materials into the video format can open up a whole new dimension of creativity. Whether you are transferring home movies or a multi-projector slide program, you will find it possible to create many special effects that expand the flexibility of any single-camera system.

## APPLICATIONS

Some of the most common reasons for "putting things on tape" are the safekeeping of original material, the storage and fast access of information, and the production of multiple copies for distribution. The quick playback capability of video eliminates the need to set up different types of audiovisual equipment.

### STORAGE OF SLIDE-TAPE AND FILMS ON VIDEOTAPES

A school or library can benefit from storing audiovisual materials on tape. Having multiple copies on file allows any number of people to check out the same title at one time. If a videotaped copy is damaged or lost, the original (or master tape) can be used to make a new copy. This system is especially cost-effective for popular or heavily used titles.

### INCORPORATING PROJECTED MATERIALS INTO A VIDEO PRODUCTION

Original material is often transferred to tape for editing and post-production purposes. For example, transferring original motion picture footage to videotape is very economical and wise. Editing can be done electronically on videotape, and then the motion picture footage can be conformed to the tape. Thus you eliminate having to purchase film work prints, along with the physical cutting and splicing of the work print whenever an editing change is desired. Videotape is much faster and more economical to use in this stage of production. Many programs and commercials are originated on film and transferred to videotape for editing and distribution. Some producers take this one step further: The edited master videotape is transferred back to film. The release prints are used for distribution purposes. Transfers from tape to film are on the expensive side, and the quality depends on which lab does the transfer.

## THE FILM CHAIN AND ITS USE

The professional way to transfer film and slides to videotape is with the use of a film chain. The film chain derives its name from earlier days when a studio camera and its associated equipment was known as a "camera chain," and when a movie projector and camera combined became known as a "film-chain." Usually the film chain, also called a *film island* or *telecine*, consists of one or two film projectors, one or two slide projectors, a multiplexer, and a television camera. Since the film chain is a single-camera system, much of the same flexibility is possible with your video camera and the projection techniques covered later in the book.

This particular piece of equipment is often found as a permanent fixture at television stations, large production facilities, or other large-scale users of video (Figure 7-1).

The video camera is particularly suitable for motion picture and slide reproduction. It responds quickly, and it automatically compensates for rapid changes in brightness as the film runs or as the slides change. Images from the slide and/or film projectors are focused onto mirrors in the multiplexer, and then into the camera with a special lens or prism between (Figure 7-2). The camera is in a fixed position and focused on the lens or prism. The video images from the film

145

FIGURE 7–1. Filmchain used at a broadcast television station. (Photo courtesy KPHO TV5, Phoenix)

FIGURE 7–2. A multiplier in its simple form uses a mirror and a lens to focus the projected image. The light controller has its cover removed to see the camera lens.

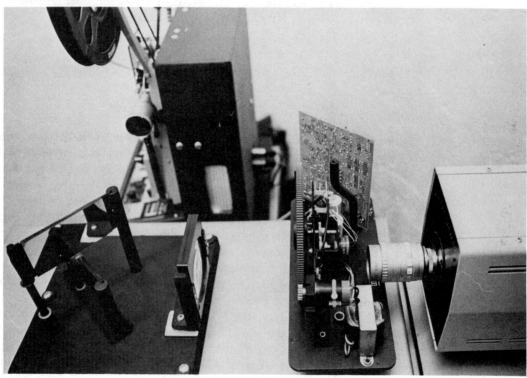

chain camera are fed into a control room of a TV studio and mixed with other cameras. In this way, the projected images can be used during a live program or during a production being videotaped and/or edited. The multiplexer is controlled from the control room as well, and switching from slides to film or between projectors is possible. This allows the director to utilize many different sources of visual material from the film chain alone.

The multiplexer, camera, and projectors must remain in critical alignment at all times. The equipment is mounted on a heavy metal base firmly attached or bolted to the floor, and this characteristic probably gave rise to the term "film island."

**35 mm SLIDES**

Color slides provide an inexpensive alternative to exterior shots, taped or filmed footage, or extensive field production. When using slides in a video production, make sure that all images are horizontally shot, evenly illuminated, and properly exposed. Slides with high areas of contrast do not work well when transferred to video. Generally speaking, however, a good-looking, well-exposed slide usually looks good when transferred to video—even though "well-exposed" means different things to different people. You quickly find out that when subjects are illuminated from the front and have a minimum of dark areas, they look better than those taken on overcast days, with heavy shadows, or with poor light (Figure 7-3). You may also find that slightly overexposed slides transfer well because they transmit more light when projected. The true test comes about when viewing the slides on your video screen. Also remember that video is a motion medium.

If you are going to use slides in a video production, shoot many different angles and close-ups to cover the subject matter. The extra shots give you something to choose from and work with. With the projection techniques discussed later, you can add motion to your slides by zooming in or out, or by panning and tilting the camera. Using enough visuals to supplement your script keeps viewer interest up.

Another aspect of shooting slides for video is that the video screen is quite small with respect to a projected image on a large screen. You will find that close-up shots, which fill the frame with the subject, are more effective than long shots (Figure 7-4). If the shot is taken from too far away, it is easily seen on a large screen, but not on video.

After transferring a number of slides to video, you'll be able to select the best slides yourself.

FIGURE 7–3. Proper lighting is very important when shooting slides for use on video.

FIGURE 7–3a. Too much contrast, uneven illumination.

FIGURE 7–3b. Well balanced lighting, good material for video use.

a

b

**FIGURE 7–4.** Close-up shots (a) that fill the frame are better suited for the video format than long shots (b).

## SHOOTING FOR VIDEO

The ability of your video camera to reproduce fine detail and color varies according to price. Less expensive single-tube cameras do not give you much resolving power, nor do they reproduce some colors accurately, such as reds and yellows, which are the hardest to reproduce. The reproduction problem is further complicated by the type of recorder you use. Although ½-inch and ¾-inch formats play back your original recording quite well, the problems, which begin with dubbing or editing, are inherent to helical scan machines. The signal, when passed along to the next machine, which has its own characteristics, starts getting "noisier" in dark areas and in areas of high color saturation. These problems can be kept to a minimum if you use material as close to original as possible.

As you work with these problems, you become more and more aware of them. The average person typically does not notice the things that make you cringe as they fly by on the screen. Be aware of the capabilities of your shooting system, and you will be able to plan around or minimize the problems.

## DISSOLVE UNITS

Multiple-camera effects—such as chroma keys, dissolves, fading in and out, keying titles, and inserting one scene over another—are done with a special effects generator (Figure 7-5). Slow pans, zooms, or tilts across dissolving slides can create a very interesting visual effect.

**FIGURE 7–5.** A large special effects generator, or switcher used to mix many sources of video. (Photo courtesy KPHO TV5, Phoenix)

This specialized piece of video gear uses two or more video cameras and requires a complex array of support equipment. Since we are working with a single-camera system, we can simulate many of these effects by using 35-mm slides with a dissolve unit, motion picture film, and a variety of projection techniques. Some of these effects, which often look better than their electronic counterparts, cost far less to accomplish. Any audiovisual supply house carries one or more lines of dissolve units.

A dissolve unit used with slide projectors and motion picture projection can open up new outlets for creativity. A dissolve unit, in its basic form, connects to two slide projectors, and it controls the light output and advance mechanism of each.

Better dissolve units, like the U.S. Maxx from Optisonics HEC Corporation (see Source Index) incorporate a cassette recorder and dissolver in one unit (Figure 7-6). Thus they make it possible to listen to the sound track and to pre-program everything from cuts to 25-second dissolves while watching the visuals. Having everything pre-programmed saves a lot of money in studio time when doing any kind of transfer work. The

FIGURE 7–6a. Dissolve control unit with two projectors.

FIGURE 7–6b. Audio cassette recorder/player incorporated into the dissolve unit.

FIGURE 7–6c. Extension speaker. (Photo courtesy Optisonics HEC Corporation)

Maxx also has a jack on the rear panel for transferring the sound track directly to the audio IN on the VTR. The sound from this unit is surprisingly clean and can be amplified with the addition of the ASA speaker/amplifier system (Figure 7-6). This capability is important, especially if you have to be some distance from the unit while it is running to perform camera movements on the slide progression. The ease and dependability of programming, along with the portability, of this unit (the Maxx, ASA speaker/amplifier and two slide projectors fit in its case) make it a lot easier to do any type of slide-tape transfer to video.

From the basic system, equipment progresses in complexity. Multiple-input and computer-controlled units can execute fast cuts, animated effects, variable speed dissolves, superimpositions, and many others. Some systems can be programmed to start and stop motion picture projectors as well. All these sources projected on one screen can offer many exciting visual effects at a reasonable cost.

## Possible Effects

In the dissolve, the light source on one projector is faded out while the other projector's light source fades in. With the two images superimposed on a screen, one slide "dissolves" into the other. Switching from one slide projector to the other without a blank interval gives you the effect of cutting from scene to scene as the projectors advance. Using the basic dissolve mode, you can also fade into and out of a set of slides by using blank slides at the beginning and end of a set of slides. If you are incorporating many slides into a video program, these techniques can save on editing time.

Dissolved units can also be programmed to change slides with audio cues, if you have a stereo or multi-track audio recorder. These *cue tones* (or beeps) are recorded on one unused channel of your audio recording, while the other track carries the audio information. When programming a set of slides you listen to the audio track(s) while you manually run through the set of slides. When you have determined where and when the changes are to occur, go back and run through the slide sequence to record "beeps" or "cue tones" on the available track of your audio recorder. Once the tones are recorded, patch the line out of the cue tone track to the dissolve unit. The line OUT of the audio tape can then be fed to the line IN of your videotape recorder (Figure 7-7). You can record the visuals with your camera, and, as they change to the command of the cue tone track, the audio is synchronously recorded on the audio track(s) of your videotape recorder.

By programming the slides before the transfer to videotape, you save yourself the frustration of missing a slide change while doing the transfer "live." Programming allows you to change slides to the beat of a music track or to change at a constant rate. One item to be aware of is that slide projectors take a brief moment to change slides, so extremely fast cuts between two projectors

are impossible. Only multi-projector systems consisting of three or more projectors are capable of fast cuts and animated effects.

## MULTI-IMAGE PRESENTATIONS

Multi-image presentations (like video) are used as an extremely effective medium in reaching a variety of audiences. Generally, these presentations utilize either a multi-screen or a single-screen approach. In both cases, many images can appear simultaneously to create a visual message.

The single-screen approach is of special interest to the single-camera video producer. Through a variety of projection techniques (covered later), you can transpose the unique qualities of multiple projection of slides to the video format. The 35-mm camera, the copystand, and the slide copier are valuable tools used in producing titles, graphics, and other visuals, all of which offer many creative possibilities.

### The Copystand

The copystand allows you to produce slides from artwork, stills, illustrations, charts, graphics, diagrams, cartoons, transparencies, and maps. In its basic form, the copystand holds a camera above a flat plane. The "copy," or artwork, is usually lit from above with lights at a 45-degree angle to either side. Some copystands also allow for "underlighting" by having a translucent stage lit from underneath (Figure 7-8).

FIGURE 7–7.

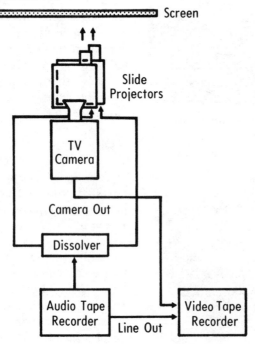

FIGURE 7–8. The copystand allows the user to photograph artwork, transparencies, and the like.

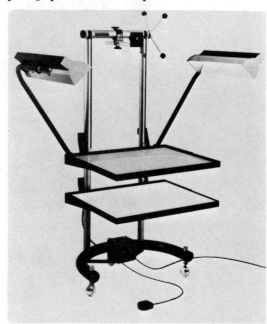

FIGURE 7–9. When programmed to dissolve from one to the next and so on, the figure moves in a flowing motion. Maintaining registration from one frame to the next is critical.

Use a 35-mm camera with through-the-lens viewing when using a copystand or when shooting material that will eventually be transferred to video. Doing so allows you to frame the subject accurately, especially when trying to build a sequence where each successive image must be in register relative to all of the other frames. For example, a dancer was photographed in a series of steps, in which her position changed in each successive frame. When the slides were programmed to dissolve from one image to the next, the figure moves in a flowing motion (Figure 7-9). To obtain the best results, keep the dancer's body in the same relative position within each frame of film.

## Registration

*Registration* refers to the precise placement of the image on the film plane of a camera with reference to the film sprocket holes. A pin-registered slide mount takes advantage of this relationship of picture area to sprocket holes. When a sequence of slides is shot and mounted in pin-registered slide mounts, the frame area falls into a consistent pattern.

FIGURE 7–10.

Pin Registered Slide Mount

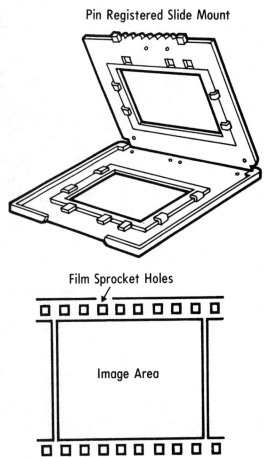

Film Sprocket Holes

Image Area

This registration system enables you to dissolve images from one to another with no loss of registration on the screen (Figure 7-10). Since in-camera registration varies slightly from one camera to another, shoot all material used within a particular sequence with the same camera.

## THE SLIDE DUPLICATOR

The slide duplicator can be used to create titles and special effects slides. The basic slide duplicator consists of an underlit stage for holding the slide to be copied and a column to your 35-mm **single-lens reflex** camera (Figure 7-11). The key elements re-

FIGURE 7–11. Slide duplication with built-in color head.

quired to produce interesting title slides and special effects with the slide duplicator are:

1. the ability to accomplish multiple exposures with your camera, and
2. the use of high contrast black-and-white negative and positive "mattes."

### Mattes

Kodalith slides, or mattes, are produced with black-and-white high contrast Kodalith film, Kodak Ortho type 3, #6556 ASA 8. Black-and-white artwork, such as titles and graphics (see Chapter 8, "Graphics") are prepared and shot on the copystand, yielding a negative of the artwork. These negatives, called *clear core mattes,* are used in turn to create dark core mattes by contact printing a clear core matte with Kodalith film in a pin-registered slide mount. Remember that since the result is a negative image, all the dark and light areas are reversed (Figure 7-12).

Producing mattes with Kodalith film allows great flexibility in that color can be added during the duplication process through the use of filters and/or gels. The Mangum-Sickles Chroma Pro is a slide duplicator that has a tungsten light source combined with dichroic filters which allow you to "dial in" a desired color. These dichroic filters also allow you to adjust the color filtration and correct any slides that depart seriously from normal color balance. When duplicating slides and/or creating titles and special effects slides, use Kodak Ektachrome slide duplicating film, #5071 ASA 8. Processing is usually available on a same-day or 24-hour basis, and it offers the very good color reproduction and low contrast necessary for duplicating slides.

FIGURE 7–12.

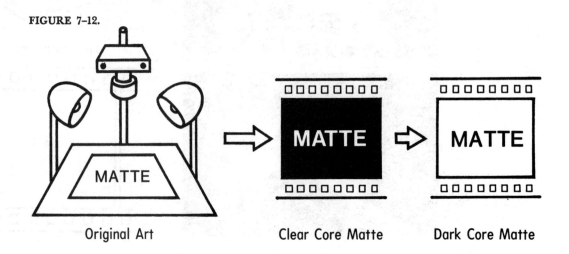

Original Art                Clear Core Matte        Dark Core Matte

## Titles

Dark core mattes for *black titles,* which are created by contact printing the clear core matte with a piece of Kodalith film, can be sandwiched with an original slide in a slide mount and then either projected directly or duplicated on the slide duplicator. Dark core matte titles are used mainly to add black titles in light areas of an original slide (Figure 7-13).

FIGURE 7–13. Sample of dark core matte sandwiched with original slide.

*White titles* are created through a double exposure technique. The first exposure is of the original slide (use Kodak 5071 slide duplicating film), and a second exposure is made using a clear core matte title. The white light shining through the clear core matte burns through the previous exposure yielding a white title over the background or original slide. It is important to align the clear core matte over dark areas in the original so that the burn-in reads well on the finished slide (Figure 7-14).

Similarly, white titles can be added to colored backgrounds by exposing them first to a desired color of light and then burning in the title by using the clear core matte with white light. As a variation on this technique, add the desired filter pack when you place the clear core matte into the carrier of the slide duplicator. The result is a colored title on a black field.

Colored titles require a clear core matte and a pin-registered dark core matte. The dark core matte is sandwiched with the original slide for the first exposure. Next, the clear core matte is introduced and the filter pack is added for the desired color. The clear core matte must be registered with re-

FIGURE 7–14a. Original clear core matte.

FIGURE 7–14b. Original background slide.

FIGURE 7–14c. Turn-in title over background (final slide).

lation to the position of the dark core matte, so that the second exposure yields a colored title over the background. Note that the dark core matte holds back exposure, while the colored type appears, thus allowing the proper exposure of the background.

**The Neon and Other Effects**

1. To get the *"neon" effect,* place a piece of diffusion material, such as white translucent plastic, between the clear core matte and the camera lens. First, the clear core matte is placed in the slide carrier and a desired color is selected for the "glow." The diffusion material, situated slightly above the type, "spreads out" the image from the clear core matte. The first exposure is made, and then the diffuser is removed along with the filter pack. The second exposure burns in the information from the clear core matte. The result is a white title with a colored "glow" on a black field. Some possible diffusion materials for neons are: tracing paper, frosted acetate, opaline plastic, ground glass, and milk-white plexiglass.

A wide variety of filters can be used in place of diffusion material to create an equal variety of effects: star filters, diffraction gratings, fog filters, multi-faceted filters, and/or any other material that passes light. The main idea is to experiment with a number of different effects. The exposure procedure is the same as for neons: The effect filter is exposed first, then the title is burned in with white light (Figure 7-15).

FIGURE 7–15a. Original clear core matte.

FIGURE 7–15b. Neon effect (final slide).

2. A *drop shadow effect* is created in much the same way as neons. The dark core matte is sandwiched with the original for the first exposure. For the second exposure, the light core matte is inserted into the slide carrier, color is added, and the carrier position is shifted slightly up and to the left. This shift causes the dark core and light core mattes to misregister slightly, leaving a black line to the right and below the colored (or white, if you choose) type (Figure 7-16).

FIGURE 7–16.

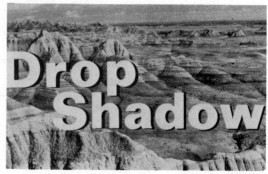

By moving the slide or camera focus during exposure, you can accomplish many "streaking" effects. Moving the artwork during exposure creates the "streaked" effect. Usually, a second exposure of the slide in its final position establishes the subject matter.

3. *Slit scan effects,* or *zoomers,* are created by moving either the camera or the lens on the bellows during exposure. Once again, the motion can be colorized while the final position is exposed a second time to establish the subject matter.

4. Rotating the artwork during exposure results in a *spinning effect.*

Any of these can be done in multiple steps as well, adding different color filtration at each step (Figure 7-17). And they are all merely a sampling of what is possible with the slide duplicator. When used in a sequence of slides and programmed for single-screen projection, they open up many possibilities for the video producer.

FIGURE 7–17a. Zoomer.

FIGURE 7–17b. Streaker.

FIGURE 7–17c. Spinner.

## SUPER-8 AND 16-mm FILM

When you have to obtain remote or on-location footage, you can use the motion picture camera in place of a portable video camera.

### COST FACTORS

Super-8 film and cameras are relatively inexpensive compared to the cost of a color portable video camera, although the difference will probably close in the near future as video technology continues to bring the cost of video down. For the present, however, Super-8 is a good alternative to the video camera in that cameras can be purchased for less money and are less expensive to repair or replace if an accident should occur.

### SHOOTING FOR VIDEO

Shooting film for eventual transfer to tape follows the same general rules as still photography. Learning the basics about the type of film you are using and judging the correct exposure both result in good looking video transfers. Although you can adjust the levels and colors during the transfer to video, most low-priced video cameras are quite limited and often cannot compensate for the errors made on your original film. So if you remember only one rule, it would be that *you should practice and learn to expose film properly.* There is no substitute for well exposed film.

A good way to take the guesswork out of shooting film for video is to shoot a test reel and take good notes. When transferring the film with your particular video camera, notice which colors reproduce the best, which film stocks work best, and which light conditions render the best video image. You'll probably find that avoiding scenes that are high in contrast or that are back lighted gives you a good video image. High-speed film stocks are "grainier" and higher in contrast as well. When you have to use these films in low-light conditions, you have to make compromises in some situations. After working with a few different types of film and noting the results with your video camera, judge which combination works best for you.

Another tip is to keep the subject evenly illuminated from the front and the action toward the center of the screen. The left and right sides of the projected image are cut off during the transfer to video tape, because the aspect ratios of the film camera and video camera frames are different (more on this in the next chapter). So the scene in your film camera's viewfinder is not how it looks on the TV screen after the transfer to tape. You must compose your shots keeping this difference in mind.

### SOUND SPEED

Normally, film should always be shot at 24 frames per second, because this is the speed at which you will project your film during the transfer to video. Since it is also the speed at which you should record sound on film, 24 frames per second is also known as *sound speed.* Shooting film without sound is much easier to shoot, but recording the sound while filming can make the picture information more realistic, especially if the sound is relevant to the visual information. Having that sound track available is always a good idea even if it is used only as background "wild sound" mixed in with other audio.

## SOUND WITH FILM

There are basically two ways to record sound with film:

1. In the so-called *single-system sound recording,* the sound head inside many film cameras is used to record synchronized sound. A magnetic sound track that runs down the side of the film records the sound, and a thinner "balance stripe" running along the opposite edge compensates for the extra thickness of the magnetic coating. The magnetic stripe is not affected during the developing process of the film.
2. The other method of recording "sync sound," called *"double-system" sound recording,* is to synchronize a separate audio tape recorder to the film camera. Although the sound quality of the double system is much better than the sound-on-film technique, it is harder to find a double system,

or interlock projector, for the transfer to videotape.

You are better off shooting with single-system sound, because a number of Super-8 and 16-mm projectors can handle magnetic sound films. Super-8, however, is generally not available with an optical sound track, although most 16-mm prints from outside sources have it. With an *optical sound track,* the sound, recorded on the film during the printing process, varies in area of density along the edge opposite the film perforations. In the projector, the optical track passes by a light emitter or exciter lamp, at which point a photoelectric cell converts the light changes into electric energy, which is in turn amplified and sent to a speaker. A *magnetic track,* on the other hand, passes over an audio head, which picks up the signal much like audio tape, amplifies it, and sends it to a speaker. To feed the audio from your projector to your videotape recorder, you need to patch the line OUT on the projector to the line IN of your video recorder. Not all projectors have a line OUT jack, but they do have an external speaker jack. So you just feed the speaker OUT to the line IN of your video recorder, but the volume control on the projector has to be set at a very low level (Figure 7-18).

FIGURE 7–18. If your projector does not have a "line-out," you can use the speaker OUT along with an attenuating patch cord.

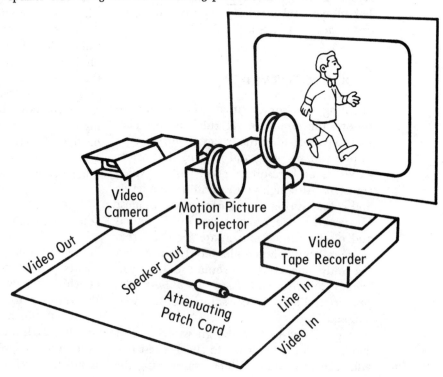

The best way to handle a speaker OUT feed is to use an attenuating patch cord, or *pad,* between the projector's speaker OUT and the line IN of your video recorder. The function of this pad is to match the impedance of the speaker OUT to line level. Most electronic stores have an attenuating pad, which should cost only a few dollars. The type of connectors you need depend on the type of projector and video recorder you have. If you have any question on how to hook it up, explain what you are trying to do at the electronic parts supplier. The solution is usually quite simple.

## PROJECTING FILM FOR TRANSFER TO TAPE

In any case, your film must be projected on a projector that is modified to synchronize the 24-frame-per-second rate of the film to the 30-frame-per-second rate of your video camera. This conversion is most easily accomplished with a projector fitted with a five-blade shutter. As the projector and camera are operating at the same time, the first film frame is scanned twice, the second is scanned three times, the third twice, and so on. This five-blade shutter does not adversely affect the projector for normal use, and it eliminates the "flickering" effect you

see if using a standard projector. Many projector manufacturers have models specifically designed for television use. Regular projectors can be retrofitted with a five-blade shutter, but it is a good idea to purchase one with the proper shutter already installed.

Another way to synchronize the film during the transfer is to use a variable voltage regulator to adjust the voltage going to your projector. The voltage should be varied only by a factor of plus or minus 5 to 10 volts. Beyond this point, the bulb may burn out and/or the color temperature of the lamp may change. By varying the voltage, you are able to speed up or slow down the film while it is running. This feature helps when you're working with the old regular 8 projectors. Super-8 and 16-mm also work with this method, but you may not want to affect the running speed when projecting film with sound. As you change the speed of the film, the pitch of the audio track changes.

If you are not inclined to do them yourself, Fotomat outlets and many video retail outlets offer film and slide transfers suitable for the home user; they transfer your material to either Beta or VHS tape formats. Television stations, production facilities, universities, and schools are also all good possibilities for transferring your footage to tape.

## ADVANTAGES OF FILM OVER VIDEOTAPE

The motion picture camera lends itself well to a variety of techniques that are very costly to do on videotape. Since motion photography or a "movie" is merely a series of successive still frames, you can speed up or slow down time, create artificial motion with inanimate objects, and study events not normally visible to the naked eye in real time. Understanding and using these basic concepts can expand the capabilities of any video system.

## DISTORTION OF TIME

Distorting and manipulating time on videotape is very costly for the average user. But using the motion picture camera and transferring the results to videotape is a very

cost-effective approach to achieving special effects.

If you film at a speed greater than the normal 24 frames per second and then project at normal speed, motion is slowed. The higher film speed lessens any objectionable vibrations and camera movements. Projected at normal speed, film has greater spacing between movements, and the picture appears steadier. At even higher camera speeds, the projected images appear to move in slow motion. This technique is often used to study the motion itself or to analyze the action of an event. It is especially useful when filming from a moving object, such as an automobile or airplane, when using a telephoto lens, or when shooting hand-held.

When filming at speeds faster than 24 frames per second, you need to determine your exposure more accurately. Since the film is traveling through the camera at a higher rate, the exposure time decreases and the f-stop has to be adjusted to let in more light. The adjustment on the f-stop, in turn, affects the depth of field. Higher ASA-rated film stock may also be necessary, depending on the frame-per-second rate and on the amount of light available.

If you film at a slower-than-normal speed, the projected images are speeded up. Speeding up the motion often has a comical effect. Movies from the earlier days of film were shot at slower speeds, so when we see them projected at today's normal speed, they appear to move faster.

## ANIMATION TECHNIQUES

By using single-frame techniques, you can put inanimate objects into motion. To create movement, you separate drawings or moves for each position of movement throughout the action. When projected, the action appears to be continuous. Animation can produce effects unobtainable in live-action motion pictures or in video production. In many cases, it is more effective than live action. The method enables photographing three-dimensional objects, artwork, drawings, or cutouts one frame at a time. You can also project the action in reverse to create illusions and situations unobtainable in any other way. The art of animation really incorporates the worlds of graphic arts and cinematography. Since the images are hand-made, their composition, color, and movement are determined by the artist. The technical process of the cinemagrapher ties the two worlds together.

## LINE DRAWING BUILD-UP

Similarly, to make a line drawing build itself up, you project an image on an artcard and, with the film camera focused on the image, you expose frames of film as you draw lines, using the projected image as a guide. You have to cover the projector lens during exposures with the film camera. As you "trace" more and more lines from the projection, frames of film are exposed until the drawing is complete. When the film is projected, the drawing appears to build and grow to completion (Figure 7-19).

FIGURE 7–19. A line drawing can appear to "draw itself." By drawing a few lines, exposing a few frames, drawing more lines and exposing more frames, the resulting image grows and builds to completion.

Through careful planning, the rate at which the drawing grows can be predetermined since we know that one second of projected film equals 24 frames. With a little arithmetic, we can judge how many lines to add and how many frames to expose to achieve the desired duration of the action.

## THREE-DIMENSIONAL OBJECTS

Three-dimensional objects—models, clay figures, sets, and props—can be manipulated step by step through a motion in a similar fashion. The basic technique is to move the object slightly, expose a frame of film, move the object again, expose another frame, and so on. This can be modified so that objects "pop" onto the frame. Likewise, they can also be made to disappear. (Figure 7-20).

Planning the action is extremely important:

1. Shoot a test to check the lighting and the camera angles.
2. The objects themselves need to be stable and capable of withstanding the heat from the lights. Having your key character or object fall over or melt after hours of tedious work can be very frustrating. Generally speaking, manipulating large characters and objects is much easier than handling small ones. Close-ups and fluid movement are easily produced and the weight of large objects lends to their stability.
3. Devise a shooting procedure so that your hand is not caught in one or more of the frames when making exposures.
4. Using a heavy tripod and cable release is equally important.

FIGURE 7–20. Three-dimensional objects can be photographed a frame at a time creating a smooth, fluid motion. Here the wooden model is shown in various positions, each frame part of the sequence.

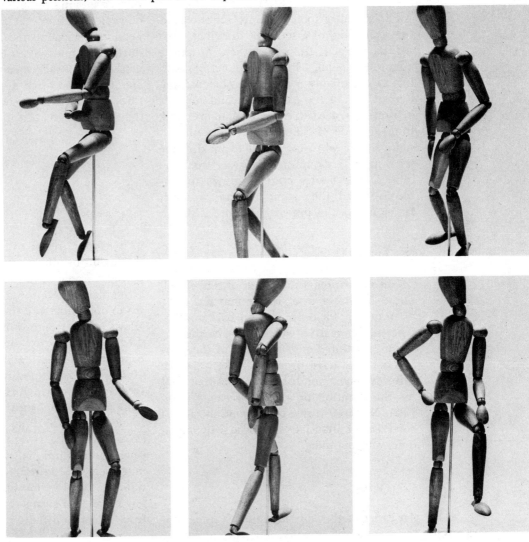

FIGURE 7-21. It **is much** easier to make a character walk from one side of the screen to the other than to walk toward or away from the screen plane.

## ANIMATED CARTOONS

An animated cartoon is simply a motion picture consisting of a series of drawings, each slightly different from the other. To create a repeated action, a limited number of drawings can be used over and over. *Dimensionality* can add to the complexity and number of drawings needed: Having a figure walk from one side of the screen to the other is quite simple when compared to making the same figure walk toward or away from the camera. The figures must be drawn in perspective, and the action requires a much larger number of drawings (Figure 7-21).

## CEL ANIMATION

In cel animation, transparent sheets of cellulose acetate or of a similar material serve as an overlay for drawings and backgrounds. The subject matter, which is to be the key action, is painted onto the back of the overlays and registered over the background. In this way, a common background can be used for the duration of a given scene (Figure 7-22). Needless to say, cel animation takes a good deal of financial support, artistic talent, time, and planning.

## CUTOUTS

An easier method of animation is using cutout photos and artwork. The cutouts can be positioned on a background and given motion by moving the pieces and exposing each movement a frame at a time (Figure 7-23). Zooming in and panning across the subject during an animated sequence can be done by marking off small segments on the zoom ring and pan head with a piece of tape. Look through your viewfinder, plan your moves, then measure off the increments you need.

## TIME-LAPSE

"*Time-lapse*" refers to a technique whereby the action of an event is compressed by exposing a frame of film over a length of time at regular intervals. Slowing down the camera to one frame at a time over a long period allows you to record events that move so slowly that they are not perceptible to the naked eye. Besides having a camera capable of single-frame exposure, you also need an *intervalometer*, which is a timing device that allows you to shoot a subject at a selectable frame per unit of time. Some intervalometers can also turn lights on and off. By using the time-lapse technique, you can record the movement of a flower growing and blooming, watch a parking lot fill up and empty, or any number of events that can be compressed from hours to a matter of seconds.

**160**

FIGURE 7–22. Once again, each element of action must be (in this case) painted in on acetate overlap. Here both the character and toothpaste tube are separate cells, each changing as the action develops.

FIGURE 7–23. In this chart, cutout lines are added. When projected, they "pop-on."

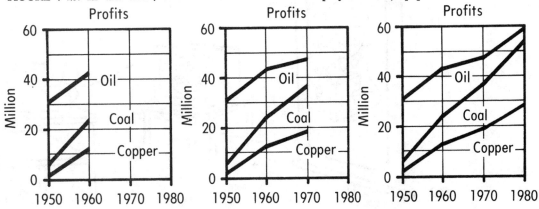

The projection of slides, film, and other transparencies for transfer to videotape can be done in a number of ways, depending on your resources. For front projection, you can use many different surfaces including a white card, a white wall, or a glass-beaded, lenticular, or "daylite" screen.

## THE WHITE CARD

A white card should have a stiff backing and a matte finish, which gives you even illumination and cuts down on any glare from the projector bulb. Avoid a highly textured surface since it shows up in your video transfer. An adjustable easel makes a good support for the card. Obtain a cart or table high enough to position the lens at approximately the same height as your video camera on its tripod.

### Keystoning

Alignment is very important. Position the projector at a 90-degree angle to the projection surface to minimize "keystoning." Keystoning results when the projector is at an angle other than 90 degrees to the screen. If the projection is not "straight on," the image compresses to one side.

## Projection Size

Since you are going to point your video camera at the projected image to transfer it to tape, the size of the projection should be kept relatively small. A small projection size also gives you a brighter image, which is beneficial because most video cameras work their best at fairly high light levels: the brighter the image, the better the quality of your video transfer. The size of the projected image is determined by how close you can focus in with your camera. A close-up lens, which is also known as a "diopter" lens and which can be attached to the front of your camera lens, allows you to focus down on a very small projection size. The projection size can be easily adjusted with the use of a telephoto or zoom lens on the projector(s).

## SETTING UP FOR FRONT PROJECTION

With your camera mounted on its tripod, position it as close to 90 degrees to the projected image as possible (Figure 7-24). Viewing the output of your camera on a

FIGURE 7–24a. Proper positioning of projector(s) and video camera are necessary.

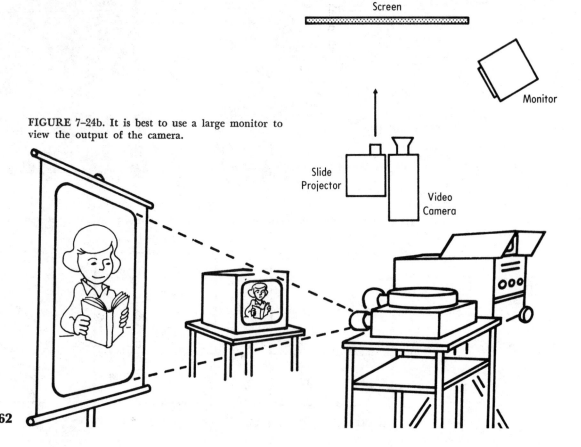

FIGURE 7–24b. It is best to use a large monitor to view the output of the camera.

162

large monitor allows for optimum focusing and approximates what the final recording will look like. As you fill the monitor with the image, you see that the projected images are slightly cut off on the sides, top, and bottom. You also note why the material had to be shot originally in the horizontal format, so as to fit the aspect ratio of the TV screen. The white balance (if you have a color camera) can be set by projecting the light source directly at the card, making certain that the iris is closed down to accommodate the brightness of the light. Run through part or all of the material to check the video/audio levels and color balance as well as to make adjustments. Good results are obtained when using the automatic iris or level control, depending on the design of the camera. Any projection screen or even a white wall can be substituted for the white card.

## USING A BEAM SPLITTER

The most important things to remember are alignment and image brightness. In this respect, a beam splitter mirror and a special reflective projection screen help to avoid problems. A *beam splitter* is a specialized type of glass that is coated to reflect and transmit light in differing percentages. Beam splitters can be ordered to whatever specifications you require. For our purposes here, we suggest one that transmits 50 percent of light (which also reflects 50 percent). The recom-

mended screen material, called Scotchlite or Kodak Ektalite, has unique properties of reflecting light directly back at the source. The material comes in rolls and is available with adhesive backing. You have to determine the screen size needed.

Since the screen reflects light directly back at the source, the equipment must be set up so the camera "sees" the projected image through the beam splitter. The beam splitter is positioned at a 45-degree angle to the screen surface. The projector, in turn, is positioned at a 90-degree angle to the screen and uses the front surface of the beam splitter to throw the image on the Scotchlite or Ektalite screen. With the camera positioned behind the beam spliter, the screen material reflects the image back through the beam splitter, and the image is transmitted into the camera lens (Figure 7-25).

The unique qualities of these screen materials are such that they can be used to achieve optical *chroma key* effects. You can light a narrator or objects in front of the screen without "washing out" the projected image, since the screen reflects light coming directly from 90-degrees back at the source. This characteristic effectively masks any shadows cast by objects in the projector beam. The projected image may be so bright in relation to the subject, that a neutral-density filter may have to be used on the projector lens to cut down the amount of transmitted light.

FIGURE 7-25. Basic set-up using beam splitter and highly reflective screen.

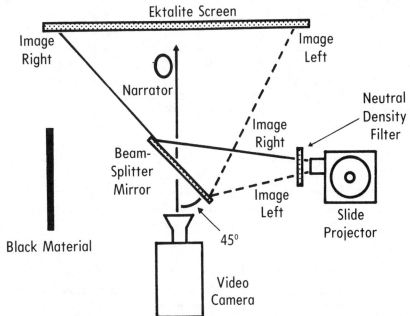

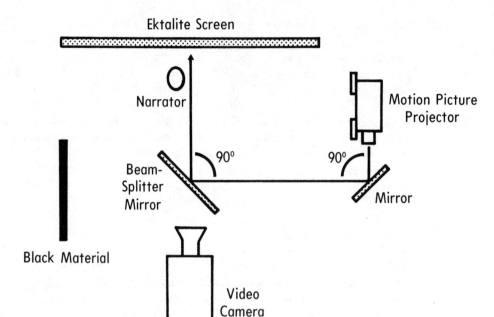

FIGURE 7-26. Beam splitter used with motion picture projector. Take care when using a "live" microphone on the narrator. Obtain a quiet running projector if possible.

Bear in mind that the left-to-right relationship is reversed by the mirror. You may have to "flop" your slides to maintain the reading direction from left to right. Also, when projecting motion picture footage (with a five-blade shutter), use footage that does not contain titling or action that looks odd when reversed. Or just use a mirror and the beam-splitter in tandem so that the image is not reversed. Right-angle projection lenses, which incorporate a mirror into the lens assembly, can also be used (Figure 7-26). The focal length of the projector lens you use is determined by the size of the projected image desired and by the distance of the beam-splitter/projector apparatus to the screen. Experimenting with this method of projection yields some of the most interesting results obtainable through projection.

## REAR PROJECTION

Rear screen projection involves the use of a specially designed sheet of rear screen material, which can be made of glass or plastic. The viewer (or video camera) looks at the frosted or dull side of the rear screen, while the projectors are positioned to throw the images from behind the screen. When using the rear screen for transferring projected material to video, look for a screen with fine grain on the dull side, since some extremely grainy screens can affect the image quality of your transfer. The rear screen can be used on a set during a video production, but the set must be carefully lit so that the image on the screen is not washed out.

### USING A MIRROR

Either a mirror or a right-angle lens must be used so that the right and left sides are not reversed when viewed from the front (Figure 7-27). Slides, however, can just be reversed in their trays and projected from the rear without the use of a mirror. If depth is a problem in the room you are working in, use wide-angle projection lenses for "on-the-set" projection. (Remember to use a small image size for transferring directly to video.) The rear screen technique eliminates the problem of keystoning, but you have to align the image squarely on the screen for the transfer.

### MULTIPLE PROJECTION

Multiple projection can also be accomplished using a rear screen. Motion picture footage and slides on a dissolve unit can be positioned either "full frame," or in different areas of the screen (Figure 7-28). Multiple projection and screen positioning can offer a wide range of possibilities.

**FIGURE 7-27a.** When employing a rear screen with a motion picture projector, use a mirror so that left and right are not reversed.

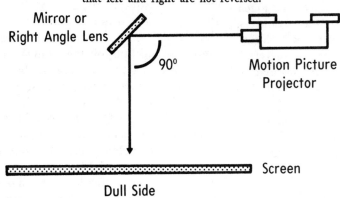

Mirror or Right Angle Lens

90°

Motion Picture Projector

Screen

Dull Side

**FIGURE 7-27b.** Slides can be turned around and projected directly.

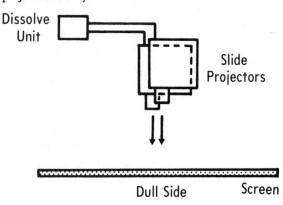

Dissolve Unit

Slide Projectors

Dull Side    Screen

**FIGURE 7-28a.** Using multiple projection can yield some interesting effects.

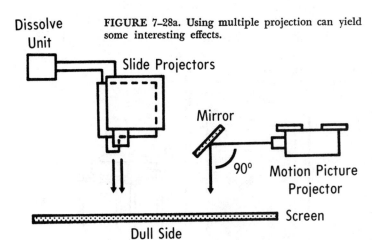

Dissolve Unit

Slide Projectors

Mirror

90°    Motion Picture Projector

Screen

Dull Side

Video Camera

**FIGURE 7-28b.** Make sure to keep the image as small as possible.

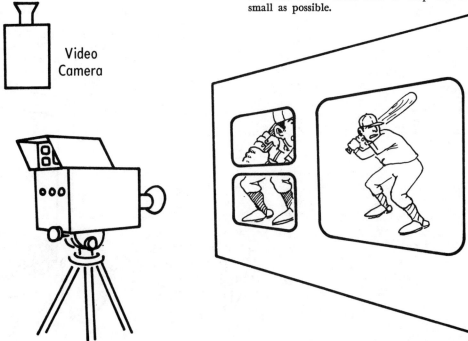

## FRONT AND REAR PROJECTION

Front and rear projection can be combined for special titling effects. Adding titles to slide sequences and film footage adds a touch of professionalism to your video transfers. Titles can be used for opening and closing sequences, as sequels to program material, and generally as added printed information to visuals. Slides, film, and other materials are projected from the rear, while title slides are projected from the front of the screen (Figure 7-29). The images are focused on the dull side (the front) of the screen facing the camera. This multiple projection approach results in effective and "easy-to-read" titling. Aligning all the projectors carefully is important. Audiovisual carts that have lockable wheels and that are the same height for all projectors are also very helpful. They allow you greater ease in adjusting the positioning of the projected images on the screen.

## TITLE WIPES

Once the equipment is positioned and aligned, an added dimension of "wiping in" and "wiping out" the titles can be achieved simply by blocking off the front of the title projector lens with a piece of cardboard. The cardboard is moved from side to side, or from top to bottom, to reveal the title on the screen (Figure 7-29). When you have determined the sequence of events, check the levels on your video camera and recorder. If the titles are too bright, use neutral-density filters on the projector lens, or remount the slides with colored gels (this is also a way of colorizing the titles). The white light coming from the projector can be projected onto the rear screen to white-balance the video camera. Remember to close down the iris!

FIGURE 7–29a. Using a rear screen, you can project images from the rear, while projecting title slides from the front.

FIGURE 7–29b. By moving a piece of cardboard in front of the title projector lens, you can "wipe on," or "wipe off" titles.

**COPYRIGHT MATERIAL**

Incorporating slides, films, and other projections into your productions enhances the appeal of your work. But remember that much of the material you use is probably copyrighted, unless of course, you originated it. In fact, you may be tempted to transfer to your own tape some of the incredible amount of visual material already available. Doing so is usually permissible, but, since much of the material you use is probably copyrighted, you cannot legally sell it or charge admission to see it. That is considered "infringing" on someone else's copyright, for which there are heavy fines. If you have any question about what you are reproducing with your video camera, seek permission in writing and find out how the regulations affect your particular application. House report #94-1476, available from the Government Printing Office in Washington D.C., answers any questions you may have.

**PUBLIC DOMAIN**

Numerous titles are categorized as "public domain" materials. One of the easiest ways to determine whether a title falls under this category is to look for the copyright notice anywhere in the program. If the notice does not appear, it is probably not protected. Outdated copyrights are another area, but it is up to you to check to see if the copyright holder has renewed the registration with the copyright office. Some distribution houses advertise public domain titles, and they are a good source of hard-to-obtain material. When transferred to video, scenes can be incorporated into a production and thus aid in keeping your budget down.

**STOCK MATERIALS**

Stock shots are available of film footage and slides. If you are in a major city, you can look up stock shot sources in the Yellow Pages. There is usually a per-foot fee for usage of the material.

Sometimes you can obtain both public domain and stock shots, transfer the footage to tape, and edit together a complete program to an audio track. The audio track can also be assembled from stock or library sources. The biggest factor is your willingness to experiment and to work with the resources you have.

**SUMMARY**

All the techniques in this chapter describe a variety of devices and equipment that are relatively inexpensive and easily obtainable. Much of the hardware can be rented, which should be considered as an alternative to outright purchase. Working with a variety of equipment and set-ups gives you valuable experience, and it results in a more effective use of the video medium.

**8**
**8**
**8**
**8**
**8**
**8**
**8**

**GRAPHICS
FOR TELEVISION**

Graphic production is the sore spot in almost all low-budget video presentations. It takes time and a certain amount of experience to produce attractive lettering and illustrations, both of which are normally in short supply, unless the videographer is also an illustrator.

There are, however, a number of ways to cut down on the time and expense, and still produce professional-looking graphics. The purpose of this chapter is to make you aware of what's available and what you can expect from them.

**DESIGN** Since video differs from all other types of media in the way it generates an image, graphics for the video medium must be designed with the limits of television in mind. The most important considerations are:

1. the style of artwork,
2. the aspect ratio,
3. the legibility of layout,
4. the color and gray-scale response, and
5. the ease of manipulation.

## STYLE

Producing artwork with style in mind is very important. Drab, unstylized artwork can ruin an otherwise superlative video production. Conversely, smooth professional-looking artwork can give even a mediocre presentation a better-than-average look.

The style of artwork should also match the mood or feeling that the production is intended to inspire in the viewer. For instance, a comedy show could be opened with cartoon lettering, or a horror mystery with drop shadow lettering (Figure 8-1).

## ASPECT RATIO

The aspect ratio of anything is equal to its length times its width, expressed in standard units. Confused? Don't be! It's easy. Measure the length (height) and then the width of your TV screen. You will find that the height relates to the width in a ratio of three units to four units; for example, if the screen is 18 inches tall, it has to be 24 inches wide— 3 to 4! So the aspect ratio of television is 3:4. The same ratio is true for the camera viewfinder and the monitor screen; they are the same basic shape—3 to 4—but different sizes. The aspect ratio refers only to the shape.

So if artwork is to fit well on camera, it should be produced in a 3:4 ratio. For example, 9 inches by 12 inches, and the standard unit is 3; 12 inches by 16 inches is a 3:4 ratio, but the standard unit is 4. All television screens have an aspect ratio of 3:4— they're always three units high by four units wide, no matter what size they are.

Within the 3:4 aspect ratio of the television screen, you also lose up to 20 percent of the picture area around the perimeter due to a variety of recording and playback

FIGURE 8–1. The style of artwork should usually evoke the same feeling that the overall production is intended to inspire in the viewer.

tolerances and misadjustments. So the area of the picture seen on a well adjusted monitor or monitor/receiver may not be the same as the picture area seen on some other monitor or home set. The image may be somewhat higher, lower, to one side or the other, or it may be tighter or looser in the frame, or you may find some combination of several of these differences (Figure 8-2).

FIGURE 8–2. Transmission and reception tolerances and misadjustments may account for up to a 20-percent misalignment of the image area around the perimeter of the receiver screen.

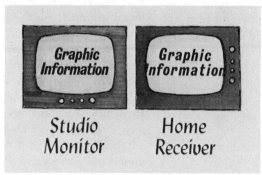

FORMAT AND SIZE

To compensate for these recording and playback differences, the 3:4 format for graphic materials should be divided into (Figure 8-3):

1. A *margin area* for handling the visual and as a buffer against edge damage if the graphic is dropped—that is, the blank edge of the visual is damaged instead of the artwork itself.
2. A *scanning area,* which the camera is framed and focused on.

FIGURE 8–3. To compensate for misalignment of the video image, prepare graphic materials in a 3:4 format divided into the three areas shown.

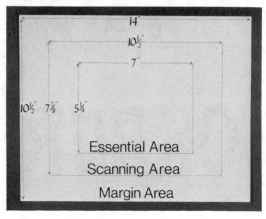

3. An *essential area* which contains the important graphics.

Since no one has standardized the terms used to refer to these different areas, they may be called by various names:

1. The margin area may be called the border area or dead border area.
2. The scanning area may be called the scanned area or picture area, the camera field, transmitted area, or exposed area.
3. The essential area may be called the safe title area, lettering area, copy area, or usable area.

In each case, the idea is the same but the words differ. To retain the proper aspect ratio and to provide ample space for each area, the dimensions of each area should be approximately as shown in Figure 8-3. Commercially produced grids are available for the same purpose.

FIGURE 8–4. The background of the essential area should fill the scanning area.

The point is twofold: (1) to make it easier to frame a graphic without losing part of the information when viewed on the screen of a misadjusted monitor or monitor/receiver, and (2) not to run off the edge of a graphic because it turns out to be the wrong aspect ratio to fit the screen. For this reason, all important graphic information should be included in the essential area. The background of the essential area should be allowed to spill over into and to fill the scanning area (Figure 8-4). This spill-over gives the cameraperson something to frame without "squeezing" the essential area, which may result in losing some of the graphic information on the misadjusted monitor or receiver.

Here are some tips on legibility:

1. The amount of caption information on a graphic should generally not exceed ten words. For all practical purposes, more than ten words cannot be read quickly enough, and using more than ten causes a reduction in size of the individual words to a point where they become almost unreadable. This number limit allows you to use letters at least ½-inch high. Since some screens are so small, letters should be large enough on the screen to be easily seen—even on small screens.

2. Letters should be bold and simple. Sans serif lettering is easier to read than more ornate styles of lettering, which may be pretty and artsy but completely illegible. The resolving power of the television screen is not great enough to pick up thin, fragile letters without losing detail. This rule also applies to patterns or illustrations with too much delicate detail.

3. If a moderate amount of detail is to be used, try to keep it out of the corners of the screen, which are most lacking in resolution.

4. Try not to use closely spaced horizontally oriented patterns of any type such as horizontal lines, herringbone patterns, or checkerboard designs. They interfere with the scanning process of the video camera and cause an effect known as "moire," a kind of break-up in the image.

5. A combination of upper- and lower-case lettering is generally more readable than either one or the other alone, because we are used to seeing upper- and lower-case in sentences like this.

## COLOR AND GRAY SCALES

Color cameras are set up to faithfully reproduce standard colors. But they come from different manufacturers, and their pick-up tubes, electronic circuitry, and optics often differ. So certain cameras work better with some types of colors than others. Stay with colors your camera reproduces well. Run a test with a color chart and notice which colors reproduce the best.

In general, work with "true" colors, except for red and yellow; many cameras have problems reproducing large areas of red or yellow. If you intend to use them, try to reduce the area that they are used in. Also, man-made colors, like chartreuse and hard-hat electric pink, usually change hue and become "muddy"—especially when reproduced on inexpensive equipment.

An important parallel consideration is the gray-scale response of the graphic—especially if it is produced in shades of gray from black to white. For perfection in reproduction, the black areas of the graphic should never be totally black, and the white areas should be off-white or "television white." For absolutely best reproduction, the shades of gray used in the graphic should match the shade-gradations of the card used for "shad-

FIGURE 8–5. These and similar patterns cause breakup in the video image.

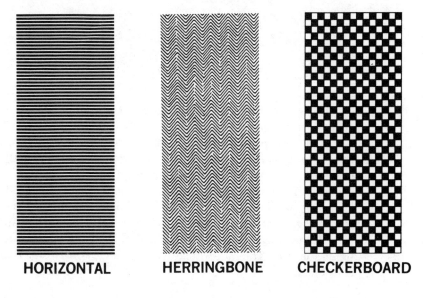

**HORIZONTAL**  **HERRINGBONE**  **CHECKERBOARD**

ing" the color camera during set-up. This requirement is fine in theory, but it finds little application in practice. (2) Contrast. It's little application in practice. The best thing to remember is to avoid glaring whites and jet-blue blacks in the same graphic.

It's the old story of television's limited range of contrast. When using white letters or line art on a black field, adjust the video level to slightly less than 100 percent, to avoid noise and break-up in the editing and dubbing of the finished program. If there is no control on your VTR to adjust the video level, switch the camera's iris to manual and "stop down" one-half f-stop. Even one entire f-stop should not appreciably degrade picture quality. If the contrast range of a graphic is too wide, something has to give —either the highlight detail or the shadow area detail. To hold both, the contrast range of the graphic has to be "compressed," by using not-quite-black blacks and not-quite-white whites or by adjusting the video level. If there is too much contrast between the visual you want to use and its background, simply cut it out and paste it on a less "contrasty" background. A light beige or light blue background works well, as does light yellow or cream.

Sometimes a visual lacks contrast. This condition can be improved by outlining areas to be emphasized with a pen, pencil, or felt marker (Figure 8-6).

FIGURE 8–6. Sometimes contrast may be increased by outlining the areas to be emphasized.

Visuals with too much contrast, if left on camera for a prolonged period, can "burn in." This type of burn-in causes the graphic image to remain imprinted on the video camera's tube, and it appears as a ghost in the following scene. If the burn-in is serious, it might never go away. So leaving high-contrast graphics on camera is not a good idea. Either turn down the f-stop or dim the lights on the graphic—whichever is more convenient.

## HANDLING AND STORAGE

If possible, use a standard size for all graphics. To arrive at a standard size, start with a standard 22-by-28 inch card stock, which, when cut into four pieces, are each 11 by 14 inches—a format very close to 3:4. One piece of the 11-by-14 card stock can be ruled and punched at the corners of each area, and then laid over the other pieces of stock to serve as a quick guide in designating the corners of each area (Figure 8-7). These corner registration dots can be used to help center the important graphic elements of each area until the graphic nears completion —then the dots can be erased and the graphic finished (Figure 8-8).

FIGURE 8–7. One sheet of artboard can be ruled and punched to serve as a template for marking the corners of each area.

FIGURE 8–8. The corner dots of each area can be erased as the graphic nears completion.

A standard size has a number of advantages. An 11-by-14 card is large enough for the camera operator to frame and focus on, and yet small enough for easy handling and storage. Frequently, a number of visuals are used in rapid succession. If they are all of a standard size, they are much easier to "pull" for each visual change. They will also be easier to store since they will fit together in order on a standard size shelf or in a standard size file.

The different types of title cards are as follows:

1. A *simple title card* contains only a caption or caption information.
2. An *illustrated title card* contains a caption and an illustration of some sort.
3. A *super card,* made for superimposing or "keying" titles, is produced with white graphics on a black background. The information on this card is electronically keyed over footage from another source.

Since we are dealing principally with single-camera systems, we can consider taping footage in the field with titles in mind only if the right equipment is available back at the studio. Titles are added to the pre-recorded field footage by means of a studio camera and a switcher. (A character generator can also be used to add titles to pre-recorded tape, and, since the cost of good character generators seems to be falling steadily, many independent video producers may soon be able to own them.)

## LETTERING SYSTEMS

### HAND LETTERING

All three types of title cards contain some type of lettering, the least expensive and fastest of which is hand lettering. And hand styles are frequently more attractive than other types of lettering. Yet developing a good hand-lettering style requires practice and a steady hand.

Frequently, hiring *calligraphers,* who specialize in hand-lettering styles, for a short period of time to do all the lettering for a given production is much less expensive than renting a studio character generator or paying an artist to produce full-blown illustrations. Just be sure to work with the person doing the lettering so that he or she realizes video limitations and doesn't spend an enormous amount of time creating caption cards or credits that won't work. In fact, if the calligrapher reads the first part of this chapter, everything about lettering for video should be perfectly clear.

Probably the only other thing that an artist needs to know is that there are still a lot of people out there who do not have color television playback equipment. So if you're thinking of coding the parts of a drawing using different colors, you had better consider a different system, such as numbers. Numbers work in both color and black and white. Color works only in color.

### LETTERING AIDS

For those without a steady hand, a number of lettering aids are available. Each has its advantages and disadvantages, and they vary greatly in price. With a little practice, each can be used to produce lettering that is superior to a "shaky" hand-lettering style.

**Transfer or Rub-On Lettering**

Transfer or rub-on letters and patterns come in many styles and sizes. Of the video producers questioned about what they used for illustrated title cards, most responded that they use transfer letters and patterns at least part of the time. Many now use character generators, but find them to be more useful for long lists of credits or for producing voluminous captions. They prefer transfer letters for short titles and a variety of style.

Transfer letters take time to "space" and rub down. To use them, pencil in light guidelines to line up the letters horizontally. Then line up the letters with the guidelines, and rub them off the transparent acetate backing they are attached to and onto the card stock (Figure 8-9). Transfer letters are "optically spaced" horizontally as they are rubbed onto the card stock—that is, you use your eyes, rather than a ruler, to determine the spacing

FIGURE 8-9. Rubbing transfer letters onto card stock.

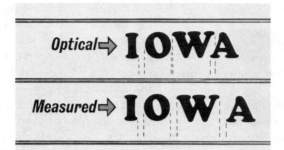

FIGURE 8–10. Optical spacing versus measured spacing.

between letters. Due to the varying width of the letters, some letters have to be spaced closer together than others (Figure 8-10).

### Rubber Stamp

Rubber stamp letters and designs, inexpensive and easy to use, have become the rage in certain art circles in recent years. Rubber stamp letters come in different sizes and styles. A guide is used to keep them properly aligned across the card stock and to estimate spacing between words, but letters are optically spaced. Each letter is inked on a pad with a slight rocking motion, and then positioned in the guide and pressed down on the card stock, again with a slight rocking motion (Figure 8-11).

FIGURE 8–11. Rubber stamp lettering.

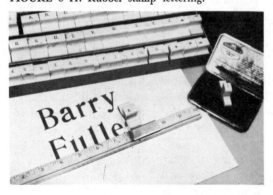

While they do not have a smooth finished look, the rough spots can be "touched up" after stamping a word, making them very attractive and effective for certain applications. Using different colored inks to produce words with a variety of colors is only one way in which they can be used. Since accuracy is not as important with rubber stamp letters as with transfer letters, they are especially helpful for hurried lettering jobs. Used in combination with rub-on designs, the results can be very pleasing.

**174**

### Wrico

Wrico lettering is done with special ink pens, templates, and guides of various sizes and styles (Figure 8-12). The point sizes of the Wrico pens must be matched with the groove size in the Wrico templates. For instance, a "B" pen must be used with a "B"

FIGURE 8–12. Wrico lettering set.

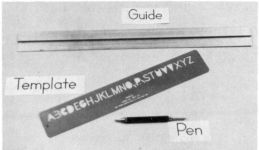

template. The guide holds the template above the surface of the card stock, because, if the template touches the card stock, the fresh ink smears. Letters are optically spaced. Various colors of ink may be used to add interest to Wrico lettering. Care must be taken in the selection of the card stock since some types of card stock allow ink to "bleed" with the result that the letters look ragged instead of smooth. If the pens are not cleaned regularly, they tend to allow ink to "pool" at the corners of letters, or they feed the wrong amount of ink to the surface of the paper—either too much, resulting in "flooding," or too little, resulting in "skips." If you keep the pens clean and take your time, however, you can do a nice job of lettering with Wrico.

### Leroy

Leroy lettering is done with a template and scriber (Figure 8-13). The template comes in different sizes and styles. Either the scriber can be filled with ink for making a few letters, or a reservoir can be mounted on it for doing a large lettering job. The scriber is then adjusted so that its inkwell just about touches the surface of the card stock. Then the scriber is placed on the template and

FIGURE 8–13. Leroy lettering set.

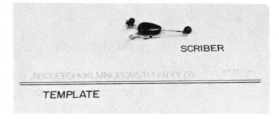

FIGURE 8–14. Leroy template and scriber being used to draw letters.

the letters are drawn (Figure 8-14). All letters are optically spaced. The inkwell on the Leroy scriber, like the Wrico pens, needs attention. It must be cleaned often to avoid pooling, flooding, and skips. The same care must be taken in selecting nonbleeding card stock.

## Rapidograph

The Rapidograph pen and template sets are easy to use. The pens come in different point widths which match the groove widths in the templates (Figure 8-15). The template, which has raised edges to lift the letters away from the card stock, is positioned as desired on the card stock and used as a guide to draw letters. Spacing is optical. All of the same things apply to Rapidograph as to Wrico and Leroy in regard to the selection of stock and cleanliness. In addition, when using a Rapidograph set, remember to use a pen and template of sufficient size to be seen clearly on the television screen. Rapidograph sets are used extensively in mechanical drawing, and so most sets have very small point sizes. A size 4 or larger works fine for video lettering.

FIGURE 8–15. Rapidograph lettering set.

## Stencil Lettering

Stencil lettering is inexpensive and comes in many sizes and styles. The horizontal lines of letters on the stencils have guide holes either above or below them. These holes are lined up with a lightly penciled guideline on the card stock. A pencil or ballpoint pen is used to trace the outline of the letters (Figure 8-16). The guideline is then erased and the letters are filled in with ink, colored felt markers, or, if you are patient, with paints.

FIGURE 8–16. Outlining stencil letters.

Stencils are relatively fragile compared to other lettering systems. People who aren't familiar with the proper way to use them tend to use them like silk screens: They hold them in place, cover them with ink or spray paint, lift them up, and expect a clean-looking letter. Paper stencils just don't work that way. If you want them to last very long, you've got to use them only for making outlines, and avoid getting them wet with paint or ink.

## Three-Dimensional Letters

Many word games and toys come with their own sets of letters. These letters may be used as quick lettering aids when there is very

FIGURE 8–17. Many word games and toys come with sets of letters.

little time to be spent with other types of lettering systems (Figure 8-17). Their only disadvantage is that they usually aren't designed to be attached to anything, so they can't be used on card stock standing upright. Since trying to aim the camera at something flat "on its back" is a hassle, glue small magnets, Velcro strips, or tabs to the back of each letter. Then a magnetic surface or a felt board can be used to display them in an upright position.

### Menu or Spaghetti Boards

Most menu boards are made of black felt with some type of backing material, which has uniformly spaced grooves to accept lines of letters. The letters themselves, although usually white, do come in colors and have protruding parts on the back of them, which fit into the grooves on the board. The letters can be arranged and rearranged as desired. Since they are usually white on a black background, they can also be keyed (or superimposed) over another scene in the same way as captions from a "super card."

### Magnetic Letters

Magnetic letters are three-dimentional letters that come with small magnets attached to the back of them. They are usually used on a sheet of metal or magnetic board. But, if the magnets are strong enough, a piece of card stock can be taped or glued to the magnetic surface for color changes, and the magnetic letters can be "attached" to it; the little magnets have to be pretty strong for this to work. Some are and some aren't. The only problem with magnetic letters seems to be their magnetism: After a period of use, they don't want to stay in place—even on a magnetic surface. Older makes of magnetic letters seem to work better, since they have better magnets.

### Custom Lettering

Many other types of lettering—like ceramic, wood, styrofoam, and the like—are normally too large to use for video lettering except in special applications. For example, a client once wanted an ad for his pool-cleaning invention called "Down 'n Out" to start with a slow zoom in on the words "Down 'n Out" floating on the surface of a pool, and then dissolve to underwater footage of the "Down 'n Out" cleaning the pool. Well, even with no perceptible breeze, the surface tension of the water made those letters float away in all directions. We ended up using custom-cut wooden letters tied together and anchored with transparent fish line. Even then, letters didn't want to float level, so we had to make styrofoam "pontoons" and glue them under the letters. Then we placed each letter in the water, and kept trimming the pontoons until they floated almost level. Many other types of materials, such as foamcore, cardboard, and plywood, are used for custom lettering purposes.

### Typewriters

If your video camera has close-up capabilities, or if you have access to a 35-mm C adaptor and a 35-mm macro lens or to close-up adaptor lenses, you can set up your camera so that it can focus close enough to pick up titles from 3x5 cards. Typewriting is, of course, the most inexpensive method mentioned thus far. Normal type styles may not be very interesting, but IBM Selectric typewriters with various styles of type can be used for variety. A primary typewriter, which has the advantage of larger letters than on ordinary typewriters, can also be used (Figure 8-18). Small typewriting errors and flaws in the surface of the card stock or typing paper are amplified using this method.

FIGURE 8–18. With close-up lenses, ordinary typefaces may be used for lettering. Primary type is much larger.

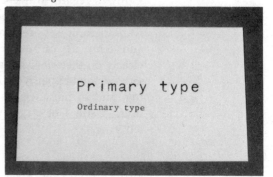

### Letteron

In the Letteron machine, metal templates "kiss-cut" letters of different styles and sizes from a specially designed, adhesive-backed tape. The tape comes in different colors. The letters may then be rubbed onto card stock, posterboard, or just about any surface. The process is fairly slow, and the cost relatively high, but the results are good. The advantage of Letteron over conventional types of transfer lettering is that you cut only what you use. You don't end up with a sheet of letters with no *es*, but nine *is*.

### Embossograph

The Embossograph works something like the Letteron, but, instead of cutting out letters, it presses letter shapes out of a colored material that looks like wax paper. The colored part comes off and is pressed onto the card stock. Sometimes you have to peel unwanted lettering material off the card stock and touch up the results. Sizes and styles of lettering are not too varied, but the system is relatively inexpensive.

### Hot Press

The hot press works much like the Embossograph, but it uses a heat process for sticking on the letter instead of contact pressure. The sizes and styles of letters are more varied than the Embossograph, but the process is about as slow. Both are most suitable for short captions or credits.

### Typesetting

Typesetting is one of the easiest and fastest ways to produce titles and credits for a production without spending a lot of money for a calligrapher or artist. Just about every offset printing establishment of any size has at least one typesetting machine, since the printer uses typesetting to produce copy for offset printing purposes. With such a machine, you can line up and space letters of many sizes and styles. As the operator types the copy, it is automatically transferred to photosensitive paper. The paper is run through a special processor, and the copy comes out as black letters on a white background. Using a simple *reversal PMT* process, you can get white letters on a black background for "keying" titles.

If the printer is producing titles for video for the first time, you have to educate him or her on the limitations of the medium. And, since there are so many styles and point sizes to choose from, you have to undergo a little education yourself. Once this initial period of communication is complete, you should get what you want without having to explain everything again.

Ask the printer if the image is developed on resin-coated (RC) paper. If so, you may consider it permanent. If it is developed on stabilization (S-type) paper, then it is susceptible to fading. On S-type paper, the processing chemicals are not washed off the surface. As a result, they continue to process the image, at an imperceptibly slow rate, to the point that it eventually disappears. So if the printer supplies S-type and if you plan to use the typesetting over a period of weeks, tell the printer to be sure to "fix" the image extra well. If the image is not run through a chemical fixer, it will begin to fade and turn brown within a few weeks—even days sometimes.

When choosing type styles, be sure to follow the recommendations mentioned earlier in this chapter regarding size, the number of words per card, boldness, case, and so on. All these recommendations are based on the past experience of a number of video producers, and you are a giant step ahead if you observe them.

### KroyType 80™ Lettering Machine

All the other lettering systems have some type of problem associated with them. Either they take a long time to use, are not very neat and accurate, get messy, or are prohibitively expensive. The KroyType™ lettering machine, however, from Kroy Industries, Inc. (Figure 8-19) is much faster than either hand or mechanical lettering, produces professional-looking letters, is absolutely clean (requiring no messy chemical developers or drying time), and is relatively inexpensive.

FIGURE 8-19. A KroyType 80™ lettering machine. (Photo courtesy of Kroy Industries, Inc.)

The lettering comes in many sizes, colors, and styles for many purposes. The KroyType 80™ lettering machine produces sizes of up to approximately one-half inch high, and the KroyType XL™ gives you letters of between approximately ½ and 2 inches high. Of special importance to the video producer is the fact that the lettering styles can be produced in reverse or white on black. This makes it possible to strip up the lettering on a black card and "key" the lettering over pre-recorded tape for video titles, credits, or any other purposes. Its features make the Kroy-Type lettering machines the best low-cost alternative for graphic lettering that we are aware of (see Source Index).

### Character Generators

Character generators electronically transfer letters typed on a keyboard to the television screen (Figure 8-20). Many features enable more expensive character generators to produce horizontal crawls, vertical rolls, drop shadow, various styles and sizes, and other special effects, such as reverse lettering, bordered lettering, flashing words, arrows, circles, squares, and the like. Many also store information that is frequently used or edited only slightly for repeated use. The editing can, in some cases, be done without retyping anything but the edited sections. The advantage of character generators is therefore their speed and efficiency. No paper or art materials are needed. With a little training, almost anyone can operate them. Their disadvantage is that no matter how many features they have, they won't always do what you want them to. They are also

FIGURE 8–20. A 3M model D-3016 character generator. (Photo courtesy of 3M)

relatively limited as far as font styles are concerned. Many have only one font style.

The price of comparatively good character generators, however, is now within range of some independent producers. A character generator, used in tandem with other graphics to provide more variety, is a hard combination to beat. New developments in electronics are making it less expensive to manufacture character generators, driving their prices down even more.

## SIMPLE ILLUSTRATION TECHNIQUES

Simple lettering may not always be enough to make the point—to communicate the concept. Frequently, some type of illustration is necessary. Since often very little money is available for artwork, you have to be able to cut corners without sacrificing quality. And you can do so by producing simple illustrations in a variety of ways.

### COPYRIGHT-FREE ARTWORK

One of the easiest ways is by pasting up copyright-free artwork. Most copyright-free artwork is either "tear" art, transfer art, free audiovisual art, or your own photographic work. When selecting any of these materials, be sure to keep the limitations of the video medium in mind: Select bold graphics rather than extremely detailed work . . . keep an eye on color, contrast, and aspect ratio . . . and be doubly sure that the material you are using is not copyrighted. Neglecting to check copyrights could cause you problems later, especially if you intend to sell the tape in which the art is used.

### Tear Art

"Tear" art is torn from the pages of books that have line drawings of a wide range of objects, people, and situations. Frequently such books are found at offset printing establishments. They are, however, also for sale to the general public. Some of these books come with a great range of borders, which can be used to frame captions or other illustrative material.

### Transfer Art

Transfer art is similar to transfer letters in that it comes on a backing sheet and is rubbed onto posterboard or card stock. Transfer art does not have the artistic range of tear art, but it has a wide variety of patterns, borders, and frequently used symbols.

### Free Audiovisual Materials

The *Educator's Guide to Free Materials*, produced by an organization in Randolph, Wisconsin, is an index to free audiovisual materials. The materials vary from posters and printed material to slide-tape presentations and films. Some of this material is copyrighted, some not.

The Educator's Guide is not the only one of its type. Guides are also available from U.S. government agencies listing their holdings, most of which are in the public domain. Some of the most interesting media come from NASA (National Aeronautics and Space Administration). Space footage of earth makes a great opening for many types of presentations.

### Photographs (Self-Made)

If you intend to shoot photographs or slides to be used in your video presentation, be especially careful of aspect ratio: The aspect ratio of slides is 2:3, while video is 3:4. So slides have to be shot in the horizontal format and, when transferring slides to videotape, you lose a little more of the slide's image on both ends than you do on the top and bottom. In other words, shoot slides horizontally and a little "loose" in the frame. Don't crowd the edges of the slide with any important information, because it may be lost in the transfer to videotape. (See also Chapter 7's section on slides.)

## TRACING

Tracing is one of the simplest illustration techniques. It can be used either alone or in combination with any type of copyright-free artwork. All you need is tracing paper, carbon paper, and something to be traced.

### Flat Artwork

Just place the tracing paper over the artwork, and trace the important lines with a pencil (Figure 8-21)—either one particular image or parts of several images. Once you have finished tracing the important lines, lay the tracing paper on the carbon paper, which is positioned on the card stock. Retrace the lines on the tracing paper (Figure 8-22). The resulting carbon outline on the card stock can then be redrawn with ink or colored in (Figure 8-23).

Tracing can be made very creative by using only those elements of existing graphic material that you desire. It is also useful because excessive or delicate detail can be left out. Dropping detail saves time and can be taught to an artist, which saves the artist's time as well.

The important point is *don't duplicate existing work.* Duplicating work exactly is at best plagiarism and at worst a violation

FIGURE 8–21. Tracing an image.

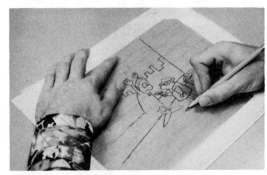

FIGURE 8–22. Transferring the image to artboard using carbon paper.

FIGURE 8–23. Coloring in the transferred image.

of the copyright law. Usually the process of tracing itself changes the appearance of the traced work to such a degree that it could not be considered a violation of copyright.

## PROJECTED IMAGES

When tracing flat artwork, the illustration may be the wrong size or aspect ratio to fit in the essential area. Sometimes you can use projection equipment to enlarge or reduce artwork for tracing purposes.

## OPAQUE PROJECTORS

If the illustration or photograph is too small, place it in an opaque projector for enlargement (Figure 8-24). The illustration, or what-

FIGURE 8–24. Graphic materials may be enlarged to fit the essential area with an opaque projector.

FIGURE 8–25. The graphic is projected onto the essential area for tracing.

ever part of it you desire, is projected directly onto the scanning area of the card stock and traced (Figure 8-25). The tracing can then be inked in or colored.

Some type of opaque projectors are designed to be clamped to a drawing table so that the projected image can be positioned, sized, and focused for tracing on almost any size area. Some types also project small three-dimensional objects on a drawing board. The size of the object can be enlarged or reduced to fit into the scanning area of the artboard. This capability eliminates having to photograph the object before tracing it, thus saving time and money.

### Slides and Negatives

Sometimes you may want to transfer graphic information from a slide, a color negative, or a black-and-white negative to the scanning area. Slides are most likely mounted in a slide mount before you get them, but you may have to put color or black-and-white negatives into slide mounts before projecting them. Then the slide or negative is projected onto the scanning area of the card stock or paper. The main lines are traced and the illustration is then colored and captioned. Surprisingly you can do so from color or black-and-white negatives, since you need only the main lines; it doesn't matter whether the projection is positive or negative.

### Overhead Projectors

Tracing from color transparencies or black-and-white negatives can also be done with an overhead projector. The projected images of 35-mm slides or negatives are relatively small, but, depending on the size of artboard you are using, the projected image may be large enough to fill the scanning area. Larger transparencies or negatives such as 2¼ by 2¼ work better since they project large images. The projected image of standard-size transparencies, color or black-and-white, may be too large to fit entirely into the scanning area, but parts of it may fit.

## REPRODUCTIONS

Sometimes you can produce an eye-catching illustration by reproducing artwork from magazines or books of tear art on black-and-white or color Xerox machines. Such an illustration can be used either alone or in combination with others produced through other means—either tracing or projection—to create professional-looking graphics.

### Xerox

On many color Xerox machines, a slide projector is mounted so that slides can be projected onto the copy surface of the Xerox machine and a color copy made directly from the slide. Small three-dimensional objects can also be placed on the copy surface of the Xerox machine and reproduced. Such visuals are usually quite interesting, and they don't require a great deal of time or money to produce. Reproductions of prints, slides, and other flat artwork can often be combined to create artistic montages.

## MONTAGE

A montage with a caption makes a very interesting title card for background art during openings, closings, station breaks, or other pauses in the program. Montages created for this purpose should be fairly simple and straightforward. For this reason, don't get carried away with the number of pictorial elements included in the montage. Too many "clutter" the video image and most likely introduce too much detail.

Otherwise, the rules for producing montages are the same as for other types of television graphics. Keep it relatively simple and bold. Watch contrast and color.

If an illustration or photograph is the correct size, it can be glued or dry-mounted directly onto the scanning area of the card stock or art paper.

### KEEPING AN ART FILE

Keep a collection of promising illustrations and photographs for a "tear sheet" file. If you intend to use any illustrations or photographs from outside sources, secure written permission from the publisher before you use them—especially if you do not intend to change them enough so that they cannot be recognized. Try to select matte-surfaced illustrations' and photographs for the file, since glossy-surfaced graphics sometimes reflect light in strange ways when on camera, especially if they have been folded at one time or another. The reflections then appear along the creases in the paper. The fold may not be noticeable otherwise, but as soon as it's placed in light, the little shiny areas show up. Sometimes you can correct this condition by changing the lighting on the graphic.

## LIGHTING GRAPHICS

First, make certain that the graphic is ready for shooting. Since it's easiest to work with graphics in an upright position, place the graphic on an easel (Figure 8-26). Make the graphic as flat and smooth as possible. Usually doing so is no problem with a photograph or some typesetting, but, with a visual montage, glue or dry-mount the many visual elements to the scanning area of the posterboard, so that the edges remain flat. Curly edges look rough and cast shadows.

Usually a single, broad source of light is adequate for lighting a graphic, because it tends to "play down" minor imperfections in the graphic and to "flatten out" inconsistencies in the graphic's surface. It won't solve basic flaws or imperfections in the graphics, but very minor problems will disappear if lighted correctly. If you don't happen to have a broad source of light, a point source of light reflected from an umbrella or reflector also works. If one source of light doesn't seem to light the graphic evenly enough, use two sources at 45-degree angles to the surface of the graphic (Figure 8-27). A shallower angle than 45-degrees tends to amplify surface flaws by throwing shadows, while a greater angle may bounce light back into the camera's lens causing reflections.

To locate the optimum distance where

**FIGURE 8-26. One type of easel.**

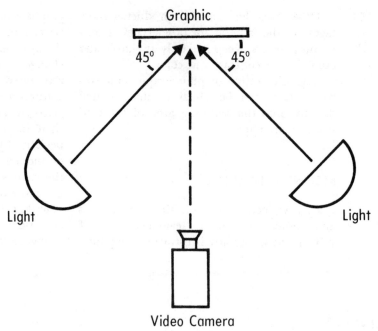

FIGURE 8–27. Lighting graphics.

the light is adequate without producing hot spots, you have to experiment. If any source of light you use seems to cause "hot spots" on the graphic, redirect the light beam so that the hot spot is off to the side, out of range of the camera's viewfinder. This technique is called *working off the edge* of the light. If possible, you may also physically move the offending light farther away from the graphic to "soften" the light. The unhappy side-effect of moving the light away from the graphic, however, is that the intensity of the light (the amount of light) falls off very quickly as the source is moved back.

**SHOWING A SERIES OF GRAPHICS**

If a series of graphics has to be shown using a single-camera system, there are several ways to accomplish smooth transitions from one visual to the next. If editing facilities are available, you can first shoot each visual for several seconds and then edit them into a smooth sequence.

If you have no time for editing, arrange the graphics in order on the easel and "pull" them at will. "Pulling" graphics on camera requires patience and a little skill. First, all the graphics have to be the same size, and the information on each one has to be fairly closely registered to the information on all others, so that when one graphic is pulled, the caption or illustration on the next graphic will be properly framed in the camera's viewfinder. Of course this requirement presents no problem if you follow the directions for standardizing your graphics. Attaching a paper or tape tab to the top or side of each graphic makes it a lot easier to separate them before pulling them out

of the scene. (Figure 8-28). The "pull" should be done with a snappy jerk. Done correctly, it looks like a cut. The only problem with "pulling" is that graphics may want to cling together, or the whole easel or graphic support may want to move. But if you are careful not to use too much adhesive or glue when producing your graphics, they shouldn't stick together. And taping the easel down or steadying it with bricks or books should prevent it from moving during the pull. With a little practice, this method works very well.

Another way to show a series of graphics without editing is by using the *drop-in* method, using either a flip chart positioned on an easel or a Tele Display Titling System:

1. Using a *flip chart and an easel,* let each successive graphic drop in on cue. All you need is someone to stand next to the easel and turn the pages of the flip chart. If posterboard is used as the backing for

FIGURE 8–28. Tabs on graphics make it easier to separate them for "pulling" from the scene.

FIGURE 8–29. The Tele Display Titling System. (Photo courtesy of Reynolds-Leteron Co.)

each graphic, each visual drops quickly, approximating a cut. If a lighter weight art paper is used, each visual tends to "float" an instant longer, looking more like a fast dissolve.

2. The *Tele Display Titling System,* available from Comprehensive Video Supply Corporation (see Source Index), is a variation of the simple flip chart and easel

system—with several advantages. It comes with cards that are pre-cut and laid out for the video medium. It also includes a foot pedal and 12 feet of cable so that each successive graphic can be released on cue from the camera position. This control is helpful when no one is around to turn the pages of the flip chart (Figure 8-29).

## ADDING MOTION TO GRAPHICS

There are three basic ways to add motion to graphics:

1. move the camera,
2. move the graphic (or part of it), or
3. move both at the same time.

### CAMERA MOVEMENTS

Camera movements on graphics can be done in fairly standard ways—pans, tilts, zooms, or a combination thereof—but these movements are usually not practical for graphics designed with a standard format and aspect ratio. For example, if a graphic is very long and thin (stretched horizontally), pans are not only creative but necessary. To fill the whole screen with a static shot of a long horizontal graphic forces you to pull back so far that you leave a lot of dead space above and below the graphic. Seeing any detail at all on the graphic itself would be hard since you would be so far away from

it. The only solution is to fill the screen with part of the graphic and pan along its length, a solution that eliminates the dead space and vastly improves legibility. The same basic treatment works for graphics stretched vertically; the only practical way to handle them is to tilt along their lengths. Very large graphics also have an advantage since you can add movement by panning or tilting across them, by zooming in or out on them, or by some combination of all of these movements! Their size lets you make these movements without running off their edges.

If a long, thin graphic stretched horizontally or vertically has words written on it, a pan or tilt can be used to produce a horizontal *crawl* or a vertical *roll*. (Sometimes a roll is called a vertical crawl.) If you pan the camera right across a horizontal graphic with words, the words appear to travel from right to left across the screen. The speed of the crawl depends on how fast you pan the camera. Doing smooth crawls and rolls, especially when they have to be slow and smooth, takes some practice. A good tripod with a fluid head helps a lot—but unfortunately the better fluid heads are quite expensive.

## MOVING GRAPHICS

Moving crawls and rolls can also be done by moving the graphic instead of the camera. One of the easiest ways to move the graphic is to make slots on both ends of a thick piece of posterboard with an Xacto knife or razor blade, and then to feed the end from a roll of computer paper through the slots (Figure 8-30). You're all set up to crawl titles, appearing and disappearing graphics, and other designs on the paper. As you pull the paper through the slots, the graphics appear, stop, disappear, or crawl across the board, depending on how quickly the paper is pulled through. If the paper binds in the slots, just widen them a little. For rolls, just draw everything for the vertical format and set the posterboard on end. This method of producing crawls and rolls works very well and costs almost nothing. It takes only one extra person to steady the slotted posterboard and to pull the paper through. At slow speeds, the graphic can be pulled more steadily than the camera can be panned or tilted.

Very nice crawls can also be done by finding an old turntable, and fitting a large circular piece of cardboard over the turn-

FIGURE 8–30. An inexpensive method to produce crawl titles.

table platen. If the turntable has controls that interfere with the size of the cardboard, place the cardboard on top of a short cylinder so that it can be as large as physically practical. Then fashion a short wide cylinder from posterboard and tape it to the circular cardboard base. Computer paper, with graphics drawn on it can then be attached to the outside wall of the cylinder (Figure 8-31). When the turntable is turned on, the graphics begin to crawl, the turntable speeds governing the rate of the crawl. Sometimes you have to help the turntable get started because most are not equipped to handle very much weight, a fact that should be a consideration in the design of the base and wall. Try to keep them as light as possible so that the turntable can turn under the weight. Vertical rolls can't be done with this apparatus unless you can find a way to lay

FIGURE 8–31. Using a turntable to produce smooth crawls.

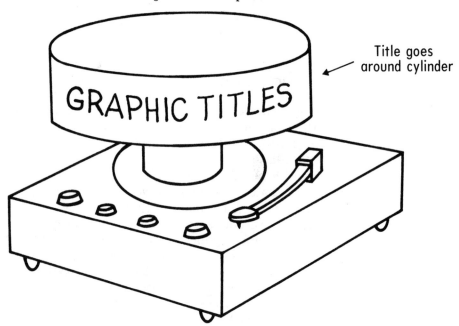

Title goes
around cylinder

GRAPHIC TITLES

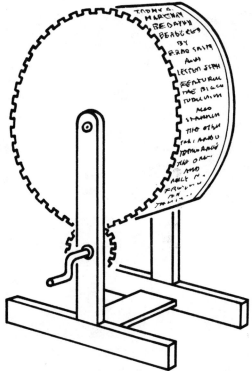

FIGURE 8-32. An inexpensive method to produce rolls.

the camera on its side, which is not recommended.

You can do vertical rolls by bending a long strip of paper around any kind of cylinder, and then turning the cylinder by hand or motor (Figure 8-32). The design of this apparatus varies, but keep two things in mind before running to the welder. First, make sure the cylinder is mounted through its exact center. If it's not, it moves slightly up and down as the roll progresses, making the roll look amateurish since it's evident how it is being done. Second, be certain that the drive mechanism is smooth—whether it is hand-cranked or motor-driven. A stuttering drive mechanism also spoils the effect. You should design and build something this complicated and expensive only if you have to produce a lot of vertical crawls. It doesn't work for horizontal crawls.

## OTHER MOVING ARTWORK

A creative mind can come up wth many more ways to move artwork:

1. You can achieve a kind of animation by producing a background on artboard, and then using animator's inks to paint a foreground subject on acetate. The acetate is then pulled across the background to add motion to the graphic (Figure 8-33).

Flat or diffuse lighting will eliminate reflections from the acetate.

2. Design graphics so that parts of them can be manipulated—like a moving bottom jaw on an otherwise immobile face to simulate talking, or moving legs to simulate walking. This movement adds life and appeal to them without resorting to expensive and time-consuming animation techniques.

3. A radio-controlled toy van pulls up to the curb in front of a cardboard box painted like a place of business—a great way to start a story or an ad.

4. Puppets, dolls, and other objects can be set into motion by using object animation techniques. With more, and more editing controllers, making clean accurate frame edits possible, you can take object animation directly to video without intermediate film production. Just move the object, shooting one or two frames per movement for thirty or fifteen moves per second. Play it back to check what you've done. No waiting for film processing. It's wonderful. Flat animation and line animation can be done the same way.

Another way to produce moving artwork so that it looks like animation is through the use of a Motionmaster™ machine. The machine, produced by Frank Woolley & Co., Inc. (see Source Index), is a large box with a rotating rear-lighted polarized disc inside. The speed and direction of rotation of the disc can be adjusted by controls on the side of the box. Pressure-sensitive polarized sheets of acetate, called Polarmotion and attached to the back of line negatives of artwork, produce various patterns of motion. Colored gel material is added over the polarization material. When the disc inside the box is

FIGURE 8-33. Using an acetate overlay to produce a moving graphic.

FIGURE 8–34. The MotionMaster machine creates moving artwork through the use of polarizing materials. (Photo courtesy of Frank Woolley & Co., Inc.)

rotated, the artwork moves in any desired direction, in any one of seventy different stock motion patterns. Movement in the opposite direction is achieved simply by reversing the direction of the disc's rotation.

Startling effects, which otherwise would cost thousands to produce using the computer graphics approach, can be created and transferred to videotape or film for just a few dollars.

## COMPUTER GRAPHICS

Any chapter on television graphics would not be complete without at least a mention of computer graphics. Computer graphics are produced in basically two ways: either by analog or by digital computers. Both ways have their pros and cons.

*Analog systems* are hardware-dependent. In other words, their kinds of effects depend on the type and capabilities of the hardware involved. If the hardware can do certain things and not others, then the artist's concept must be made to match what the hardware can do, rather than vice-versa. Most analog systems produce beautifully smooth motion in real time so that the artist can experiment with scenes and match the timing to music or to other action. The look of most analog-originated graphics is abstract and electronic.

*Digital systems,* as well as hybrid analog-digital systems, are more software-dependent. In other words, the hardware with the new LSI (large-scale integrated) circuitry is capa-

ble of almost anything, but you have to have the appropriate software programs to tell it what you want. With graphics tablets and lightpens—two different systems—you can literally "paint" the video screen. Other systems enable you to manipulate parts of the image—to change color, rotate, enlarge, reduce, compress, expand, or replicate whole images or image parts. These manipulations can then be stored and used later. Digital graphics, which require pre-planning, are not done in real time like analog graphics. A description of the digital graphics look cannot be generalized: It can cover the whole range from absolutely real-looking to spacially surreal. It really depends on the imagination and experience of the artist.

If producers are using single-camera systems to create commercial-quality video, they should explore the field of computer graphics more fully. The possibilities are just beginning to be felt, and they are enormous.

## VISUAL EFFECTS LIBRARIES

Cascom, an enterprising commercial production company from Tennessee specializing in 35-mm animation (see Source Index), has developed an approach to video graphics that may be of great interest to independent single-camera producers. They compile a videotape and film library of animated 35-mm visual effects that were originally created as by-products or out-takes from their completed commercials. The effects vary greatly: star bursts, comet trails, star and planet fields, moving line drawings, and so on. All of them, when combined with other graphic information or titles, can add an extra dimension to low-budget productions. The library, which is continuously updated, is available on a rental basis from Cascom.

## VIDEO FEEDBACK

Video feedback to produce graphics with a single-camera system is a very under-used technique. Not only is it fast and inexpensive, but it can produce extremely interesting effects. In many cases it looks exactly like computer graphics. Just glue, or otherwise attach, letters or shapes to a piece of acetate, and then tape the acetate over the screen of your monitor. After aiming the camera at the monitor's screen and adjusting the camera angle, you can use your zoom, contrast, color, and other controls to create sweeping hall-of-mirror effects, as well as colorful multi-color glows and numberless other special graphics. You can do this in real time to the beat of music or to the meter of other action. The design of the graphic material attached to the acetate determines how flexible the feedback can be. Adjusting the brightness, contrast, and color of the monitor provides more control over the appearance of the image. Three-dimensional objects can also be suspended in front of the monitor screen for feedback effects. You can produce other effects by turning your monitor on its side for feedback and using a special effects generator or character generator in combination with the feedback. The results possible are almost unlimited.

When using feedback, be careful that the video level doesn't get too high, and also avoid burning in the camera's tube by prolonged exposure to the bright monitor.

## SUMMARY

The design, production, and use of graphics in video don't have to be expensive and time-consuming to be done well. Simple lettering and illustration techniques, as well as motion and feedback, can be employed to add life and sparkle to video presentations, which otherwise might lack eye appeal. Creating graphics is one of the most enjoyable and interesting aspects of video work. Experimenting with some of the techniques in this chapter can, in itself, provide an enjoyable way to experience the phenomenal range of possibilities in video.

# 99999

# INEXPENSIVE SET DESIGN FOR TELEVISION

Whenever anyone says "set design," most people immediately think of Hollywood and large cash outlays. Most independents, consumers, and even corporate and educational video producers don't have the kind of resources to create large production sets. Even if they did, there is some question as to how appropriate such sets would be. For many types of television production, spectacular or costly sets aren't as practical as inexpensive ones. Most of the time, the location itself serves as the set, but in some cases the location has to be changed or "dressed" slightly to create the desired effect. For the most part, the "desired effect" is simply to enhance the mood or intent of what is being communicated. But in some cases, the set is designed to clash purposefully with the message or action for a special effect—to create tension or suspense, comical incongruity, abstract reference, or other impressions. Most of the techniques we discuss can be used in the studio (or in a controlled setting), as well as on location (which may or may not be controlled).

There is really no formula for set design.

No one comprehensive set of procedures imbues a set with the evocative appearance that pleases everyone. Set design, like graphic design, is often more representative of the available time and money than of the limitless aesthetic possibilities. But within the constraints imposed by taste, budget, and time, you still have enough latitude to do a better-than-average job of set design in most situations.

While many items used in set design can be purchased from theatrical supply houses, as well as from display or party supply outlets, most have to be specially designed or fabricated. To make sets, you don't need so much construction experience as you do resourcefulness and ingenuity. The purpose of this chapter is therefore to help you more fully develop these traits as opposed to "teaching" set design, by explaining a number of specific techniques, and by showing you examples of how they are applied. From that point, you should be able to embellish and streamline the basic techniques to fit any personal applications you have in mind.

## LIMBO

The easiest and least expensive set is none at all. In the so-called *limbo* or a *limbo setting*, only light and shadow are used. The limbo setting is effective for long monologs or in certain dramatic situations (Figure 9-1).

FIGURE 9–1. The limbo setting works well for monologes, dramatic situations, or some types of solo musical works.

Limbo is applied for the most part in situations that are intended to be eerie. Inasmuch as "limbo" means a place or condition of oblivion, everything around the subject in this sort of set is black, obscure, or "hellish." The limbo setting can be used very effectively to depict malevolence, mania, wickedness, or the "darker" side of the personality. Moving patterns and flashing lights can be added to the limbo setting to symbolize mental aberrations, hallucinations, and the like. Opening up the pool of light and adding other subjects or props can tone down this effect until a feeling more like drama prevails. Yet often just a limbo-lighted close-up of an evil face carries the entire scene.

## CUTAWAYS

A limbo setting may also be used for a *cutaway*, which is normally a "fill shot" to help the editor with scene transitions—a cut away from the main action or a change in action. To use a limbo setting as a cutaway, interject the limbo scene into other action. For instance, the wicked witch in limbo laughs into her mirror as, in the main action the lovely princess falls victim to her inscrutable spell. Then the handsome prince breaks the spell with a kiss, and back in limbo the wicked witch shrieks in rage. Again, although the limbo setting does not have to be eerie or wicked, as you can see, it lends itself well to such applications.

## STUDIO OR LOCATION SETS

The studio alone can be a most interesting set with a little planning. Most people don't have the foggiest idea of what goes on in a studio—they just think it's mysterious, marvelous, and wonderful.

### BACKGROUND EQUIPMENT

Arranging a few pieces of lighting and production equipment against a wall or backdrop says "TV" to them. Such a setting, if lighted appropriately, can be interesting without being overly obtrusive. It is also very widely applicable in that it supports almost any kind of main action activity—whether a commercial, a talk show, or an entertainment special. The control room, or any of the other engineering areas of the studio, are also getting an increasing amount of exposure in news and talk programs, as well as in any scenes in which "high technology" is represented. For example, sporting events frequently have cutaways in which commentators, guests, or others discuss and analyze the action on the court or field—and they do so almost always in an announcing booth or control room.

### BACKGROUND LOCATION OR ACTIVITY

On location, the "set" may consist of the background or of an activity in the background, if it is not too distracting. (Often you have no choice.) Usually, you can change the type of shot (long, medium, or close-up), the angle of the shot, and the part of the background shown in the shot enough to present the viewer with the most interesting part of the setting, without adding a lot of confusion to the scene.

You can use the existing lighting conditions and camera focus to play down a distracting background. For example, if the background is extremely busy, and if you have to work with areas of light and shade, shoot the main subject or action in the area with the higher light level and use the shaded area as the background. A busy background in a comparatively low-lighted area does not seem as busy. As for camera focus, try to drop focus on the background by adding neutral-density lenses to force an increase in the lens aperture. A distracting background is not nearly as distracting when it's out of focus. Shooting against a background that is lower in light level or slightly out of focus increases the odds that viewer interest will stay on the foreground where it normally belongs.

Sometimes the background is so important that it has to be well lighted and in focus so that the camera shot can be changed quickly from foreground to background. If so, and if you don't want the confusion or action of the background in the foreground shot, just frame the foreground shot more tightly until it has to be changed or "opened up" to the background.

## BACKDROPS

Backdrops generally provide a more neutral look than backgrounds. Most often backdrops are used in a studio or in a place that serves as a studio.

### CYCLORAMA

The most common type of backdrop is a large section of fabric or plastic called a *cyclorama*, or simply a *cyc.* Sometimes the cyc can be opened, closed, or adjusted like a curtain, but it is often permanently stretched on a framework and tied into place (Figure 9-2). A cyclorama is designed to give a neutral illusion of distance. Sometimes, with the appropriate lighting, it is used to represent the sky or heavens (Figure 9-3).

Cycloramas are sometimes beige or light brown, but they are more often medium blue, which is supposed to be the best background color for flesh tones. The blue is also used in chroma-keying; that is, the background blue is replaced with the signal from a second camera. Hence anything from the second camera can be placed, or *keyed,* behind the foreground subject. In a single-camera system, footage shot against a **blue** backdrop can be keyed in post-production. Keying comes in very handy in commercial work.

Since only light colors are used for cycloramas, cookie patterns projected from ellipsoidal spots are very legible on cycs. In the absence of a cyclorama, you can use just a plain wall, as long as it's relatively smooth and painted a medium off-white color (usually blue). With a painted wall as a backdrop, you save both in terms of the dollar cost and of studio space. On the other hand, suspending a backdrop a few feet out from the studio wall provides a practical storage area for other types of background or props.

FIGURE 9-2. A cyclorama (cyc) curtain. Some types of cyc are stretched on a framework and tied in place.

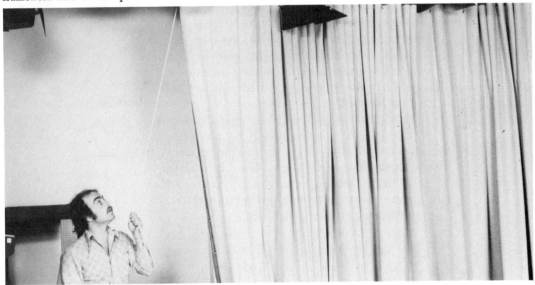

FIGURE 9-3. A cyclorama is intended to give a neutral illusion of distance or to represent the sky. Blue cycs are also used for chroma keying.

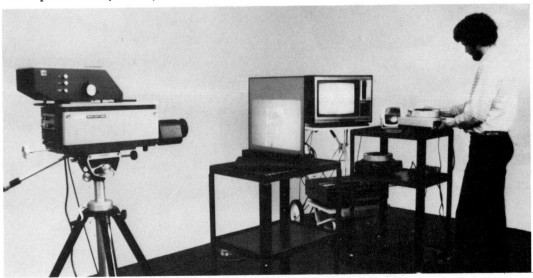

Sometimes, when shooting close to the studio floor or at an angle that exposes it to view, it's helpful to conceal the area where the cyc and floor meet. You can do so by means of a *cove,* which joins the background to the floor in one continuous line. It may be flat (Figure 9-4) or curved.

## FIXED BACKGROUNDS

Some studios construct a fixed background in a continuous piece that curves gently from the floor, continues up the wall, and curves into the ceiling. When the floor, wall, and ceiling are painted one color, you lose distance reference altogether. These backgrounds are called *bubble cycs* or *infinity cycs.* If you need a distance reference in a studio with an infinity cyc, the easiest thing to do is to project patterns from an ellipsoidal spot or slide projector onto the background, thus breaking up the background and making it seem "closer" (Figure 9-5). For the best effect, the projected pattern should be colored with a "warm" colored gel: orange, bronze, yellow, or red-orange. Of course, other colors like purple or mauve can be used to fit whatever mood is intended. If only a small area needs to be covered in a shot, a king-size blue bed sheet works as a temporary cyc.

## CURTAINS OR DRAPERIES

Depending on their color and pattern, curtains or draperies can also serve as a neutral background. The best type to use are draperies with a solid neutral color rather than patterned ones. Patterned draperies tend to draw attention away from the talent or action.

Fine- or tight-patterned draperies are an even more serious problem because they cause the video image to "vibrate," "hum," or "sing." This incredibly distracting side-effect should be avoided not only in backgrounds, but also in props and costumes. Any type of tight horizontal, herringbone, or checkerboard pattern is especially prone to such problems. It's not always easy to tell which patterns will cause the humming. If you suspect a pattern will cause such mischief, try it out on camera: If the monitor sings, don't use it; if not, there's no problem.

FIGURE 9-4. A cove is used to cover the space between the cyc and the studio floor. Some coves are curved.

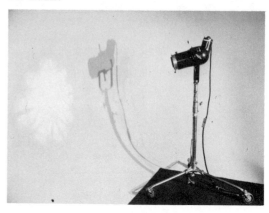

FIGURE 9-5. Patterns projected on cycs break up the background and add a sense of dimension to the studio.

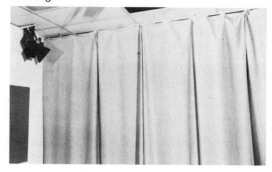

FIGURE 9-6. Curtains with widely spaced vertical patterns can be used in place of cycloramas. Other types of patterns may cause problems with video scanning.

Most draperies have pleats or folds, which are just about impossible to smooth out. Sometimes, rather than trying to smooth them out, accentuate them by side-lighting them. This type of wide vertical shadow pattern causes no problems with video scanning and provides a simple, neutral background (Figure 9-6).

Inexpensive fabric for making drapes can be obtained at remnant stores. When choosing a fabric, keep weight as well as pattern in mind. The fabric should be relatively heavy to resist movement from drafts or air conditioning. A gently undulating background can be almost as distracting as one that "vibrates." If no appropriate heavy material is available, hem a chain or bar into the bottom of light-weight fabrics to resist movements from drafts.

## SEAMLESS PAPER

Seamless paper, another type of background, comes in many colors and patterns. Most seamless paper comes in rolls 9 by 36 feet. However, some rolls may be longer, and black- or white-colored rolls come in 12-foot widths.

Seamless paper can be used in a number of ways: It can be taped to a wall with duct tape or suspended from a wooden pole or pipe (Figure 9-7). Or, if a large area of the background has to be covered, you can unroll it horizontally and tape it to a wall. Since it is so inexpensive, it can also be used on the floor, and, when soiled, turned over and reused, or discarded. Large pieces of off-white seamless can be used for making supergraphics or other set decorations. More on that later.

FIGURE 9–7. Seamless paper can be used in place of a cyclorama.

## FLOOR TREATMENT

Most studio floors are made of smoothly finished concrete that is either painted off-white or gray, or covered with tile or linoleum. Frequently the tile or linoleum is painted as well. The advantage of a smooth, painted surface is that it can be repainted according to the needs of a given production. It's durable, and moving equipment around on it is easy.

### DESIGNS

The floor can also be decorated with radial lines or abstract designs, or it can be covered with any of the new floor coverings that look like wood, tile, or brick. Various widths of multi-colored tapes can be added to appropriate floor coverings to produce futuristic-looking spatial patterns and perspective lines.

## CARPET

Various types of carpet are also used on the floor. Usually indoor-outdoor carpet is the best if equipment has to be moved over it. But you may also use shag and other more texturous carpet if you can roll back or tuck under the corners or edges, out of the way of the camera equipment. The advantage of carpet is the realistic effect it produces, and its noise-dampening quality.

If you can find older, used floor coverings that are in good condition, especially carpets, use them. Borrow floor coverings from someone who doesn't care what happens to them, rent them, or buy them second-hand or at a reduced price. Why not get the best? You *can*, of course, purchase the better brands of new carpet, but it won't be new for long. Video work destroys carpet in short order.

Video production is very hard on floor coverings. For example, twice during a memorable three-day shoot, quartz lights blew up in a 4,000-watt softlight, spewing molten glass on a new 12-by-20-foot rug. The liquid-hot fragments burned holes through the weave and backing right down to the floor. Normal wear and tear is also intense since the floor covering is in the center of the traffic area.

## SET MATERIALS

Sets that aren't too complicated and that require only fabric backdrops are called *soft sets*. More complicated sets, called *hard sets,* include flats, risers, and other special-purpose staging materials and construction techniques. Flats for television work are usually made of either "softwall" or "hardwall" materials.

### SOFTWALL FLATS

Softwall flats are made of muslin or canvas stretched over a 1x2 or 1x4 frame. The muslin or canvas may be painted or otherwise decorated. Softwall flats weigh considerably less than their hardwall counterparts, and they cost less to construct, but they are also less durable. For this reason, of the two types, hardwall flats are used more frequently in video.

### HARDWALL FLATS

Hardwall flats are almost always framed with 1x2s or 1x4s, and they are usually 4 by 8 feet in size since almost all hardwall materials come in sheets of that size. All flats are made to provide the maximum strength and surface area while keeping the weight to a minimum. Depending on how strong or durable they have to be, most hardwall flats are made of:

1. cardboard,
2. foamcore,
3. feltboard (Upsonboard),
4. masonite, vinylboard (Marlite),
5. paneling,
6. plywood, or
7. vacuum-formed plastic.

### Cardboard

Cardboard is inexpensive and can be purchased from suppliers in large unblemished sheets. Easily painted with rollers or brushes, it can be quickly attached to a frame with a staple gun. However, it is difficult to cut smoothly and tends to crease when bent. For its weight, it is very strong, but it does not stand up well to punctures or scrapes with sharp objects. Despite the fact that its surface can be painted, if moisture or water gets inside its corrugation, it gets "mushy," eventually drying scaly or deteriorating altogether.

### Foamcore

Foamcore, also inexpensive, comes in 4x8 sheets of several different thicknesses. It is easy to paint with rollers or brushes, and, since it comes with a smooth white surface on both sides, no base paint is needed as in the case of cardboard. Foamcore is not only very easy to cut smoothly with a single-edge razor blade or utility knife, it is also easily stapled to a frame. Although it can be bent slightly, it creases if bent too far. Contact with sharp objects dents or punctures it, but it stands up well to moisture and water. Overall, it is as light-weight and strong as cardboard, but it cuts easier, bends more, and is more water-resistant.

Since it is called different names in different parts of the country, you frequently have to describe it rather than ask for it by name. A good way to describe it is: "Material that comes in 4x8 sheets, with a white, smooth, and vinyl-like surface, sandwiching a white foam center layer."

### Feltboard (Upsonboard)

Feltboard, also called Upsonboard or bulletin board, is usually surfaced on one side, so it can be painted. It's made of a pressed fibrous material that can be either stapled onto a frame with a heavy-duty stapler, or tacked on with large-headed tacks. If small-headed tacks or finishing nails are used, they might pull through the board, remaining in the frame. It usually must be cut with a jig saw or band saw. Since it is fibrous, it doesn't cut cleanly—usually with a ragged edge. It can be scored and broken quickly, but the edge will be ragged. It can be bent quite far without breaking, but it doesn't take well to moisture or water. More puncture-resistant than cardboard or foamcore, it dents and scrapes fairly easily. Its strong point is that things can be easily pinned to it like a bulletin board, and, if you use common pins or other thin shafts, the holes are practically invisible from a few feet away.

### Mansonite
The name "masonite" is fairly universal. You can ask for it by name just about anywhere. Masonite is strong, bends quite easily, can be cut smoothly with a jig saw, has a smooth finished surface on one side and a rough surface on the other. Both surfaces can be painted. It is durable, resists punctures and scrapes, and can be nailed firmly to a frame with small-headed tacks or finish nails.

### Vinylboard (Marlite)
Vinylboard isn't called vinylboard anywhere. Depending on which brand name your local lumberyard carries, it may be called any number of things. One of the most widely distributed brand names is Marlite.

Vinylboard has a vinyl-covered, masonite-like surface, which comes in many colors and designs. It is used to customize shower enclosures and in some cases countertops around kitchen and bathroom sinks. The surface is one-sided—usually smooth and shiny—which can cause problems with lighting. It is durable, resists punctures and scrapes, can be bent quite far, can be washed, and passes as metal or plastic in the construction of futuristic-looking structures. It can be cut smoothly with a jig saw, and it stays on the frame if nailed with small-headed tacks or finish nails.

### Paneling
Paneling, a masonite-like material with a wide variety of surface designs, is ubiquitous.

The surface designs may be raised or flat, and they may look like wood grains, stone, brick, or tile. Prices vary depending on how real the surface looks. Sometimes, however, an inexpensive surface may be made to look more real with the simple addition of shadow lines or shading. Paneling may be bent, cut with a jig saw, and nailed with small-headed tacks or finish nails. It is water-resistant, can be washed or wiped off, and resists punctures and scrapes.

### Plywood
Plywood, which comes in different thicknesses and surface grades (qualities), is used everywhere. Some types may even be used outside. Plywood can be cut with a jig saw, is very strong, takes a lot of paint to cover, and bends easily (at least the thinner sheets do). Since plywood is pressed together in layers (plys), don't plan on nailing into the end or edge of it; the nails pull right out because the plys separate. This weak point, however, is also a strong point. Since it is made in plys, and since the grain of each ply runs in a different direction, you can nail into the flat side of very small pieces of plywood without splitting them. It can be nailed with just about anything from finish nails to spikes. This capability is very important in building frames for flats, which we cover later. Just don't plan to nail into the edges of it.

### Vacuum-Formed Plastic
An assortment of scenic backgrounds are available in raised-pattern vacuum-formed plastic. There are sheets that look like library bookshelves, period wallpaneling designs (Italian provencial, Castilian with pilasters, and the like), and other backgrounds. These may be combined with other paneling designs or backgrounds to add realism to the set.

**FLATS** No matter what type of "face" you put on a flat, it has to be attached to a frame for added strength, so that a number of faces can be connected together to form walls or other standing backgrounds. The best and most inexpensive way to build a strong frame is to cut the frame lumber—1x2s, 1x4s, or 2x4s—to size and then to join the pieces together with corner blocks, keystones, and at least one (better two) corner braces made of the same lumber as the frame itself (Figure 9-8). The easiest way to make the

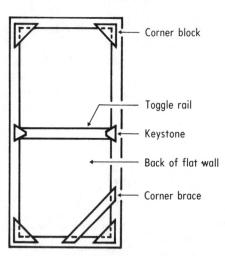

FIGURE 9–8. Frame for a flat.

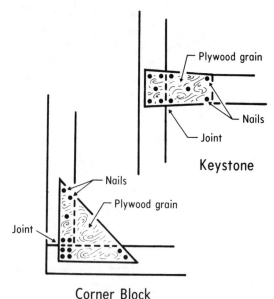

Keystone

Corner Block

FIGURE 9–9. Corner block and keystone.

corner blocks and keystones is from plywood, since small pieces of plywood hardly ever split (Figure 9-9).

Once a flat is built, it has to be supported in an upright position, usually by means of a brace and jack arrangement often called a *bracing jack*. Of the several ways to make one, the easiest is to clamp an L-shaped jack, made of two pieces of lumber nailed together at right angles to each other, to a third piece of lumber, which forms the third side of the triangle. The jack is then weighted down with a sandbag or some other type of stage weight (Figure 9-10). A brace and jack arrangement is surprisingly strong and easy to work with. The flat can be supported either

in a fully upright position or at just about any other angle.

When several flats are used at one time to simulate walls or other structures, you have to join the flats to each other in a continuous line. One way to do so is to use *lashlines*. Cleats, hooks, or eyelets are screwed into the frame of each flat 8 to 10 inches apart diagonally from each other. Then a lashline (rope) is wound tightly through the hardware and tied at the top and bottom, thus joining the flats tightly together (Figure 9-11). Another procedure is to use interlocking hinges. Half the hinge is attached to one flat and half to another. When the flats are fitted together, the hinge pin is shoved

FIGURE 9–10. Brace and jack.

FIGURE 9–11. A strong line is interwoven through hardware cleats.

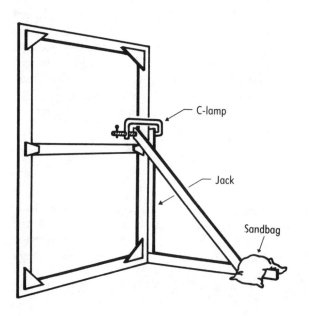

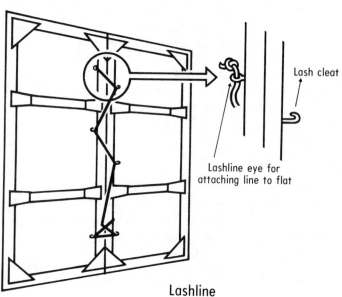

Lashline

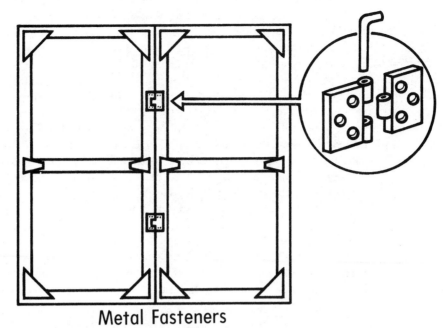

## Metal Fasteners

FIGURE 9–12. Hinge halves, which fit together where the flats meet, are locked with a pin.

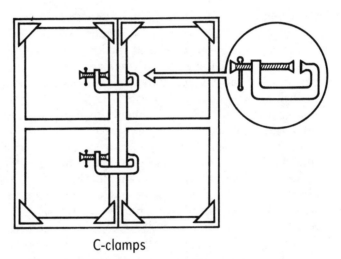

## C-clamps

FIGURE 9–13. C-clamps clamp the flats together.

into place, thus fastening the flats together. Although this is a strong way to connect flats, the disadvantage is that the hinges have to be positioned accurately on all flats, or they won't fit together correctly (Figure 9-12). C-clamps are probably the fastest and strongest way to join flats together. They are, however, comparatively expensive, and they do not allow the flat to bend in angles (Figure 9-13). Each arrangement has its advantages and disadvantages, but a combination of them should suffice for joining just about any type of flat to any other.

**RISERS** Risers are used for raising areas of the set above the stage or floor level. Risers are used a great deal in school drama classes and plays, as well as in little theater and music groups. In television work, risers are just about always necessary for talk shows, panel discussions, or any other sit-down type of presentation, because studio cameras are usually operated at eye level. If the people sitting down are not elevated, the camera would be shooting down on them. Since this angle is rather unflattering, risers are used to raise everyone about 8 to 10 inches off the stage or studio floor.

Since they have to hold considerable weight, risers are often constructed of plywood with 2x4, 2x6, or even heavier frames. (Whenever something has to hold greater-than-normal weight, it has to be constructed of heavier materials. Even flats or other structures on the set are made heavier if they have to support a greater amount of weight than usual.) Risers are frequently made 4 by 8 feet long, but often 4 by 4 footers are constructed, as well as 2 by 4 and 2 by 8 footers. Several of each type can be stacked and joined together in a modular fashion to create multi-level sets for dance, dramatic, or musical productions. Usually risers are painted matte black so they won't be visible through other types of temporary coverings, but sometimes they are permanently covered with carpeting to help dampen the hollow sound they make when walked on.

Risers are a lot easier to borrow than flats, so instead of paying a lot of money to construct and transport them, try borrowing them first. Since flats are usually custom-designed and painted, and since a greater amount of time is spent constructing them, they are harder to borrow. In general, the best thing to do is to try to borrow the risers and construct the flats yourself.

## SKELETAL SETS

Once you build or borrow the basic flats and risers, you can use them in a number of ways, depending on time and budget, to create skeletal or full sets. (Full sets are discussed later in this chapter.) Skeletal sets, in their most basic form, may not even have flats or risers. For example, a camera close-up, low-angle lighting, and an appropriate costume can be combined to create a setting that symbolizes a jail cell (Figure 9-14). In Figure 9-15, the basic elements of the scene are shown. Had a more realistic skeletal set been desired, a flat with a stone wall and barred window painted on it could have been placed behind the actor. Since the actor is the center of attention in the shot, such a flat would not have had to have been too detailed, since it would have been slightly out of focus anyway.

## GOBOS

Skeletal set scenes are frequently established by using a *gobo,* which is anything that creates the illusion of a scene by being a foreground when seen through the camera. In Figure 9-15, for example, the gobo is the jail bar assembly. In Figure 9-16, the camera shoots through a window in a door to create the feeling that the viewer is outside looking in. If the scene were being shot live, a second camera picks up the action from a different angle closer to the talent, which gives the impression of moving inside. After the second camera picks up the action, the gobo is moved out of the way of the first camera (Figure 9-17). When shooting with a single-camera system, the action would have to be delayed until the camera could be moved to the new location and angle.

FIGURE 9–14. A skeletal set.

FIGURE 9–15. Skeletal set elements.

FIGURE 9-16. A gobo is anything placed between the subject and the camera to establish place or time.

FIGURE 9-17. The gobo is moved when cameras are switched or, with a single-camera system, when the gobo scene is finished.

## PROJECTED IMAGES

For an even more interesting and effective skeletal set, projected images can be used in conjunction with gobos, flats, and risers. Slides or filmstrips may be still-projected or projected in succession from a single projector or by means of a programmer and dissolve unit arrangement. Motion picture footage may also be projected. The projectors themselves typically have to be hidden and soundproofed.

### Front Screen

Front screens can be made by using a flat painted bright white, or by using commercially produced high-reflectance screen materials. (For more on front and rear projection, see Chapter 7, "Putting Slides and Film on Video.")

### Rear Screen

Rear screens can be used when rear-projecting images. Projecting images from the rear is advantageous since the projector is off stage, out of the way of the action and away from the microphones. One of the most common uses of projected images is background scenes. If a set has a window or a door, it's really easy to set up a front or rear screen and project an image that is seen through the window or door in the set.

Since video requires quite a bit of light, use the brightest, highest-power projectors available, or use the projector lamp with the highest safe wattage rating. When the image is used primarily to fill the background, however, it really doesn't have to be extremely bright or legible. A conventional projector and bulb can be used for such an application.

## CREATING SETS THROUGH LIGHTING

Sometimes more abstract images or patterns are used on a skeletal set with cookies, ellipsoidal spot lights, or pattern projectors.

### Cookies

The word cookie, derived from Cucaloris (also spelled Cookalourus or Kukaloris), is used to describe any of a variety of large patterns made of wood or metal, which are held or positioned in front of a light to cast patterns on a set or background (Figure 9-18). Wooden cookies work well if their patterns don't have to have fine-focused detail. Since they are held out in front of a lighting unit, the pattern cast is very soft around the edges, an effect that is often very desirable.

FIGURE 9-18. A wooden pattern being used to cast a shadow.

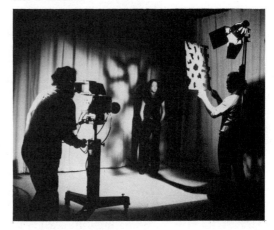

### Ellipsoidal Spots

Ellipsoidal spots enable you to fine focus patterns of different types on specific areas of the set or background. Obtaining the type of pattern desired is often difficult, especially if you rent the ellipsoidal unit (usually people who rent lighting units have a very

**FIGURE 9–19.** Patterns that can be projected onto a background by an ellipsoidal spot. (All designs copyright The Great American Market)

limited variety of patterns on hand). A good source of a wide variety of patterns is The Great American Market (see Source Index), from whom a free catalog of patterns is available. Some of the patterns offered are designed to work together, from two or more light sources, either in sequence or superimposed. Many can be sandwiched together and, with the addition of color gels, used to create very interesting backgrounds for any type of set. The patterns come in sizes to fit any ellipsoidal spot, and, if you need a pattern of your own design, they can make it for you. Figure 9-19 shows several of the patterns available from the catalog.

## Pattern Projectors

Pattern projectors are large, heavy-duty spot lights that project patterns over large areas from a greater-than-average distance. They are useful in large staging areas inside or out. Although their patterns are similar to those used with the ellipsoidal spot, some pattern projectors—such as the Scene Machine and other projection systems from the Great American Market—are capable of moving effects. For most applications in a small studio or production facility, the ellipsoidal spot is a more practical tool, from the standpoint of size, mobility, and power requirements.

**SUPER GRAPHICS** Sometimes the images projected onto areas of the set or background have to be more permanent. And sometimes lighting units are not available for projection purposes. In either case, you can draw or paint projected slides, negatives, or other types of flat art or transparency material directly on the flats, risers, or other areas of the set or background. The image is simply projected and drawn on the desired surface material. The type of projection device used depends on the medium from which the drawing is made. The technique is fundamentally the same as that used in creating graphics by tracing projected images. The advantage is that more inexperienced people can help in the design of the set.

**200**

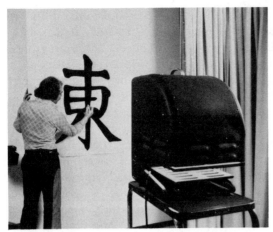

FIGURE 9–20. Large drawings or monograms can be projected and traced from opaque flat art.

FIGURE 9–21. Projected drawings work well with other elements of a simple set.

## MONOGRAMS

In Figure 9-20 a large monogram is drawn on a piece of off-white display (butcher) paper, which can be used instead of a flat for many types of large graphics or banners. Many bold designs or cartoon figures, traced or drawn on this type of paper, can be used as a given production's monogram and only decoration. Or they can be combined with projected patterns and other super graphics (Figure 9-21).

## POSTERS AND PICTURES

Appropriate posters and pictures, as well as other large graphics, can be framed or mounted on rigid backing and hung on a backdrop, flat, or easel to set the mood for a scene or production (Figure 9-22).

## CUTOUTS

Using the projection-drawing method and flat materials, first trace a projected image or lettering and then cut it out. The resulting cutout can be hung in front of the cyclorama and, with the proper lighting, used to set the scene. In Figure 9-23, a simple cutout, made of black construction paper, serves to symbolize a cityscape. (The lights were turned up on the set to photograph the cutout.) When the cutout was in use on the set, it was backlighted through the cyclorama for a very realistic effect. Cutouts from wood, cardboard, and other materials can be made inexpensively, by people with little or no experience.

Styrofoam lettering is becoming very widespread because styrofoam is easily shaped

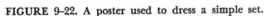
FIGURE 9–22. A poster used to dress a simple set.

FIGURE 9–23. A cutout used as a cityscape.

and very inexpensive, and because the lettering styles are as limited only by the imagination of the person doing the cutting. Cutout letters are made from polystyrene (styrofoam), spray painted, and glued to backgrounds made of colored display paper. Styrofoam can be cut easily with a jig saw or utility knife. Sometimes the utility knife does not make completely clean cuts, but either way works satisfactorily. Styrofoam, on account of its versatility, can also be used for many other types of cutouts, such as interlocking abstract forms and many types of gobos. Styrofoam is extremely light-weight. In fact, its only disadvantage is that it is susceptible to puncture and edge damage, but this drawback can be minimized by careful handling and storage.

## MISCELLANEOUS EFFECTS

Another way to establish a distinctive look for a skeletal set is to shoot scenes through various fabrics or filters. Depending on the color and texture of the fabric, the scene is affected to a less or greater degree. In Figure 9-24, for example, a man is being shot through a piece of silk stretched on a frame. The silk's texture "softens" the scene, causing

it to take on a diffuse quality. When the silk is rotated, it acts like a grid or starburst filter transforming highlights into soft stars. Tipping the silk at an angle to the lens causes distortion and some prismatic effects. In some areas of the scene the light shifts to a different shade of color. Many scenes of this type can be made more bizarre by making things float in space, by suspending objects from the ceiling on transparent fishline.

In Figure 9-25 an inflatable plane is suspended in space as part of a comical sketch in which the main characters travel to another location by plane. The plane is suspended on fishline from the lighting grid in the studio while an ellipsoidal spot projects a cloud pattern on the cyclorama. By moving the ellipsoidal spot slowly across the cyclorama and slowly tilting the wings of the plane, first one way and then the other, we achieve a feeling of motion.

In this case, moving the projected background was much easier than trying to move the plane across a stationary background because the plane was unstable and getting it to look at all believable was hard. The cyclorama, partially backlighted to make the "sky" glow behind the cloud projection, at first appeared somewhat realistic, but upon second look it was an obvious sham—to the delight of the viewers.

FIGURE 9-24. Shooting through a fabric "softens" and adds a hue to the scene. Visual special effects may also be produced.

FIGURE 9-25. Suspending objects on transparent fishline makes them appear to be floating in space.

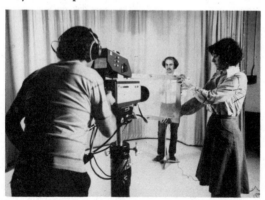

**FULL SETS** Constructing full sets is just a matter of combining all the techniques mentioned so far. Full sets consist of more than just flats and risers. Figure 9-26 shows, for example, the creative use of flats, risers, and other types of staging on a studio set. Although it looks very solid and substantial, it is only a facade. Behind the flats is nothing but

backstage space. (Remember that some areas of the set, such as a staircase or suspended porch, must be constructed to support extra weight for the safety of the actors.)

On theatrical sets, large pre-constructed backgrounds can be lowered or rolled into place for scene changes. These large backgrounds may be constructed—similarly to

FIGURE 9-26. A full set.

flats, by means of projection drawing, painting, or other methods—and then suspended from a pulley system on the ceiling or propped up on a dolly so that they can be rolled into place when needed. Usually dollies, as opposed to pullies, are used in television studios. Figure 9-27 shows how various backgrounds are hung from the ceiling on theatrical sets. When the scene is to be changed, the appropriate backdrop is lowered into place, and other props of furniture are placed on the set to add realism or symbolism.

Many of the elements that go into making up full sets are available from exhibit and display houses. Uni-Set® Corporation (see Source Index) offers pre-made, modular, geometric shapes, which can be combined to produce three-dimensional sets for almost any purpose. Each of the life-sized shapes comes with a correspondingly small, model-sized shape so that you can build and study a model of the intended set before moving the larger, heavier forms into place. With the addition of set dressings and props, many very attractive and interesting settings can be designed from the basic forms supplied (Figure 9-28).

FIGURE 9-27. Theatrical set elements hung from the ceiling.

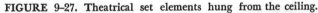

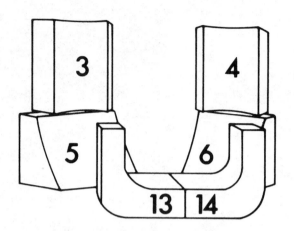

FIGURE 9-28. A news set consisting of pre-made, modular, geometric shapes. (Photo courtesy of Uni-Set Corporation)

Many of the books available on staging and prop design for the theater contain information that is applicable to television work, as long as detail, color, contrast, and patterns are kept in mind. Many of these books deal with such assorted subjects as making swords and shields, masks, make-up, replicas of muskets, and the like. They also usually give detailed construction directions, as well as sources of materials for construction.

## PROPS

There are three types of "props," or "properties":

1. *Set props* consist of any items or objects used to enhance or add detail to the set. In the case of a living room scene, for example, the set props might be bookshelves, books, knick-knacks, pictures, wall hangings, and even a fireplace.
2. *Hand props* are any items that the performers must use in the course of the production. Common hand props are books, clothing, eating utensils, food, telephones, guns, and the like.
3. *Practical props* are any props that have to function the way they do in reality: sinks, stove, washers, fireplaces, and so on.

## BUILDING PROPS

Depending on the kind and purpose of the set being built, there are a number of ways to build set props. Cardboard, for instance, can be used to create interesting free-standing objects such as shrubs and trees (Figure 9-29).

FIGURE 9-29. A cardboard tree.

A great variety of three-dimensional objects can be made from papier maché over a chicken-wire frame. Papier maché is very inexpensive to work with. Flour, water, chicken wire, cardboard, and spray or poster paint are all you need to make almost any type of object or prop. Figure 9-30 shows how large an animal you can make this way. This 4-foot rabbit, used in children's fairy-tale productions, was built for less than $10. First the chicken wire was shaped into a basic rabbit form. Then the papier maché was applied to the frame (in several stages because the wet papier maché was too heavy for the chicken wire to support all at once) until the rabbit was complete. Once the papier maché dried, it was spray-painted matte white. Then the face and ears were painted on. The whiskers were made out of pieces of broom, spray-painted black.

FIGURE 9–30. A papier mache rabbit.

FIGURE 9–32. Milk crates covered with brick-patterned linoleum paper for a brick wall facade.

Papier maché can also be used to make light-weight substitutes for boulders and rocks (Figure 9-31). Its only disadvantage is that it is relatively fragile and must be handled and stored carefully to avoid damaging it.

Many other types of props, such as walls or fireplaces, can be simulated by covering interlocking milk crates with paper, fabric, or cardboard. Since they interlock, the resulting structure is fairly strong and stable. Other props may be set on this structure or combined with its design for a more realistic appearance (Figure 9-32). For example, when working on a production about the land of

FIGURE 9–31. A papier mache rock.

the "Little People," a number of large cardboard boxes were cut and painted to serve as "Little People Houses" (Figure 9-33). Still other types of props can be made by covering stacked ice cream boxes with paper. Columns of ice cream boxes are free-standing but not very stable. Gluing them to a larger base made from masonite or a thin sheet of plywood makes them much less apt to tip over. Carpet-packing cylinders of various sizes may serve as pipes or columns (Figure 9-34). They can also be cut, interlocked, and formed into many types of abstract structures. They are not only relatively strong, and lightweight, but also, if constructed correctly, then can be easily disassembled and stored.

FIGURE 9–33. A cardboard box converted to a house for "Little People."

FIGURE 9-34. Ice cream boxes taped together and covered with paper to form columns.

If not, the next best way is to rent. Many furniture outlets rent display furniture for a percentage of new cost. If you need a number of pieces of furniture, this approach can add up to a fairly substantial expense. So keep the number of pieces of furniture on a television set to a minimum; a cluttered or overdressed set makes it very difficult for talent and crew to move around (Figure 9-35). Also, as you add more props, the lighting becomes more difficult. Something is always casting a shadow where it shouldn't or where it looks incongruous with the direction of other shadows.

Other set props—such as pictures, wall hangings, calendars, and the like—can usually be borrowed or purchased from second-hand stores. If you are working on a tight budget, like many independents, borrowing is the best way to get the props you need. Sometimes retail stores lend props just for a credit line at the end of the production. Some retailers even pay a small amount for the benefit of the television exposure.

## FURNITURE

Many sets require some type of furniture. Again, borrowing is the best way if possible.

## COSTUMES

Costuming really isn't a part of set design, but it should be mentioned because certain costume characteristics can affect the operation of your video equipment.

First, most independent video producers using single-camera systems typically have less expensive cameras than those used in television studios. In this case, avoid white in costumes, as well as in large areas of the set. Inexpensive cameras have problems with large contrast ranges. If the automatic video level control or auto iris sees a bright white area, the control or the iris may close down to compensate, thus darkening the scene suddenly. If the camera's ability to compensate for the bright areas is overridden

FIGURE 9-35. Furniture is usually kept to a minimum on a television set.

by switching the controls to manual, the camera's tube may be exposed to damage. At the very least, the image might "lag", or "burn out," resulting in a hot white area with no detail in that part of the image. To avoid this problem, use off-white colors like cream, beige, or gray, thus keeping the contrast range within the capabilities of even the most inexpensive camera.

Besides white, the next greatest area of concern in costuming is patterns, as it is in set design. Horizontal lines, herringbone, small checkerboard, and other tight patterns with regularly spaced horizontal lines should be avoided since they frequently result in a "flutter" or "vibration" on the screen. Again, when in doubt about the effect of a pattern, try it on camera.

## SPECIAL EFFECTS

Most effects, since they are "special," are relatively difficult to do well and reliably. Many are dangerous to some extent and require "special" attention so that they can be executed without injury to someone or damage to something. Special effects should therefore be handled only by competent parties, who know what they are doing and who have a good record of performance without causing injury or damage.

Usually a special effect is not very effective by itself. It requires the close attention of the talent and technical personnel involved in the production. The technical personnel frequently have to supplement the effect with the creative use of sound, lighting, or both. So make one or more persons responsible for the effects in a production so there will be no doubt about who has the responsibility for making an effect work smoothly and safely.

Much is written on creating illusions through the use of special set effects. Although an almost limitless number of effects can be considered "special," let's examine only those that are most frequently used:

1. breakaway props and furniture,
2. rain,
3. smoke and fog,
4. fire and explosions, and
5. snow and ice.

### BREAKAWAY PROPS AND FURNITURE

In every good barroom-brawl scene, at least one bottle is broken over someone's head and a chair is smashed against someone's back, shoulders, or head. Usually at least one person is thrown through a window or sent crashing through a railing. Break a bottle over someone's head in real life, and you either kill or hospitalize the poor soul.

Equally deadly is hitting people with a chair, knocking them through windows, or throwing them through railings. Yet the actors in the brawl scene get up and walk away after a combination of these things happen in a single fight. This is because these things never really happened to them at all.

All these special effects involve breakaway props and furniture. The bottle was made not of glass with sharp edges, but of a synthetic material or hardened sugar-water, which breaks extremely easily and has dull edges. The sound of breaking glass was also an effect, probably added during the post-production sound mix. The person flying through the window hit a relatively harmless substitute for glass, and the shattering sound was added later. You can break the bottle or the window without the sound effect, but the illusion is not the same since it doesn't sound the same as real breaking glass.

Breaking wood can be done without the sound effect too, although it usually sounds as though the wood is weak or rotten when it breaks. Usually the chair or railing is pre-broken and glued back together using light-duty glue so that the joints can be broken easily on contact. Any protruding screws, nails, or sharp edges are, of course, removed. Breaking the chair or railing at this point might result in a convincing visual effect, but it might not *sound* very accurate. So small pieces of balsa wood are glued at the joints to add a convincing splintering sound.

Even if the visual and sound aspects of the effect work well, the actors must execute the effect believably or the entire illusion is lost. Since actors who are to be hit with a breakaway prop tend to shy away from the actual contact unless they feel protected, "block" out the action so that the actual contact takes place on a part of the body that is protected but that looks convincing. Stay away from the eyes and face! Have the actors pad their bodies or wear padded hats to protect the point of contact. Above all, be careful. Even well-trained stunt men are often injured through an accident or recklessness. Untrained people can be seriously hurt simply through ignorance.

RAIN

There are a number of ways to create the illusion of rain. In each case, water must be conducted through a hose to either another perforated hose or to a length of plastic pipe with holes drilled in it. Usually the pipe is preferable because handling a piece of it is easier than handling something as flexible as hose. If the hose or pipe can be moved or shaken from side to side as the water escapes from it, the effect is more convincing than individual straight lines of falling water.

The fallen water then has to be caught in something. If the rain has to cover a relatively small area, such as a set window, and if the vessel to catch the water can be hidden, collect the "rain" in something like a children's wading pool. If the rain has to cover the width of the entire set, then special catching vessels—such as wood troughs lined with plastic sheeting material—have to be hidden in fake scenery or plants.

The only problem with water is the mess. Be sure that the troughs are properly positioned under the rain pipe, or most of the water will end up on the floor of the set. Make alignment marks on the floor so that the troughs can be positioned quickly and accurately under the pipe. No matter how thorough you are, you usually have at least one leak or spill. So the area around the leak or spill has to be cleaned and dried meticulously, or you run the risk of injury to an actor or to anyone else using the set.

Like other effects, rain needs more than just water to carry the illusion of a storm. Sound effects and lightning have to augment the effect. Of the several standard ways to create the sound of rain, one is to place metal shot in a tray with a wire-screen bottom and move the tray back and forth. Another is to place the shot in a wire-screen drum and rotate it. Thunder is created with a device known as a thunder sheet, which is simply a suspended rectangle of sheet metal that is shaken offstage. Theater supply houses can supply many of these items at a nominal rental fee. Lighting can be created by bouncing light from a reflector above the stage. Usually the flash of light should be followed by the thunder. By changing the intensity and frequency of the thunder and light flashes, you can conjure up a convincing storm.

SMOKE AND FOG

You make smoke and fog either by dry ice or by smoke machines.

Dry ice works well for low-hanging, thick fog, but it presents several problems. First, if you don't handle it with well insulated gloves, it can inflict severe injury to the hands. If a very large area of the set has to be covered, it takes a large amount of dry ice. Also, the dry ice has to be put into very hot water to be effective, and, since the dry ice is so cold, it quickly cools the water. As a result, you have to recycle the hot water almost continuously if the fog has to last very long at all. Lastly, dry ice in hot water makes a loud bubbling sound, and you need fans to propel the fog in a given direction; either of these additional noises may be undesirable. Theater supply houses have special dry ice drums with water heaters and built-in low-noise fans that make the job a lot easier.

Smoke machines heat oil to make a more general vapor-like smoke. Some oils work better than others. Again, the theater supply house can help with the machine and with the type of oil. For covering small areas, a hot plate and vegetable oil may work fine. Smoke of a different sort may be required for fire and explosions.

FIRE AND EXPLOSIONS

The safe way of produce the effect of fire is, of course, to use little or no fire at all. For campfires and fireplaces, burn a can of Sterno under fake logs that do not catch fire but that look as if they are burning. Lighting personnel can help by playing red and orange lights on nearby props or people to add to the effect. If the fire effect is small enough and far enough away from the camera—such as a fire seen through a window—hang a piece of Saran Wrap behind the facade of the window. Then move it slowly by hand or with a fan, and play red, orange, or yellow colored lights on it from below. Also obscure the effect with plenty of smoke from a smoke machine, and supplement it by fire sound effects. You can also use a fan from below the window to blow fire streamers into view.

Neither of these methods is as effective as using the real thing. Fire is obviously a very difficult effect to control safely, because the only convincing fire is fire itself. When you do use fire, it is absolutely mandatory to obey local fire codes as well as to have proper safety equipment and qualified personnel on hand when working with fire. For producing controlled flames, theater supply houses have devices that regulate the length of the flame and its direction. The diameter or width of the flame varies with the shape of the device producing it. This method of producing fire is somewhat safer and more dependable than using Sterno, and it is much more flexible. Just remember that all these methods are potentially hazardous and must be handled very carefully by qualified personnel. With less-expensive video cameras, you must also be careful not to burn in the camera's tube by staying focused on the fire for more than a few seconds.

Producing explosions is at least as dangerous as producing fire—and the same warnings apply. Of the many different ways to produce explosions, one way is to use a low-amperage fuse without its glass cover to ignite flash powder. Depending on the size of the flash-powder charge, the resulting flash and smoke are smaller or larger. Usually some sort of additional sound effect is needed, since flash powder really doesn't sound like a dynamite explosion. The problems with this technique are many and significant. Since a thorough knowledge of electricity and explosive charges is necessary, the explosion can be provided only by an expert. Don't even begin to try something like this yourself.

Theater supply houses carry safer, more sophisticated devices for creating explosions called *mortars,* some of which make loud booms and spew smoke. Others flash, sparkle, and make smoke, while still others just flash and smoke. Usually a variety of mortars, set off at the same time, provides the desired effect. Mortars, fire, smoke, and sound effects, used together, can be very dramatic.

## SNOW AND ICE

Falling snow is typically one of two things: plastic granules or paper confetti. Theater supply houses carry granular plastic snow, which, since it is plastic, you can use many times over. Granular plastic snow appears somewhat more believable than paper confetti, which is made from paper hole punchings, but both have the disadvantage of having uniformly sized granules, unlike snow which is very random in size. So neither looks very realistic when gently falling to earth. If, however, a large fan is used to propel them across the set, they do a good job of approximating driven snow. Whichever type is used, it is usually either dropped from ladders by stagehands, or, if a larger area has to be covered, slowly spilled from an overhead trough made of muslin. The muslin trough is gently rocked from side to side for a uniform, continuous snowfall. A little more realism can be introduced by using handheld fans to interrupt and swirl the snow as it falls, since snow, in real life, seldom, if ever, falls uniformly.

Ice and icicles can be made to look quite real by treating white styrofoam with acetone. The acetone melts the styrofoam into irregular shiny forms that look like ice. Styrofoam can also be used for making ice blocks, packed snow, or snow structures like igloos. Its light weight and relative durability make it an excellent choice for this type of set construction.

Frost and surface ice are easily produced by using aerosol cans of decorative frost sold commercially for use during the Christmas season. Since aerosol frost looks more like snow than frost, apply it very sparingly when using it for frost. Otherwise the result looks like a build-up of sprayed-on snow—very unrealistic.

In general, incidentally, the application and use of a product is more important than the product itself. It may be capable of looking startlingly realistic, when used properly, or terribly campy when not. Of course, you can argue that realism is not always necessary. Perhaps the campy look *is* the desired effect, such as for comical incongruity. So experiment with the capabilities of a product so that you know *how* to employ it in a given situation.

Miniatures have been used for years to create relatively inexpensive substitutes for full-sized sets, but the art has been perfected only recently. Everyone has seen at least one foreign-made Godzilla movie and marvelled at how awful the miniatures are. But most people are totally unaware that most of the *Star Wars* saga is done in miniature. With the advent of *Star Wars, The Black Hole,* and other movies involving a great number of special effects, the art of using miniatures has reached a new height. Now, whole books and periodicals devote themselves to the production of miniatures and miniature set effects. Since a great deal of this information is of interest to anyone attempting to produce believable video on a low budget, let's discuss a few of the available alternatives.

## DIORAMAS

Since usually it isn't practical to spend a lot of time building your own miniatures, you may wish to take advantage of miniatures that are already built. *Dioramas*—used a great deal for commemorative purposes, for displays, and in advertising—are basically miniature sets in the form of partially or wholly three-dimensional still-life scenes. If you have ever visited a large museum, you have probably seen at least one good diorama. Depending on the time, money, and effort spent in their construction, they can be more or less convincing. If realism is not an issue, dioramas can be used for many purposes, including comedy sketches and children's programming.

Unless the diorama is very large and extremely well designed, it probably cannot be used for anything other than cutaways or for establishing shots if realism is an issue. To set a scene or to establish an environment, you may be able to use quick cutaways to footage of dioramas. Foreground action or graphics may be keyed over footage of a subtly lighted diorama. Or do the same over footage that has purposely been shot slightly out of focus to give the effect that the diorama scene is far away, thus creating an impression without drawing undue attention to the diorama itself. Of course, you can in many ways embellish or add realism to dioramas, if their owners don't object. For example, a diorama showing how the pyramids were constructed would be more realistic without the little plastic slave figures.

You could add movement by placing a small bush in the foreground and using a fan to gently agitate its leaves. If done well, the overall effect would be to establish an Egyptian or biblical setting, just before you cut away to other action.

## SCALE MODELS

Scale models—of everything from pre-World War I airplanes to architectural scale models of buildings and cities—can be very useful on small sets or as supplements to dioramas. Displays showing the proposed layout of subdivisions or shopping centers, for example, are often very well designed, and they can be used much like dioramas if the proper background is available or can be built. Many scale models are "working" scale models, that is, they are capable of functioning much like their actual-sized counterparts. Engineering firms and schools of architecture are good sources of building scale models. Government planning offices often have scale models of planned subdivisions or of other large-scale projects, such as flood control planning models. Scale models of almost anything else are available in hobby shops and model train supply stores. Usually you have to spend some time searching for the type of model that best fits your needs. Generally, the longer the model remains on camera, the more convincing it has to be.

## TOYS

Although many toys seem to have declined in quality and workmanship, some still can be used in video production. Well made toy doll houses can be employed with an appropriate background, good lighting, and sound effects. Some of the newer radio-controlled toys have already been used in advertising and in public service announcements. The incredibly popular electronic games and teaching devices can be used for many purposes in video production. Depending on the purpose of the production, you may have to "dress" the toys slightly to create the desired effect. Other times you can use them "as is," such as for animation or other purposes.

Protect yourself. Some video games and teaching devices are copyrighted, so check with the manufacturer before using any of them. Also if you plan to use toys exactly as they appear off the shelf for a long, costly production, as a courtesy let the manufacturers know how the toys are to be used. If you don't and if the manufacturer can prove that you represented the toy in a way that damaged the market for it, you may find yourself the victim of a lawsuit. Whenever using anything from outside sources in a video production, ask yourself whether you're interfering with the market for the item. Consider too how you would feel about how the item is represented if you manufactured it. If you would not like to see the item represented the way you plan to, you had better not use it that way.

On the other hand, if you intend to use the item in a way that can only benefit the manufacturer, consider asking the manufacturer for some sort of support. The firm may either wish to be mentioned in the credits in return for the item itself or offer even more backing. This type of negotiation clears the air about how the item or toy is used, and it provides a clear statement of each party's responsibilities in the matter. Also, it prevents problems from arising at a later date.

### SMALL-SCALE SETS

Small-scale sets may be fabricated from scratch like full sets, or they may be assembled from available dioramas, scale models, and toys. Sometimes they can be partially fabricated and partially assembled. More often than not, low budgets make it necessary to draw on what is available and,

if possible, to build around it. The possible uses for small-scale sets are as limitless as the approaches to construction. Usually the problem is not in the set, but in the setting. In other words, what should the background look like? How can it be inexpensively and effectively constructed?

Figure 9-36 shows what can be done with available scale models, toys, and other material. Two 4-by-8 particle boards were placed next to one another on a large table. The resultant 8-by-8 working area was just large enough for the desired set. The two pieces of particle board were covered with black background paper. Then pieces of green model-railroad "grass" were cut and glued on the background paper in the shape of roadways. White curbs and center lines were added with thin white tape. Next, streetlights from model-railroad sets were added. Once wired, they could actually be turned on and off, or higher or lower in intensity. Then model-railroad bushes, trees, and mountains (in the background) were added. To finish off the set, the light blue backdrop behind the set was streaked with dark blue paint. This gave the illusion of clouds and sky when seen through the camera. The toy car in the foreground was a miniature of a Honda. The little creatures with eyes were hairy pom-poms to which stick-on eyes were added. Although the picture of the set looks flat on a page, it looked quite interesting when seen through the camera lens. This set was used in a 30-second car-pooling spot for the Department of Transportation.

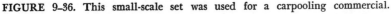

**FIGURE 9-36.** This small-scale set was used for a carpooling commercial.

Although paper backdrops can be drawn or painted to make backgrounds, they seldom look very real. If realism is the objective, then two other alternatives are: projected slide backgrounds and, for some purposes, star fields.

## PROJECTED SLIDE BACKGROUNDS

Slides can be projected onto either rear- or front-screens positioned behind the set. Rear-screen projection may work with an extra powerful slide projector, but light used to illuminate the set may wash out the image on the rear screen. To avoid this problem, use a highly reflectant screen made of Kodak Ektalite or 3M Scotchlite material, which has the unique quality of reflecting only the light that strikes it at close to a 90-degree angle. In other words, lights used to light the small-scale set, which are usually at a 30- to 45-degree angle to the screen, would have no effect on the projected image; they would not wash it out. In fact, the projected image is often so bright that you have to use neutral-density filters over the lens of the slide projector to lessen the intensity. (The set can't be lighted as bright as the projected image.)

For example, Figure 9-37 shows an architectural model in front of a Scotchlite screen. An oceanside scene is projected behind the model, but none of the slide image shows on the model itself because it is being lighted from the side with other large lighting units. Despite the intense lighting on the set, the image on the screen is clearly visible and not

washed out. A close-up of approximately what the scene looked like through the video camera is shown in Figure 9-38. The depth of field of this photograph is much more limited than the actual video image, and more of the building and background were in focus in the video scene. When used as a quick cutaway, however, the image was very convincing.

## STAR FIELDS

With the advent of space-related movies, many people have become interested in how to produce outer space sets to evoke the feeling of being in space. One of the easiest and most inexpensive ways to do so is by creating a moonscape-like set and placing a star field behind it (Figure 9-39). The set consists of papier mache made from paper towels and painted gray on a cardboard base. The star field is black backdrop paper with holes punched in it, nebular fashion, and lighted from the rear. By waving one's hand or a book back and forth through the beam of light, you can make the "stars" seem to twinkle when viewed from the front. Again, the set seems a little flat when viewed from this angle, but on camera it looked very good. When our space creature (Figure 9-40) "landed" on this outer space location called "Xena," we were able to continue our action inside the spaceship. The moonscape-like set and the star field not only did a good job of establishing the action, but they also worked well for opening and closing credits.

FIGURE 9–37. Using a projected background behind a scale model.

FIGURE 9–38. A through-the-camera look at a scale model with a projected background.

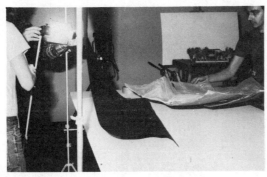

FIGURE 9–39. Papier mache moonscape being placed in front of a star field—a black piece of backdrop paper with holes punched in it and back lighted.

FIGURE 9–40. Space creature was an actor with a mask. The wall with a porthole in it is a gobo. The scene in the porthole is a NASA slide of earth projected onto a Scotchlite screen. To give the effect that the creature is circling the earth, the slide projector was slowly moved to the right.

**SUMMARY**

Set design, like graphics and lighting, adds to the overall sense of mood and professionalism of a video production. A set does not have to be expensive to be good. Very creative and effective sets can be constructed for very little money and often from available materials. Since many video productions are meant to transform the viewer's sense of place or time, some sort of set or set dressing is usually necessary. In the absence of any formulas or rules, just experiment and try things out on camera until you produce the desired effect. Sometimes this transformation can be done with a few props and skillfull lighting. In other circumstances, more complex procedures, as outlined in this chapter, are necessary. Either way, set design is one of the more interesting opportunities for creative work in video production.

# 10
# 10
# 10
# 10
# 10
# 10
# 10

**SUPPORTING
YOUR VIDEO HABIT**

Going into business for yourself is in itself a big step. You have to be personally prepared to do the work and to make the sacrifices necessary for success. Any number of fine books can help you get yourself organized for starting up a small business. They can help you make the important decisions regarding financing, marketing, personnel management, accounting, taxes, and legal matters.

But committing yourself to a video production business is committing yourself to a highly distinctive lifestyle: long hours, challenging clients, but total satisfaction. This chapter is devoted to helping you gather the tools of this trade in a manner consistent with your means.

If you do indeed decide to enter the business, or perhaps have already, then you have our congratulations on becoming a "vidiot"! Anything is possible in the video field, as long as you have the knowledge, the drive, and the money. One thing you must do—and there is no way of getting out of it—is to have a goal! You have to plan and map things out very carefully. You must know in which direction you are heading. Your goal plays an important part in how you design your video system, your business, your staff, and your location. For example, if you want to pursue the commercial market, shoot local commercials, and work with advertising agencies, you should have a location that is within a 10- to 15-mile radius of the main hub of business. This location is more of a convenience to your customers than anything else. Your equipment should be of good quality, industrial ¾-inch, or broadcast-quality 1-inch all in a healthy state. Your business should represent professionalism. So you probably could use an answering service or a receptionist to handle incoming calls. A word of advice: Have an impressive demo tape to show clients. Make sure your representative, if you have one, can communicate with the agencies.

## GETTING WHAT YOU NEED

The "tools" in this business can be very expensive and the maintenance only adds to that expense. How much expense you should incur comes down to what your target market is. Keep in mind what the finished tape will be used for. The "home video enthusiast," the "industrialist," the "broadcaster"—all these names relate to levels of sophistication in video production. They should also give you a clue as to which types of equipment each category needed. For example, the home video user who wants to shoot the family wedding could use a single-tube portable camera and a ½-inch recorder. But this same equipment would be out of the question if you were shooting a broadcast production, because it doesn't meet broadcast standards (see Chapters 1 and 6).

With those limitations in mind, you can decide what is necessary to buy and/or to rent. Some items should be purchased outright, while services and high-dollar equipment can be leased on a long-term basis or rented for a short term.

## PURCHASING EQUIPMENT

A few basic pieces of equipment are needed to "set up shop": tape stock, at least one VTR and monitor, some cable and adaptors, one or two slide projectors, an audio cassette recorder, a light box, basic lighting equipment, and a 35-mm still camera.

When purchasing your equipment, shop around. Make sure you get several different bids from dealers. Hunting them down may take some time, but it pays off. Use the Yellow Pages, production directories, and trade magazines to find various dealers and manufacturers. Tell them your exact needs so they can supply you with the most efficient system within your budget.

While shopping around, don't just go for the best prices. Look for the suppliers that can back up their equipment with service! Be sure to check out the dealer to see if they have an engineer on staff, to answer questions and to install equipment. If you do not have "hands-on" experience in system layout, hire a freelance installer to get the job done properly—one who can check out the system. A word of warning on buying used equipment: Some pieces are great buys, but most of the time you are buying somebody else's problems. Make sure you know what you're getting into.

## TRADEOFFS

Tradeoffs are fine if you know someone personally who has the equipment you need, and the two of you can come to your own terms on exchange. For example, you might have a video camera and need to do some editing. You know of someone who has an editing system but no camera. You could offer to exchange time on the editing system for time using the camera.

## RENTALS

You can rent almost anything: camera lens, scopes, lighting equipment, dollies, audio equipment and ¾-inch portable recorders. In fact, you can rent a whole portable system for a day, for a week, or for months at a time depending on your cash flow and budget. Studio space can be rented. Services can also be rented: audio time, editing time, camerapersons, VTR operators, production assistants, audio operators, grips, gaffers, writers, food stylists, make-up artists, caterers, carpenters, artists, and so on. (When "renting" talent, always get talent releases.)

When starting out, you usually need rental equipment on a large scale. For example, cameras should be rented because different jobs call for different cameras with varying capabilities. The cost of purchasing all or perhaps even one would cut into your cash flow quite a bit. As you grow, you'll begin to notice certain pieces of equipment and services that you are using more and more. This is the time to consider purchasing those items and services.

Equipment rental houses in your area that service the professional market should have most of the basic equipment you need. The larger rental agencies have much more, and most of them have catalogs. Try to establish credit with them. Check out the equipment you are going to rent. If you have equipment shipped, be prepared to pay for the freight charge and insurance fee. There is usually a two-day minimum charge too. If you rent a large amount of equipment you should receive a discount—so ask for it. As for damage, if you break it, you pay for it.

## HOME VIDEO ENTHUSIAST

A home video system, such as the single-tube camera and ½-inch VTR, offers a wide range of possibilities. The work is out there if you guide yourself toward taping weddings, reunions, bands, small business meetings, test commercials, school and sports events, "video pals," and insurance documentations. You can build a healthy business in this area in a professional manner. Advertising in your local papers reaches your target market much faster than cold calling.

## WEDDINGS

Anyone can shoot a family or a friend's wedding, and it looks fine. To do so the right way, you need to be creative, not just record the happening. If your clients want a number of copies made from the finished piece, you should be mastering on ¾-inch, and then dubbing down to ½-inch; the quality is better. Also be sure to check with the client on the format needed for the copies—Beta, VHS, or ¾-inch.

Now for the creativity! To make an entertaining piece out of the tape, get old photographs or film (home movies) from both families and transfer them to tape. Edit this along with the wedding footage, add some music, and you have a nice piece of work that you can show to clients. And you'll have a happy and satisfied customer—the best advertising you can have.

## REUNIONS

Call your class president, call the colleges, call the high schools, talk to the principals and vice principals of schools, and let your services be known. Use old yearbook photographs and other visual materials from a particular class, along with the recording of the reunion, to make an amusing tape. Making copies available to the alumni and to the library could increase your business. This venture won't make you wealthy, but offering a number of services in related areas can.

## BANDS

Videotaping bands can be profitable if you are in an area that has enough professional bands to support your company. In this case you need higher-quality equipment because you are dealing on a higher professional level. For shooting the local bands, your equipment can be less than broadcast, but you are going to need a wider client range to support your company. Just shooting local bands is not enough. In any case, your service can offer the bands solid looking demo tapes and shorts for cable TV. Remember, budget sets the mood.

## SMALL BUSINESS MEETINGS

Taping small business meetings means a lot of cold calling and leg work. The jobs don't come easily, because most small businesses can't justify the cost of videotaping a meeting. Those that can often find it more economical to purchase their own 1/2-inch systems, do it themselves, and save money. (The low cost of 1/2-inch systems is what keeps this service from accelerating!) If you get this type of answer, mention that you can make copies of the tapes. You could get your foot in the door with this service.

## TEST COMMERCIALS

Advertising agencies, talent agencies, and manufacturers use test commercials for testing a product, checking out new talent, and judging performance. A single-tube camera and a 1/2-inch VTR can cover this area very well. Again, although most large agencies and manufacturers can afford to purchase their own equipment, you can offer a duplicating service to them.

## SPORTS

Sporting events are great. But going out with your 1/2-inch system, shooting cold, and anticipating sales from the participants and spectators is crazy. You need to pre-plan just like anything else. You can videotape individuals, such as golfers who want to study their drive. In that case, hit all of the golf courses, but be sure to check with the management (that goes for any event). By calling the producer of the event you can find out if there is interest in getting the event documented. You could do very well in this area.

## VIDEO PALS

The idea of "video pals" is like pen pals. You exchange information with other vidiots on videotape cassette. The problem arises when you receive a Beta tape and all you have is your 3/4-inch or VHS videotape recorder. It takes planning, but it is fun. There is a publication called the *Satellite Video Exchange Society,* telephone number (604) 688-4336. They are located in Vancouver, B.C., Canada.

## INSURANCE DOCUMENTATION

Some people are making it by documenting insurance records visually, and they are doing it on 1/2-inch equipment. They record the contents of the homes, office, school, or any place covered on the policy. Then they give one copy to the policyholder and one to the insurance company, and they hold on to the master.

You can work either with insurance agencies or solo. When work picks up, get a few more 1/2-inch systems and some hired help, so you can cover many clients in an area in the same day. Besides offering records you can offer services such as vault storage and record updating.

**NONBROADCAST
VIDEO**

The industrial video user usually takes on a larger area and has a bigger budget to work with. The format used in many cases is 3/4-inch and sometimes 1-inch. In venturing out in these fields you need stamina, some capital, a professional appearance, and a true knowledge of your video capabilities. You can build a fine business catering to the industrial clientele, but, unless you have your marketing strategies planned very carefully, watch out!

The nonbroadcast market includes:

1. education,
2. the medical field,
3. business,
4. government, and
5. cable TV.

## EDUCATION

In the educational market, the budgets for videotape production are unstable. You have to get on many bidding lists. So get to know the decision makers. Try contacting educational publishers, who have areas that sometimes call for videotape programs. Contacting the local schools to videotape their Christmas plays by third-graders, or shooting a musical the university is performing adds variety, but the pay is usually very low. This sort of service is just a way of getting out there and letting them know who you are.

Producing your own educational material is terrific after you have found what to produce. If you do produce a marketable educational tape, your returns on it can last anywhere from one to five years.

## MEDICINE

The need for video producers in the medical field is growing, and individual programs are taking off. The use of audiovisual materials in hospitals is extremely varied: trainig tapes for doctors, nurses, interns . . . in-house patient education tapes . . . outpatient clinics . . . in-service personnel . . . patient entertainment . . . patient observation and surgery documentation. The field is wide open, and you don't need a medical background, although some practical knowledge of the medical field is helpful. Although hospitals are getting their own audiovisual facilities and producing their own programs, they are also using outside production companies. With their heavy workload and their need to produce high-quality work, they sometimes turn to outside companies.

## BUSINESS

In the business world the applications keep increasing, with new and different programs created for the many areas that business touches: sales training, marketing, production performance, orientations, in-house video magazine, and numberless others. To get in the door of industry, you have to be "business-like." You have to know the rules and play the game. They deal with large budgets, and they are not going to hand it over to someone who doesn't give the impression of professionalism or who does not know his or her own business.

## GOVERNMENT

Contracting government jobs is difficult. There is a lot of paperwork—piles upon piles of paperwork! If you can get through the paper, you could possibly make some good money, because the jobs are there. So contact your local government, contact Washington, DC, and get on the bidders list. Directories are available that provide listings of minority and ethnic groups. So if you are represented in any of these areas, get your name on the list and tell them what your company can offer.

## CABLE TV

Cable TV is like a giant who has a huge appetite. It needs good, solid programs like shorts and features to keep it alive. Since this is no secret, the cable market has been inundated with a variety of programs, most of them of low quality. So it needs high-quality material. Producing your own programs for Cable TV is a marvelous idea, and it makes you some money. If you can create quality programs, you have a very good chance of selling them to the cable market.

Each cable company or distributor has a different contract. There are no standard forms; each contract is customized for each property, depending on whether it is for nonexclusive or exclusive use, nontheatrical versus theatrical, and so forth. The best and first thing to do is to call the distributors, and see how they work. Get to know their names. Then call the cable companies to see what they're buying. One thing they all say is, "Show us something you have produced." There is no way around it! You must produce.

If you are just starting out and you have no heavy capital, take it easy and wait. Cable will still be with us later on. If you have some capital, great! Do the research and create a quality piece. Then send it to the distributors.

As for the equipment you use, make sure it meets their standards. It can be on ¾-inch or 1-inch.

## BROADCASTING

In comparison with the industrial market, the broadcast market has greater possibilities and usually much bigger budgets.

When shooting for broadcast productions, use broadcast equipment. If for some reason you can't shoot with a 1-inch system and you have to go with a ¾-inch system, make sure you have a good three-tube camera and a decent ¾-inch VTR. You can transfer ¾-inch tape to 1-inch tape in post-production. The reason for the transfer is that, if you are shooting for broadcast, cable, local TV, or national TV, and you make a great number of copies and you are going to need every bit of beginning quality you can get to eliminate technical problems with picture quality, such as stability and resolution.

Producing for broadcast involves shooting:

1. documentaries,
2. PSAs (Public Service Announcements),
3. commercials, and
4. full-length productions.

### DOCUMENTARIES

The term *documentary* refers to a technique, not to a type of videotape. When you make a documentary, all you do is record real situations with little or no script. You can use actors, nonactors, a narrator, or nobody. In some cases just going out and shooting an event can work, but other times you can fall flat on your face! Documentaries necessitate a lot of pre-production planning and finding out whether your program is marketable, as well as getting production licenses and releases from on-camera talent and proprietors.

The types of programs are endless. All you have to do is use your imagination and do some research. Contact your Chamber of Commerce to see if they would like a videotape history on their city to be used by their public relations department. You could do a short on an extraordinary person or place,

"how to do it" tapes on fixing your car or learning to cook, or travelogs on interesting places throughout the state. Any of these ideas should start you thinking of the many different things that can be produced for cable, local, and national television.

### PSA/COMMERCIALS

Shooting PSAs for local organizations and local governments is fun, but the pay is moderate. But PSAs for national organizations and government can make for a much larger porduction and a commensurate budget. You have to contact the individual who is the decision maker and get on a bidder's list. All you have to do is call up and ask questions. Be sure to have a demo tape to show them.

If you've never shot a commercial, watch television—a lot of TV! Start to get the feel for how scenes flow together. Keep the sound *off* and just watch. Study the number of camera moves. This exercise can't hurt even if you have been shooting commercials for ten years.

For local commercials, the budgets are not very big. National ones are much bigger. Your "rep" has to go out, meet with the advertising agencies, show them your most outstanding demo tape, convey to them that you will deliver the goods on time, and guarantee a high-quality production. Be competitive in price. Most agencies know, or at lease have a rough idea, of their budget. If at all possible, get them to tell you their approximate budget. By knowing their budget you can design a production they can afford.

Find out what you are responsible for: talent, music, shooting, editing, transfer, or duplicating? All of these points should be resolved and a contract signed before production begins! Discuss this with your attorney.

If you have a blockbusting idea for a feature and no capital, start looking for an executive producer to finance your program. But be sure you have a solid contract. There is nothing like naively working your tail off, then being kicked off the production! This should tell you something. If you decide you want to do a full-length production, you'd better have had a lot of experience in the video world—from knowing about financing to picking the right staff. Working on a crew for someone else's large production, to see what actually goes on, is valuable experience.

The marketing of the production is just as important, and in some cases much more. You should seek outside help.

Whether you're producing for yourself or for a client, you need a lot of pre-production planning and then some. You have to be organized, with clear, well-thought-out production plans. The script must be mapped out for the director, lighting, cameraperson, set designer, talent, and audio. Your staff should be able to get along with one another besides pulling for the production. If you're using equipment from out of town, make sure the supplier is a reputable outfit. When you are planning a budget, allow for Murphy's Law: where there is a *way*, things *will* go wrong.

## GETTING THE WORD OUT

You have to get the word out, or you won't make it happen. The first three years are very intense work. By the end of that third year, if you have not noticed an increase in your business, then you are doing something wrong. The video business may not be your field, or being independent may not suit you.

Exposure of your company must be consistent. Some types of advertising take hardly any money, but the more involved kind can entail great cost. So you're going to need some capital to start all this wonderful exposure. Getting the word out entails all sorts of manuevers: talking about your company, phone calls, referrals, advertising in newspapers, trade magazines, television exposure, brochures about your company, and attending some software add hardware tradeshows. You are going to have to concentrate on all these areas because no one thing gets you on top.

### WORD OF MOUTH

Another way of getting the word out is through your clients. If they are happy with your service, they will tell others. Word-of-mouth advertising is extremely rewarding because there is nothing like positive feedback from a satisfied client.

A sales/service representative can keep word of mouth going by seeing to your old clients, keeping in touch with them, and helping to execute their upcoming jobs. The "rep" can also call on potential clients, follow leads, and inform the decision makers on how your company can service them with the finest quality available.

### TALK, TALK, TALK

When talking about your company, let people know that you are out there to service their needs. Take advantage of using the phone and other situations that let you speak about your company.

You don't have to overkill with your boasting, but talking about your business does have a positive side effect. People can mingle and exchange information within networks and organizations like NAFE, BPW, IABE, UIC, AWRT, PGA, ASTD, Chamber of Commerce and others, many others. Attending meetings is trying, but keep your dues up so you can receive information that could help your company. You are going to learn to "read people" from encountering so many of them, an ability that broadens your scope.

### USING THE TELEPHONE

The phone covers a lot of ground. By using the phone, you can ascertain which advertising agencies and companies use video, which are thinking of using video, or which have no interest in video at all. From this information you can determine your plan of action. You can make appointments to show your demo tape or have clients come to your studio and see your facilities. They may want you to send a brochure and keep in touch. Or you may want to dismiss some prospects altogether.

When using the phone you need to have a rapport with the party on the other end. The phone can work for you and it also can work against you. You can turn off a potential client just by the tone of your voice, or by the way you answer your phone. Instead of just saying, "Hello," mention the company's title and give you name. That sort of greeting is much more effective, and callers know exactly whom they are speaking with. You can even turn off the party with the manner in which you relate to them. (Let's face it, you may be technically competent and extremely creative, but you may not relate well with people.) If so, then hire someone to represent you and your company.

Remember to contact the person who is the decision maker! Deal only with the responsible people in client firms or organizations. Contacting new clients is endless. When calling ad agencies, speak with the art director or the creative director. At industrial companies speak with the director of training, sales manager, marketing director, purchasing director, director of personnel, or all of them. When calling hospitals search out the public relations director, in-service education department, or the outpatient education department. When contacting these departments and directors, find out what audiovisual services they need and use.

## REFERRALS

After you have been in business a while and you have built a good reputation, you can expect to receive referrals. A client may pass your name on to a business associate/friend, or a client may introduce you directly to a new lead. Referrals happen only if you have happy clients. Happy clients are kept happy when the work you have completed is of high quality, backed up with impeccable service. Other referrals can come from anyone who knows you, or who knows of your work. It could be a friend who heard of a bid open in the Department of Education. Referrals can come your way anytime from anyone, so always present yourself and your company in a professional way!

## LISTINGS AND ADVERTISING

Besides telling the world about you and your company with the word-of-mouth system, you can also use the *printed word*. Advertising takes a little money, some money, or a lot of money depending on where you place your ads. Some listings are free, such as local directories like the Chamber of Commerce, or you may belong to organizations that have free listings. The listings in some trade magazines and media directories are relatively inexpensive. The full-blown ads in the heavy-duty directories—such as the *Black Book, On Location,* and the like—are expensive but they do target their market very well.

When you decide to place a listing or an ad, you have to justify the price because it costs you heavy money. Also run it a number of times—a half-year or a full year. If you run it two or three years, the price really goes down. But be consistent—that's the key.

## NEWSLETTERS

Your chances of acquiring a healthy clientele from advertising in newsletters are slim. What these newsletters can do for you, besides give you some inexpensive exposure, is keep you in contact with what is going on in the organizations publishing the newsletters. The artsy newsletter, for example, gives you information on local arts, state-of-the-art video equipment, techniques, and programs. So, do keep in touch in this area.

School newspapers are a good way to keep informed as to what is happening in the schools. Maybe a teacher or two will notice your listing and might call you for your services. Very few teachers, however, have the authority to commission a project, although the head of the Educational Department might see the listing and give you a job. For the small cost, it's worth keeping in touch.

Business newsletters are a much better source, and you may benefit greatly from them. The price to advertise is not expensive, and decision makers do read the publication. By reading those business newsletters, you have a handle on departments that would be receptive to your services.

## INTERVIEWS

A publicized interview can help you if it is flattering. Getting such an interview, however, depends on how interestingly you present yourself and your company. Getting one in your local paper is easier than getting one on the local television station. You may think that all you have to do is call them up, sell your services in an irresistible way, drop a few names—and you're on the front page or the afternoon talk show. This approach may work if your stars are in the right place, but otherwise forget it.

But what you really need is a public relations person. The PR person can get you interviews in print and on television, which add to your professional reputation. PR people know the right people. They can drop the right names because that's their job, not yours. With this type of service you are talking dollars! You are paying for intensive exposure, which takes talent. But if your PR person is good, the service should pay for itself.

## LOCAL NEWSPAPERS

Local newspapers may or may not be the way to go for you, depending on the nature of your clientele. If you are doing weddings and insurance recordings, then the local paper is a great source for reaching your market. However, if you are doing educational training tapes, then the local paper is not: You will totally miss your target audience. Look for journals and magazines that reach trainers and educational departments.

As soon as you open your doors, send the business editor at your local newspaper a clip about your company. Mention who is in charge, the services, and the location. This is free public relations. The papers are always looking for this type of information. If you hire a rep, send in a clip on the rep too.

Again, if you decide to place an ad, be sure to check whether the audience can use your services. Be consistent: If you do place an ad, run it more than once.

## BROCHURES

A good way of introducing yourself and your company is the brochure. A necessity for all business, it is especially warranted in the video business. Your brochure should make a statement. It should say something about the company. Stress that the people who work there are committed and that they are experts in their field. Tell about the facilities and the services offered. Appeal to client needs by mentioning how you will work with their time constraints, how you are willing to meet program objectives, and how you will work with their budgets. Be honest in your presentation: If you "fabricate the truth," it will catch up with you.

The brochure should follow the KISS approach: Keep It Simple, Stupid! All sorts of characters are going to read your brochure. Don't lose their interest by cluttering it up with too much print. The brochure should be pleasing to the eye. If you can't come up with a total image for your company, then hire a design firm to create it for you. They can create your company logo, as well as the letterheads for your stationery and business forms. Before you commit yourself to any design firm, first ask to see the work they have done for other companies.

## DOING IT RIGHT

In general, the key is to do it right, and to do it in style. Presenting and marketing your company to important clients (certainly all of your clients should be important to you) takes a lot of hard work. Since people make judgments on first impressions, your office, facilities, staff, and you should convey an image of total professionalism.

When you come right down to doing the job, doing it right means you need to know:

1. how to price your services competitively,
2. how to budget a production, and
3. how to offer consistent quality.

## PRICING YOUR SERVICES

Coming up with a formula for pricing your services is not easy. First you must find out what the market will bear, by learning what your competitors in the area are charging. Then you must decide whether your prices can be competitive with theirs, while still making a profit.

If you have to rent most of your equipment and you subcontract a lot of outside services, you are going to have to add your creative fees to the equipment and service costs. For example, say your production expenses for equipment and other services are running about $3,000. For you to make your fee, you can either tag on 20 percent or add up your hours spent on the job and charge an hourly wage. (Costs plus 20 percent is a standard charge in the production industry for most types of work.) Again, the cost to the customer depends on what the market will bear. When you come up with a price, try to keep it consistent.

## BUDGETING

The planning and actual writing of a budget bring you invaluable insight into the production itself. The budget organizes you and the production, and it obliges the client to focus on what is essential. It also gives you a more-than-adequate idea as to where the production is heading in terms of cost.

The presence or absence of one element has a tremendous impact on the budget price: If you are hired to do a production by a large distribution entity, such as network television or a cable company, you are required by union regulations to employ union people on that production. To find out about these regulations, call your local union office and/or check into the appropriate unions, such as:

1. Directors Guild of America (DGA),
2. Teamsters and United Scenic Artists,
3. American Federation of Television and Radio Artists (AFTRA),
4. American Federation of Musicians (AFM),
5. Screen Actors Guild (SAG),
6. International Brotherhood of Electrical Workers (IBEW),
7. National Association of Broadcast Employees and Technicians (NABET), and
8. International Alliance of Theatrical Stage Employees (IATSE).

Books on each union explain all pertinent information.

**CHECKLISTS** Always use a budget checklist when planning a production, no matter how small. Having a checklist for each aspect of the production insures that your budget is accurate and all but eliminates the possibility of overlooking an item. Of the many types of budget checklists, we will tlk about the checklist for the small- or medium-sized production company. When your productions grow into the "megabuck" category, you will then need a megabuck checklist.

For each of the following categories, examine the items possibly needed and estimate the costs involved:

1. script,
2. studio or remote location,
3. talent,
4. support services,
5. equipment,
6. post-production,
7. production personnel, and
8. miscellaneous services.

## SCRIPT CHECKLIST

The script is sometimes provided by the client, but in other cases you are responsible for it. In both cases, you need a checklist. If you are responsible for writing the script, however, you must charge for that service along with your other services.

1. Is the script clearly laid out, and does it follow a standard format?
2. Is there creative input? Cost?
3. Correct length?
4. Mapping out script for production—cost?
5. Number of copies of script? Cost?
6. Which video format is required?
7. To be shot in single-camera or multi-camera style?
8. Narration or not?
9. Live audio or not?
10. Talent or nontalent?
11. Studio and/or remote?
12. Music bed?
13. Special effects/props?

## STUDIO OR REMOTE LOCATION CHECKLIST

Most locations are dictated by the producer. If the script calls for a studio set-up and/or a remote scene, the cost of it has to be approved by the producer. Forgetting to investigate each of the many details in studio and remote production can be a great embarrasment, as well as an expensive one.

The following lists for both types of location can be much more involved, but they basically give you something to think about when you are considering a location:

### Studio Checklist

1. Size needed (measurements of the studio: width, height, and length)?
2. Is there a cyc (permanent or not)?
3. What is the flooring?
4. Rate for the studio—by the hour, day, or week?
5. Operating hours and overtime?
6. If you use their crew, what are the rates for shooting, gripping, gaffing, construction, and so on?
7. Are they union/nonunion? Which union?
8. Who is responsible for charges for electricity, bulb replacement, telephone, insurance of property, plus elements involved with the studio, taxes, and other details?
9. What power supply is available? Where are the electrical outlets?
10. What equipment is included in the rental of the studio?
11. Does it have easy access for loading and unloading?
12. If it has a freight elevator, what size?
13. Does it have a working kitchen?
14. Are there adequate make-up, hair, and wardrobe dressing rooms?
15. What about restrooms?
16. Check out water facilities (hot/cold).
17. Are there work areas for construction?
18. Chairs/tables needed? How many?
19. Catering arrangements—cost?
20. Lighting grid available?
21. Charges for painting studio? Cost?
22. Will security be needed to stay with equipment over night? Cost?

### Remote Checklist

1. Permits needed and their cost?
2. Number of locations or locations of remote shoot?
3. Are there neighborhood restrictions?
4. Is there a fee for the location? Cost?
5. Are the locations easily accessible?
6. Sign the location releases. Cost?
7. Will security be needed during production and/or at night to stay with the equipment. Cost?
8. Are the police needed for crowd and traffic control? If so, how much will it cost?
9. Is there a sufficient power supply available?
10. If shooting in deeply remote areas, do you need backup equipment: generator, power packs, batteries, and so on? Cost?
11. Where are the telephones? Cost?
12. Do you need a motor home? Cost?
13. Is there a need for hair, make-up, and wardrobe dressing rooms? Are vans needed? Cost? What about the space they use? Is there room?
14. Are there restrooms or do you need portable sanitation? Cost?
15. Number of chairs and tables needed? Cost?
16. Catering arrangements necessary? Cost?
17. Awnings to protect equipment and people from sun, rain, wind, you name it? Cost?
18. Have you checked out the sun's position during the day for setting up shots at that particular location?
19. Do you have enough transportation for one and all—meaning crew, talent, equipment, and all others who are needed to make the production work? Cost?
20. Will gas be available at the location or do you need to bring it? Cost?
21. Insurance for damage to equipment, sets, and so on.

## TALENT CHECKLIST

When talent is used in small- to medium-sized productions, a question pops up now and then, "Can we find someone who walks and talks at the same time?" Again, that sort of question depends on the size of your budget. You have to have qualified actors, extras, stunt people, animals and animal trainers, and an excellent casting director to ensure a quality performance.

1. Do you have enough talent releases? (Make sure anyone who is used in your shots signs them.)
2. Number of on-camera talent needed?
3. What types of characters are needed?
4. Number of off-camera talent needed?

5. What types of voices are needed (female, male, young, old, and so on)?
6. Number of extras? Female/male?
7. Talent agencies?
8. Agent's fee?
9. Talent union, which one, and the rates?
10. Talent nonunion, rates?
11. Animals, types you will need? If you need them in numbers, make arrangements. Cost?
12. Talents, clothing, sizes, shoes, hats, and the like?
13. Overtime fees?
14. Are they willing to do rehearsals and what is the fee?
15. Extra payment for talent when altering their hair by having it cut or removal of facial hair, and so on?
16. Special talents that may be needed: riding a horse, swimming, playing tennis, driving a car, handling snakes, speaking a language, and so on?
17. Do you need professional stunt people? Use only the professionals! The amateurs may have lower rates, but stunts call for a professional to do them.
18. Know the number of talent on location for each production day.
19. Production insurance for talent.

## SUPPORT SERVICES CHECKLIST

Support services—there is an array of them. The first thing you have to do is get to know your script inside and out, to know exactly which services you need. Support services play many roles in your production, and the cost can mount up. So be very accurate in choosing services, and consult the experts if you have questions.

1. Simple artwork (TV title cards, cue cards, and the like)?
2. Design and illustration? Cost?
3. Animation: cel/computer/3-D? Cost?
4. Set design artist/carpenters? Cost?
5. Props house? Cost?
6. Wardrobe house? Cost?
7. Hair stylists? Cost?
8. Make-up stylist? Cost?
9. Food stylist? Cost?
10. Teleprompter typist? Per hour?
11. Special effects house? Cost?
12. Production services house? (They do everything from finding your location sites to handling the paperwork on pension, welfare, and payroll taxes.) Cost?

## EQUIPMENT CHECKLIST

Equipment budgeting takes some basic knowledge in equipment performance. Knowing how long the shooting will take is the deciding factor in determining the actual budget for equipment. When you produce a small production, you act as the producer, director, cameraperson, lighting director, and soundperson. Coming up with the exact amount of equipment needed takes a great deal of planning and thought. You should know how the production will turn out, given the budget. If you are not sure as to what some equipment can do for the production, then consult the experts in the respective fields.

1. Cameras (single-tube/three tube)? Cost?
2. Number of cameras?
3. Number of VTRs? Which format—3/4-inch or 1-inch? Cost?
4. Switcher if needed? Cost?
5. Tape stock? How much?
6. Tape format—3/4-inch or 1-inch?
7. Microphones? How many? Cost?
8. Types of microphones (wireless, boom, lavaliers, or whatever)? Cost?
9. Lighting equipment (plus reflectors)? Cost?
10. Grip equipment? Cost?
11. Cranes, booms, dollies? Cost?
12. Extra cable? Cost?
13. Extra bulbs? Cost?
14. Monitors? How many? Cost?
15. Tripod? Which type? Cost?
16. Mounts? Which type? Cost?
17. Number of lenses? Which kinds? Cost?
18. Generators and batteries? Cost?
19. Audio mixer? Cost?

The post-production costs can be equal to, or up to twice as much as, the production expenses, depending on how many hours are used in editing, audio production, and any added special effects.

## POST-PRODUCTION CHECKLIST

1. Tape stock needed—3/4-inch or 1-inch?
2. Off-line editing—3/4-inch? Number of hours and cost?
3. On-line editing—3/4- or 1-inch? Number of hours and cost?
4. If you recorded on 1-inch with time code, do you need 3/4-inch copies with time

code window for decision editing? Cost per hour of transfer?

5. Number of copies needed? Format? Cost?
6. Audio production needed? Cost?
7. Audio studio? Rates?
8. Sound effects? Cost?
9. Narration? Rates?
10. Mixing? Cost?
11. Slide transfers? Cost?
12. Film transfers? Cost?
13. Character generator? Cost?
14. Computer special effects? Cost?
15. Videotape duplication? Cost? Number of copies needed? Which format?

## PRODUCTION PERSONNEL CHECKLIST

The nature of the production underway gives you an insight as to which type of crew you need. The pay also differs depending on many situations: time elements, hazardous working situations, weather, special clothing needed by crew, and insurance. The list could go on, but generally the cost depends on what is involved with the production.

You can use a small group if you are doing a nonunion production, but if it is union, look out! It gets very complicated, and you need to consult the unions.

1. Producer? Production rate?
2. Director? Day rate?
3. Assistant director, if needed? Cost?
4. Number of camera operators? Hour or day rate?
5. Number of sound engineers? Hour or day rate?
6. Lighting director? Hour or day rate?
7. Number of VTR operators? Hour or day rate?
8. Audio mixer, if needed? Rate?
9. Number of technical personnel needed? Rate?
10. Production assistant? Day rate?
11. Grip? Day rate?
12. Gaffer? Day rate?
13. Prop/set manager? Hour or day rate?

14. Casting director? Hour or day rate?
15. Script supervisor? Hour or day rate?
16. Make-up stylist? Day rate?
17. Hair stylist? Day rate?
18. Wardrobe person? Day rate?
19. Production manager? Rate?
20. Editors? Hour or day rate?
21. Food stylists? Day rate?
22. Carpenter? Hour rate?
23. Electrician? Hour rate?

## MISCELLANEOUS SERVICES CHECKLIST

The costs that miscellaneous services incur add up quickly. As these miscellaneous items add up, be sure to put them into the budget either as a percentage or by their hourly rate:

1. Does the production need legal advice? Attorney rate?
2. Phone calls, local or long distance?
3. Insurance: equipment, cast insurance, accident, third-party property damage, comprehensive general auto liability, props, costumes/set, extra expense insurance, and weather. What are their rates? Do you need one or all of them?
4. Travel. You will need to provide transportation for all members of the production—from cast to the "go-for." Equipment, props, and sets need transportation also. What type of transportation is needed? Cars, vans, trucks, planes, trains, mules? Do you have to pay mileage? Must you supply your own fuel? And you need travel insurance for everyone and everything.
5. Office personnel: secretaries, accountants, and bookkeepers. Rates per production?
6. Supplies: paper, forms, copies, postage, and so on?

Use these budget checklists to the fullest. They can save you from big embarrassments! No matter how creative you are at producing, your failure to handle your money properly can short-circuit your video dreams.

**GOING OUT OF YOUR WAY**

You can start by customizing your services to meet your clients' needs, time constraints, and budget considerations. But you can service your clients in numerous ways that don't cost you much money, but that make a lasting impression. The little things help, like going out of your way to deliver your client's videotapes to the television station. If your client needs information on buying a home video unit, get the best deal around. The best impression you can give your clients is honesty and respecting them and their work. Be yourself.

Consistently offering top-quality creative work in every phase of production is extremely important. Utilizing only quality equipment and staff is another prerequisite. Having impeccable service to match the quality of your production means repeat business. And we all know what that means—more business, bigger budgets, and satisfied clients!

## DOING IT    INTRODUCING MEDIA PEOPLE

In the fall of 1978, Steve Kanaba and Janyce Brisch-Kanaba moved to the Southwest to do freelance work in the Phoenix market. One of their first undertakings was to write, shoot, and edit "Single-Camera Production Techniques" in joint venture with Media Work of Arizona. Prior to their move, they had both gained over ten years of experience in the Chicago area, producing video for medical, industrial, and educational markets.

Early in 1979, Steve and Janyce formed a company called Media People, and constructed offices at their current Scottsdale location. Their facilities are located at the Scottsdale Media Center, which is an environment shared by graphic designers, illustrators, and photographers. Media People handles all aspects of videotape and audiovisual production, as well as post-production services. Their facilities include: two studios, one with a floor-to-ceiling cyclorama; slide production; multi-projector programming equipment; dark room; broadcast-quality film chain; a bank of ¾-inch videocassette recorders for duplication and distribution purposes, as well as for ¾-inch off-line editing. Media People also offer remote shooting capabilities with broadcast-quality vidoetape equipment. They have serviced many major corporations, in formats ranging from animation and motion pictures to computerized multi-media shows and videotape.

Media People attribute their success to their ability to remain flexible. Servicing client needs is the key. Offering the most appropriate solutions to fit the client's budget, program objectives, and time constraints gives Media People the competitive edge.

## INTRODUCING MEDIA WORKS

Media Works of Arizona was organized in 1973 by Barry J. Fuller, co-author of this book. Since 1975, Media Works has established an international reputation in the field of media production. Media Works' educational and training materials in sound-filmstrip and videocassette formats have been widely distributed in North America and many foreign countries. Barry J. Fuller, founder of Media Works, has won nationwide recognition as a media producer, and has conducted seminars at many regional and national media conferences. Mr. Fuller has also completed the course work for the PhD in Educational Technology, and has written many magazine articles, as well as starting an advanced text on video production.

Media Works has produced a number of national television commercials and Public Service Announcements, as well as slide-tape and sound-filmstrip presentations for major corporate clients.

Media Works' educational and training materials have been reviewed nationally by the American Library Associaton *Booklist, Media and Methods, Media Digest,* and others. A description of these materials is printed inside the back cover.

# GLOSSARY

*AC (Alternating Current).* The type of electricity found in most homes and businesses.

*AC Converter.* A device that converts alternating current (AC) to direct current (DC). DC is used to power portable battery-operated video equipment.

*Adaptors* (1). Video or audio plug accessories that, when connected to the plug you have, change it to the one you want. (2) When used in reference to lenses, is used to match the mounting assembly of one lens to the mounting assembly of a different camera.

*AGC* (Automatic Gain Control). Circuitry that electronically adjusts the strength of an incoming signal to a present level.

*Alpha Wrap.* The tape is wound once completely around the head drum (360 degrees).

*Analog Signal.* A signal that is continuously variable from 0 to 100 percent in strength.

*Animated Cartoon.* A motion picture consisting of a series of drawings, each slightly different from the other and phased so that the overall effect is that of motion.

*Animatics.* Takes the development of storyboards one step further and records them with a video camera and VTR.

*Aspect Ratio.* Any length-to-width expressed in standard units: 9 inches by 12 inches has an aspect ratio of 3:4, and the standard unit is 3 inches; 12 inches by 16 inches is also a 3:4 aspect ratio, but the standard unit is 4 inches.

*Assemble Edit Mode.* Adding scenes onto a blank videotape in consecutive fashion.

*Audio Dubbing.* The audio dubbing feature on a VTR/VCR makes it possible to watch a pre-recorded video image while recording a new sound track in sync with that image. The pre-recorded audio track is erased as the new audio information is recorded. On ¾-inch VCRs, the audio dub is usually on track one. This leaves track two open for music or other audio information.

*Azimuth.* A recording technique that allows the video information to be packed onto the videotape in a much denser configuration.

*Backdrop.* A neutral background usually made of paper or fabric. Fabric backdrops are usually draperies.

*Back Light.* Light from the rear of the subject, producing highlights on hair, shoulders, or top edges of the subject, thus separating it from the background. This eliminates flatness and gives a feeling of depth to the image or scene.

*Background Light* (set light). Any light illuminating the set or background.

*Balanced Line.* An audio line with three conductors, one of which is a shield or ground to protect the signal-carrying conductors from electrical or RF disturbance. Used in broadcast-compatible video and audio equipment.

*Barndoors.* A set of flaps placed over the front of a lighting unit to control light direction.

*Barrel Adaptor.* A barrel is used to connect two cables with like plugs in order to extend cable length.

*Barrel Distortion.* Vertical lines in the background appear somewhat curved, much like the curved sides of a barrel.

*Base Light.* The amount of light necessary to

get a well defined video image with properly rendered colors.

*Battery Belt.* Rechargeable cells mounted on a belt so that it can be worn around the waist. Battery belts are used to run lights, as well as the various types of video and film equipment.

*Battery-Operated Lights.* Lights that may be camera-mounted or hand-held and that are powered by a battery or battery belt.

*Beam Splitter.* A specialized type of glass, coated to reflect and transmit light in differing percentages.

*Beam Spread.* The width of coverage of a beam of light. Some lighting units have an adjustable beam spread and some do not.

*Betamax.* A ½-inch cassette home VCR format for recording and playing back video image and sound.

*Bidirectional.* A microphone pick-up pattern that accepts sound in a figure-eight pattern from two opposing directions.

*BNC Plug.* A type of plug frequently used on video cable.

*Bounce.* Direct light to white walls, ceiling, or reflectors, in order to break up and diffuse it before it reaches the subject.

*Breakaways.* Props, furniture, or set components designed to break upon contact with actors without injury to the actor.

*Breaker Box.* A box with circuit breakers assigned to each lighting unit, used to turn units on or off as desired.

*Bulk Eraser.* A device that generates high-frequency magnetic fields used to rearrange the magnetic patterns on recording tape, thus erasing the tape.

*Burn-In.* Permanently impressing an image on the faceplate of the camera tube, usually by exposing the tube to too much light or excessive contrast.

*Cable Wind.* The direction in which cable was wound when it was packed in the factory. To alleviate stress on the cable and tangling, rewind cable in the direction it was packed.

*Cannon Plug (XLR Plug).* A plug used on professional audio and video equipment to carry the audio signal. Since it is a balanced line, it has three conductors.

*Capstan Servo.* Refers to the regulation of the capstan as it pulls the tape through the VTR.

*Cardioid.* A microphone pick-up pattern that accepts sound from a heart-shaped area in front of and to the front sides of the mike.

*Cathode Ray Tube.* Any tube used to display visual information.

*Cel Animation.* Involves the use of transparent sheets of cellulose acetate or a similar material serving as an overlay for drawings and backgrounds.

*C.C.Eq. (pronounced "seek") Strategy.* Stands for controls, cables, and equipment. The order in which suspected malfunctions should be investigated.

*CCU (Camera Control Unit).* A device external to the camera head that holds circuitry and controls that affect the camera. Today many CCUs are integrated into the camera head.

*Ceramic (Crystal).* A specific type of microphone transducer.

*Chroma Key.* Method of electronically inserting the image from one video source into the image coming from another video source. A selected "key color" is replaced by the background shot wherever it appears in the foreground shot.

*Closed-Circuit Television.* (Sometimes Abbreviated CCTV). The signal is never sent through the air like broadcast television.

*Close-Up Lens.* Used in situations where you want to focus on an object inches away from the camera lens.

*Close-Up Shot (CU).* Zeros in on one person or object. It's used to show facial expression or certain areas.

*Cold Colors.* Colors that appear alien or unappealing as flesh tones in green, purple, or blue.

*Color Balance.* Refers to establishing a reference point for the dark and light areas in a scene and to adjusting your camera to "read" the color temperature of the light source used for the scene.

*Color Correction Filters.* Filters used to correct, add, or subtract color from the color of existing light to make a video or photographic image appear more accurately rendered.

*Color Temperature.* A measure of the proportional amounts of the primary colors (red, green, and blue) in a light source.

*Computer Animation.* Creating electronic animation through the use of computers. Can include many sources of video.

*Condenser.* A specific type of microphone.

*Contrast.* The difference in brightness between the shadow and highlight areas of a scene. The best video equipment can reproduce a difference of about four f-stops or 1:20 if detail is to be seen in both shadow and highlight areas.

*Control Track Editor.* Operates by counting frames of video according to the control track pulses on the videotape(s).

*Copystand.* In its basic form it holds a camera above a flat plane. The "copy" is lit from above with lights at a 45-degree angle to either side. It allows you to produce slides from artwork, stills, illustrations, and other flat sources.

*Cove.* A type of baseboard that joins a backdrop to the studio floor in one continuous line.

*Crawl.* Movement from left to right or right to left horizontally across the screen. If the image is unstable in this direction, the horizontal hold may stop the crawl.

*Crawl Titles.* Titles generated by a character generator or by other means that move from right to left or left to right across the screen.

*Crystal (Ceramic).* A specific type of microphone transducer.

*Cue Cards.* A prompting device consisting of a large cardboard sheet with clearly printed hand-lettered copy for the talent to read.

*Cue Track.* A track on some VTRs/VCRs used for recording time code information used in locating edit points.

*Cut.* A sudden transition from one camera angle or point-of-view to another.

*Cutaway.* A film shot to help with scene transition. It intercuts between two scenes in which the screen direction is reversed.

*Cutouts.* A technique of animation where photos and art work are positioned on a background, moving the pieces and exposing each movement a frame at a time.

*Cyc (cyclorama).* A smooth continuous piece of gunnite or plywood plastered over from floor to ceiling. It gives the illusion of infinity.

*Cyc Light.* A light used to illuminate the cyclorama or backdrop.

*dB (Decibel).* The measure of sound intensity or signal strength. Named after Alexander Graham Bell, which is the reason for capitalizing the B after the lower-case d.

*DC (Direct Current).* The type of electricity from batteries and AC converters.

*Defocus/Refocus.* A transition used for either passage of time or a change in scene.

*Degauss.* Sometimes used to mean "erasing" videotape.

*Demagnetize.* To remove magnetic charges from heads, CRTs, or other areas of charge build-up.

*Depth of Field.* The distance from the nearest point to the farthest point that a subject will be given in focus at a given f-stop.

*Diaphragm.* The part of a microphone that sound pressure waves strike to produce vibrating motion, which is converted into a weak electrical signal by the transducer.

*Diffuser.* Usually spun glass placed in front of a light source to soften light without significantly reducing the amount of light passing through it.

*Digital Signal.* A signal that is either on or off, with no gradation between.

*Diorama.* Maintains sets in the form of partially or wholly three-dimensional still-life scenes.

*Direct Color VTR.* A high-quality videotape recorder capable of recording the high frequency rate of the color signal directly onto the tape.

*Dissolve Unit.* A unit that, when connected to the slide projectors, controls the advance mechanism and light output of each. This makes it possible to dissolve or to cut between slides without a black interval at the slide change.

*Dolly.* A camera movement towards or away from an object or person.

*Drop Focus.* Defocus usually on a distracting background. In video, this may be done by using a telephoto lens or by adding neutral-density filters over the lens, and opening the f-stop, thus creating a shallower depth of field.

*Drop-Out.* A brief reduction in a portion of the video signal causing a streak on the monitor during reproduction of the video signal (from videotape).

*Dulling Spray.* Aerosol spray designed to be applied to highly reflective areas of props, set, or backgrounds to prevent comet-tailing during movement.

*Dynamic.* A specific type of microphone transducer.

*Editing.* Selecting and putting the scenes,

music, and other effects that make up a production into a pre-planned order.

*Editing Block.* In audio editing, a device with a ¼-inch groove in it to hold audio tape while cutting and placing adhesive tape on it for editing purposes.

*Editing Controller.* An electronic device that controls two or more VTRs or VCRs for editing purposes.

*Ellipsoidal Spot.* Also called a Leko light after one of the main manufacturers of the light. A type of spotlight used frequently to project patterns on the set or background.

*EIA.* Electrical Industries Association.

*EFP (Electronic Field Production).* Refers to all forms of portable equipment used other than ENG.

*ENG (Electronic News Gathering).* Style of shooting video with a totally portable single-camera system.

*Erase Head.* A head that uses a higher frequency oscillator to rearrange magnetic patterns on audio or videotape in such a fashion that they cannot be played back. Thus the erase head doesn't really erase the tape, just rearranges the patterns on it.

*ERP (Erase, Record, Play).* The order in which audio heads are arranged on a studio tape recorder. Sometimes record and play heads are in the same head assembly.

*Essential Area.* The central area of finished artwork where all essential information is positioned so that it is not lost in transmission or reception.

*Existing Light.* Natural light, the light as it exists on the scene, as opposed to auxiliary light or location lighting.

*Extreme Close-Up (ECU).* Used for dramatic effect or to show very tiny detail.

*Fade-to-Black.* A smooth transition done simply by turning the f-stop ring of the camera lens to its most closed setting.

*Fader Panel.* A panel with adjustable slide controls used to fade lights up or down.

*Feedback (audio).* The roaring or squealing effect produced when a microphone is placed too close to its own speaker. The sound or output from the speaker enters the microphone, is amplified, enters the mike again, is further amplified and quickly follows this loop, feeding upon itself until a roar of noise is created.

*Field.* One-half of one full scan of the video image consisting of 262.5 lines of information occurring every one-sixtieth of a second. It takes two fields to make a frame.

*Fill Light.* Light used to raise the level of light in shadows cast by key light or other light sources.

*Filter.* A piece of glass or plastic that fits on the front of the lens to regulate intensity and/or the color of light entering the lens.

*Flag.* In editing, a "whip" or instant of instability at an edit point. In lighting, an object shaped like a flag that is used to block light from the camera lens causing lens flare or from other parts of the scene.

*Flats.* Usually 4-by-8 flat wall components, painted or otherwised surfaced to supplement the appearance of a set.

*Focal Length.* The distance from the optical center of a lens to the front surface of the camera's pick-up tube or optical block.

*Focus.* Adjusting a ring or other control until the image is crisp and clear.

*Follow Through Focus.* The ability to zoom in or out and keep your subject in focus.

*Footcandle.* Technically, the amount of light thrown by one international candle on a square foot of surface every part of which is one foot away. It's also the measure used to indicate the brightness of light from any source.

*Footcandle Meter.* An incident meter used to measure the amount of light in footcandles from a source.

*Four-Point Lighting.* A combined use of key, fill, back, and background light—all light is a combination of these sources.

*F Plug.* A type of plug frequently used on antenna and RF cables to conduct audio and video signals simultaneously.

*Fresnel.* A type of adjustable spotlight used very widely in film and video work. It has a fresnel lens that closes over the front to focus the light emitted and an adjustable reflector inside to control the beam spread.

*Frame.* One full scan of the video image consisting of 525 lines of information occurring every one-thirtieth of a second.

*Frequency.* Tone or pitch. The number of times something happens in a given unit of time. If one undulation of an air pressure wave (or one cycle of frequency) is produced in one second, then one cycle per second (or one Hertz) is produced.

*Frequency Response.* The frequency at

which an electronic recording device can record and play back.

*F-stop.* Refers to the different iris openings that allow a certain amount of light to fall on the camera pick-up tubes.

*Gel Material (Color Correcting).* Rolls of plastic sheeting material that are colored to balance light from one source with light from another.

*Gel Material (Neutral Density).* Rolls of plastic sheeting material that are clear in color but that reduce light passing through by a predetermined number of f-stops. Used frequently over windows without outside exposure.

*Gels.* Sheets or pieces of colored heat-resistant plastic used to project colored light, to color-correct or balance light, or to cut down on the intensity of light.

*Ghosting.* Bright ghosts or trails occurring in the wake of moving people or objects. Usually caused by bright objects, but may also be caused by insufficient light. Also called lag or comet-tailing.

*Gobo.* Anything that establishes a scene by creating the illusion of being a foreground when seen through a camera.

*Ground.* A conductor, usually a wire or metal stake, that is literally fastened or connected somewhere in its path to the ground. Having a good ground makes electrical damage to equipment or injury to operator far less likely.

*Hand Prop.* Any item that performers must use in the course of a production.

*Hardwall Flats.* Flats built with walls of hard materials, like plywood or masonite, as opposed to softwall flats.

*Head Cleaning Tape.* A video or audio tape which is slightly abrasive and used to clean heads by playing it on the audio or video recorder. Excessive use of head cleaning tapes is thought to shorten head life.

*Heads.* Tiny electromagnets that convert electrical signals into magnetic patterns in the oxide of moving video- or audio tape.

*Head Drum Servo.* Refers to the regulation of the speed at which the VTR heads rotate.

*Head Room.* The space between a talent's head and the top of the screen.

*Helical Scanning System.* This system puts the video signal on the videotape in a slanted diagonal pattern.

*Hertz (Hz).* One cycle per second. Named after the nineteenth-century German physicist, Heinrich Hertz.

*Heterodyne TVR* (Also called "Color Under"). The high frequency rate of the color video information is reduced and combined with a reference signal generated within the VTR.

*Hum.* Noise in audio or video recordings usually caused by improper or floating grounds. Always ground all equipment for best recording results.

*Impedance.* A type of resistance to the signal flow.

*Impedance-Matching Transformers.* A device that matches input and output impedances. Common types are the 75-300-ohm impedance-matching transformer used at the VHF antenna leads on television sets to play back from a CTR/VCR; and hi/lo impedance matching transformers used between the mike and other video and audio recording devices to match the output impedance of the mike with the input impedance of the recording device. Matching impedances reduces noise and interference in the recording.

*IN.* The point (jack) at which power, audio, video, or other signals are sent into a piece of equipment—such as Audio IN, Mike IN, Video IN, and so on.

*Insert Edit Mode.* Recording new video and/or audio information over pre-recorded footage.

*Intervalometer.* A timing device that allows you to shoot a subject at a selectable frame per unit of time. Used on a motion picture camera.

*ips (inches per second).* A reel-to-reel tape recorder may record and play at 1-7/8 ips, 3-3/8 ips, 7-1/2 ips, and even 15 ips.

*Iris (f-Stop).* The device in the camera lens—either automatic, manual, or both—that controls the amount of light allowed through the lens to the faceplate of the pick-up tube or, in film, to the film plane.

*Jack.* The hole or receptacle that accepts a plug of a given shape or configuration.

*Junction Box.* A box with jacks in it used to patch together any of various equipment components.

*Kelvin Degrees.* Named after Lord Kelvin, a method of precisely referring to a light source's color by comparing the color of light to the temperaure in Kelvin degrees at which that color is produced.

*Key.* To electronically superimpose, or cut in, one image over another background image.

*Key Light.* The predominant source of light on a scene. It creates texture by being responsible for the darkest shadows in a scene. Key lights usually should come from one direction, to avoid creating cross-shadow effects.

*Keystoning.* A result of the projector being at an angle other than 90 degrees to the viewing screen.

*L Adaptor.* A video adaptor shaped like an L used to save space behind equipment components by making abrupt turns.

*Lapel Microphone.* A very small microphone clipped to the tie, lapel, or collar.

*Lavalier Microphone.* A small cylindrical microphone worn around the neck.

*Lead (Conductor).* For example, there are only two leads in unbalanced audio lines.

*Lens Mount.* The assembly on the front of the video camera where the lens is attached.

*Levels.* The strength (voltage) of a signal usually represented visually on a wave form monitor (if video) or on the VU meter (if audio). Several other types of audio level measuring devices are currently in use.

*Lighting Grid.* An assembly of pipes fastened to the ceiling on which the lighting units are mounted.

*Limbo.* Lighted area or setting surrounded on all sides by darkness. Usually produced by one or a combination of spot lights.

*Loop-Through.* A method used to hook more than one monitor/receiver to a VTR for playback purposes.

*Long Shot (LS, or Establishing Shot).* Encompasses a large area of the scene and establishes where the action is taking place.

*Manual (Control).* A switch or mechanism that makes it possible to bypass an automatic mechanism in favor of manual adjustment. Also called "defeat" or "override."

*Margin Area.* The area around the edge of finished artwork for handling the artwork and for protection against edge damage.

*Master.* A VTR that is recording the output signal from one or more sources of video, generating the finish product.

*Matching Action.* The technique of changing camera angles without breaking the continuity of motion from scene to scene.

*Mattes.* Black-and-white artwork, such as titles and graphics, is prepared and shot on the copystand, yielding a negative of the artwork. Used for slide preparation.

*Medium Shot (MS).* Focuses on one or two persons showing just their heads, shoulders, and upper torsos. Medium shots are relative to the other shots used in a program.

*Microphone.* An electronic device that converts vibrating air pressure waves to a weak electrical signal.

*Mini Plug.* A small plug resembling a phone plug, used to interconnect audio components.

*Mixer.* An audio device that combines two or more input signals into one or more output signals, often amplifying and conditioning the input signals.

*Monaural* Having one track, such as monaural tape recorders.

*Monitor.* Has no tuner and accepts a video signal only. The signal is fed directly by cable from a camera, VTR, or other source of video.

*Monitor Bridge.* System of routing several video and/or audio output signals to one monitor, allowing the user to switch between sources and view the output on the monitor.

*Monitor Receiver.* A TV set (receiver) that has external jacks and controls and sometimes extra circuitry for use in video production.

*Multi-Conductor Cables.* Cables with more than two signal-carrying conductors typically used to carry audio, video, and power simultaneously.

*Multi-Pin Cable Adaptors.* Adaptors used on multi-pin cables such as the 8-pin barrel.

*Needle Drop.* The number of times the needle is brought into contact with a record album. Music libraries may charge per drop, per production, or for a fixed period of time. Some sell their library outright with no drop charges or royalties of any kind.

*Neutral-Density (ND) Filters.* Filters that do not change the color of light, but simply cut down the amount of light allowed into the camera. Some newer cameras have built-in ND filters.

*Nose Room.* The space between the front of the nose and the edge of the screen in a profile shot.

*NTSC (National Television Systems Committee).* Also refers to the scanning system in North America and other countries. Based on the use of 60 cycles of electricity, 525 scan lines per frame, and 30 frames per second.

*Off-Line Editing.* One phase in the overall process of computerized videotape editing where copies of original material are made for the purpose of assembling a list of time code numbers for subsequent entry into the computerized "on-line" system.

*Ohm (Ω).* A measure of DC resistance and AC impedance.

*Omega Wrap.* The tape covers only a portion of the head drum.

*Omnidirectional.* A microphone pick-up pattern that accepts sound from any direction in a 360-degree pattern.

*On-Line Editing.* Refers to using an **entire** computer-assisted editing system.

*Oscillator.* An electronic device that generates high-frequency signals for timing, erase-head, and other purposes.

*Out.* The point (jack) at which power, audio, video, or other signals are sent out of a piece of equipment—Audio OUT, RF OUT, Video OUT, and so on.

*Oxide.* Easily magnetized particle used as a coating on a plastic backing forming various types of recording tape.

*PAL (Phase Alternate by Line).* Essentially a modification of the NTSC system using a 50-cycle power source, 625 scan lines per frame, and 25 frames per second.

*Pan.* A horizontal camera movement to the left or right to follow action or cover a shot.

*Pantographs.* Flexible accordion-like extenders that make it possible to adjust the height of lighting units by simply pulling them down or pushing them up to the desired position.

*Parabolic Dish.* A parabolic dish is used as a sort of sound collector (with an omnidirectional microphone) to capture the sound presence of outside sporting events and audience response.

*Passive Mixer.* A mixer that simply routes the signal or signals sent through it to a desired destination. It does nothing to amplify or condition the signals sent through it.

*Patch Cord.* A cable with plugs on both ends for connecting (patching) electronic components together. Patch cords may have a variety of video or audio plugs on them, or even hybrid video/audio plugs.

*Patch Panel (Lighting).* A panel fitted with jacks and patch cords so that power can be routed to lighting units in many different combinations. It makes it less necesasry to move lighting unit to hot outlets on the lighting grid.

*Pattern Projector.* A machine specifically designed to project patterns onto the set or background. The patterns may be superimposed or, in some cases, projected in motion.

*Patterns.* Metal discs that fit into ellipsoidal spot lights; also any type of cutout, usually of wood, held or suspended in front of a lighting unit to cast shapes on the set or background.

*Pedestal (Up or Down).* A camera movement with the entire camera being physically raised up higher or down lower, usually on a hydraulic tripod or pedestal.

*Phone Plug.* Standard ¼-inch plug frequently used for interconnection of audio components, both monaural and stereo.

*Phone Plug (RCA Plug).* The phone or RCA Plug has a center conductor and a metal shield ground. It's frequently used for interconnection of audio components, but it is also used to carry the video signal on some newer VHS ½-inch VTRs.

*Photo Floods.* Color-corrected lamps that look, in some cases, like household bulbs, but that have a high wattage, usually starting at 250 watts.

*Pick-Up Patterns.* The direction or directions from which a microphone is designed to pick up sound.

*Picture Monitors.* There are three types: (1) TV receiver, (2) monitor, and (3) hybrid.

*Play Head.* In audio, the head that plays back the recorded audio signal. The play head may be separate from the record head or in the same head assembly as the record head.

*Plug.* Any of various signal- or power-carrying devices that are inserted into a hole or receptacle, called a "jack," to make an electrical connection.

*Pop Filter.* A wire-mesh screen that fits over a microphone to cut down on "S"-ing, hisses, and pops in spoken narration.

*Portable System.* A video system that can be

carried but that is more often transported on a lightweight cart.

*Portapak.* A small lightweight camera and recorder used for shooting on location.

*Practical Prop.* Any prop that has to function on the set the way it does in reality—sinks, stoves, washers, fireplaces.

*Public Domain.* Titles and materials that do not have a copyright notice.

*Quality (of Light).* The feel of light whether hard (specular) or soft (diffuse).

*Quartz-Iodine Lamps.* A type of quartz lamp.

*Quartz Lamps.* Lamps specially designed to withstand high temperatures and to maintain consistent color temperature.

*Rack Focus.* Using selective focus to create a transition from one subject to the other in a scene.

*Radio Frequency.* Video and audio through-the-air broadcasts on assigned (or unassigned) channel frequencies. Unwanted RF may show up in recordings made near radio or television transmitters, radar, CB antennas, and the like.

*Record Head.* In audio the head that records the audio signal. The record head may be separate from the play head or in the same head assembly as the play head.

*Record Level.* The strength of the signal in record mode.

*Reflectors.* Anything from commercially made reflector "boards" to white paper or artboard, all used to reflect light for fill or for raising the overall light level in a scene.

*Registration.* Refers to the precise placement of the image on the film plane of a camera with reference to the film sprocket holes.

*Resolution.* The camera's resolving power or ability to reproduce a sharp, crisp image on the video monitor.

*RF Amplifier.* A device that amplifies the RF signal so that it can be sent to a large number of receivers for playback purposes.

*RF OUT.* The point (jack) at which the RF signal is sent from the VTR/VCR.

*RF Splitter.* A device (simple junction box) used to split the RF signal for playback on more than one TV receiver.

*Ribbon.* A specific type of microphone transducer.

*Risers.* Usually planking and plywood sheets designed in the form of modular staging to raise the set or actors off the floor.

*Roll.* Movement from top to bottom or bottom to top vertically on the screen. If the image on the screen is unstable, it may roll in either direction. The vertical hold control may stop the roll.

*Sandbag.* Bags of sand sewn together saddle-bag fashion and used to hold down the base or feet of T-stands, tripods, easels, or anything that has to be stabilized during a shoot.

*Scanning Area.* The area of finished artwork that is framed by the camera. Due to transmission and reception tolerances and misadjustments, this area may be much more than what is actually seen on a given receiver. Essential information must be kept in the central part of this area called the "essential area."

*Scoop.* A broad source of light used frequently to provide fill light. It is shaped like a scoop.

*Scrim.* Anything placed in front of a lighting unit to cut down or alternate the amount of light falling on a scene or any part of a scene. Metal screens or half-screens are frequently used.

*Secam (Sequential with Memory).* Television scanning system used in France and the USSR. Uses 50-cycle power sources, 625 scan lines per frame, and 25 frames per second. Differs from the PAL system in the way that color signals are encoded.

*SEG (Special Effects Generator).* Also commonly referred to as a "switcher." Creates effects such as wipes, supers, dissolves, and others.

*Semiportable System.* A video system that can be moved around on carts but is too heavy to be carried.

*Servo Control System.* Reads its own output and determines further output of the system.

*Set Prop.* Any item or object used to enhance or to add detail to the set.

*Shadow Mask.* A thin metal sheet perforated by dots or bars and positioned within the picture tube of a television receiver/monitor or monitor.

*Shielded Cable.* Cable with conductors that are surrounded by a wire-mesh or foil shield. The shield attenuates or grounds unwanted RF and electrical interference that might otherwise show up in the video and/or audio recording.

*Signal-Processing Equipment.* Electronic devices used to adjust and/or correct unstable video signals from VTRs and discs.

*Signal-to-Noise Ratio (S/N Ratio).* The ratio of the strength of the signal generated by an electronic device to the strength of the noise or unwanted signal generated by the same device.

*Single-Camera System.* Video systems using only one camera either portable, semiportable, or studio single-camera systems.

*Skeletal Sets.* Sets that are symbolic rather than realistic and that are usually comprised of relatively few set components.

*Skew.* The control on the VTR/VCR affecting tape tension. If there is a hook in one direction or the other at the top of the screen, the skew control should be adjusted until the hook disappears.

*Slave.* A playback VTR in an editing or duplicating system.

*Slide duplicator.* Consists of an **underlit** stage to hold the slide to be copied and a column to your 35-mm single lens reflex camera. It is used to create titles and special effects slides.

*SMPTE Time Code.* A standardized 80-bit digital signal recorded on an unused audio track of an audio or videotape recorder and used to assign a specific number to each frame of video. Used for computer-assisted editing.

*Snoot.* A cylindrical open-ended accessory placed on the front of a fresnel used to throw a tight spot of light.

*Snow.* Interference in the video image caused by dirty heads or electronic problems, which resembles a snow storm.

*Soft.* Light with a gentle, low-contract quality, as opposed to specular light.

*Softwall Flats.* Flats built with walls of canvas or muslin, as opposed to hardwall flats.

*Solderless Connectors.* Plugs attached to cable with crimping tools rather than solder.

*Sound Speed.* 24 frames per second on film.

*Specular.* Light composed of focused, direct parallel rays that originate from a comparatively small or "point" light source.

*Stacking.* Interconnecting several video distribution amplifiers to strengthen the video signal for distribution to a large number monitor/receivers for playback.

*Standardization.* Making similar formats compatible. For instance, ¾-inch U-matic cassette machines are standardized.

*Stereo.* Having two tracks such as stereo tape recorders, receivers, amplifiers, tuners, and so on.

*Stop Down.* To adjust the iris to a smaller f-stop.

*Storyboard.* A series of illustrations of key scenes that follow the script.

*Strain-Relief Collar.* A jack designed with a flexible plastic or rubber neck that absorbs most of the bending stress near the connection of the cable to the jack.

*Studio Single-Camera System.* A video camera tied into a switcher and other studio equipment that can be used alone but is designed to be used with other studio cameras. It is usually moved around on a pedestal and dolly arrangement.

*Subject Contrast.* The contrast that is part of or within the subject. An example would be a woman wearing a white blouse and a black skirt.

*Subject-to-Nonsubject Contrast.* The brightness difference between the subject and anything else. An example would be a light yellow car against a black backdrop.

*Subject-to-Subject Contrast.* Contrast between subjects. For example an actor standing in the shade in dark clothing speaking to another actor standing in the sun in a light-colored summer suit.

*Super Cardioid.* An elongated cardioid pattern.

*Swish Pan.* A transition to indicate a change in time or place between scenes.

*Sync Signal.* The signal, recorded on the sync track, that helps keep the VTR/VCR running at the proper speed for playback.

*T Adaptor.* A video adaptor shaped like a T, which can send the video signal to two points simultaneously.

*Take.* A concise scene or segment of a production that is shot and then reshot, if not acceptable. Frequently more than one take is necessary to complete a scene.

*Tear Art.* Camera-ready line drawings of common graphics, symbols, and scenes, that are usually purchased on a monthly subscription basis in book form.

*Telephoto Lens.* A lens that has a large focal length and a very narrow and shallow depth of field. It can be used for selective focus.

*Teleprompter.* A prompting device in which the copy is typed or hand-lettered on a roll of paper, which is mounted on motorized rollers with variable speed control.

*Television Black.* Black that reflects at least 3 percent of the light striking it. Thus it doesn't look entirely black.

*Television White.* White that reflects no more than 60 percent of the light striking it, Thus appearing more like gray than white.

*Termination.* In video, terminating the last monitor/receiver in line when more than one is being used for playback purposes. This is done, in some cases, with a built-in switch on the monitor/receiver or by soldering a 75-ohm resistor across the terminals of an adaptor that is placed on the video OUT jack of the last monitor/receiver in line. Termination cuts down on noise in the video image.

*Terminator.* A termination or an adaptor with a 75-ohm resistor soldered across its contacts.

*Test Tape.* A tape with color bars and tone or test pattern, used to help diagnose problems in the video system.

*Three-Dimensional.* Form of film animation using three-dimensional objects to create movement.

*Tilt.* A camera movement up or down, with the camera being tilted rather than physically moved higher or lower.

*Time-Base Corrector.* Device used to restore proper horizontal stabilities to video signals from videotape recorders.

*Time-Lapse.* Refers to a technique whereby the action of an event is compressed by exposing a frame of film over a length of time at regular intervals.

*Title Card.* A piece of finished artwork with lettering, illustrations, or other graphic information. It may be used for openings and closings, or other type of in-program transitions.

*Tracking.* The control on the VTR/VCR that synchronizes the timed position of the video heads with the position of the fields recorded on the videotape. If there is a horizontal band of break-up or disturbance in the video image, the tracking control should be adjusted until it disappears.

*Tracks.* The paths upon which the audio, video and sync signals are recorded on the moving recording tape.

*Transducer.* The element or circuitry in a microscope that converts motion from a vibrating diaphragm into a weak electrical signal.

*Transfer Art.* Adhesive art that is rubbed off a plastic backing onto art board or paper. Similar to transfer letters.

*Transition.* The move from one scene to another, the connecting thread in the way you develop your action.

*Transverse Scanning System.* In a quadruplex VTR, the video signal goes onto the tape at right angles to the direction in which the tape is moving.

*T-Stand.* A multi-purpose clamp stand used to hold or support flags, diffusers, reflectors, or other props or set materials.

*Tripod.* A three-legged unit to which the camera and camera head are attached for different camera heights on the tripod, regulate the leg shafts.

*Tungsten-Halogen Lamp.* A type of quartz lamp.

*TV Receiver.* Most commonly in the home. The receiver picks up radio frequencies through a tuner via an antenna. The frequencies carry video and audio signals, and are broadcast by a TV station.

*Truck.* Physically moving the camera in a left or right lateral movement.

*UHF (Ultra-High Frequency).* UHF TV channels are higher in frequency than VHF channels. UHF channels require a loop antenna for pick-up.

*UHF Plug.* A type of plug frequently used on video cables with a center conductor and metal shield ground used to carry the video signal.

*Unbalanced Line.* An audio line with two conductors and no shield. Since unbalanced lines have no shield to protect the conductors from RF or electrical interference, they tend to pick up noise, especially when recording near sources of electrical disturbance like radio and television stations, radar, electrical discharge, or RF emanations.

*Underscan.* A function on a video monitor that reduces the total image size of the video signal. It is used to examine the head switching point on helical scan machines.

*Unidirectional.* A microphone pick-up pattern that accepts sound from a narrow, specific direction while rejecting sound coming from other directions.

*VCR (Videocassette Recorder).* An electronic device that records and plays back picture and sound electronically on a cassette tape.

*Vectorscope.* Shows the proper relationship between the color reference signal (color burst) and the chroma (color information).

*VHF (Very High Frequency).* VHF TV channels are the ones normally viewed using rabbit ears or normal roof-top antennas.

*VHS.* A ½-inch cassette home VCR format for recording and playing back a video image and sound.

*Video Feedback.* Similar to audio feedback, but a visual rather than aural effect. The most familiar video feedback can be produced by aiming a camera at its own monitor. The video image duplicates itself in a hall-of-mirrors effect with flaring, multi-color trails. By adjusting camera and monitor controls, you can change the feedback effects or manipulate them to the tempo of music.

*VTR (Videotape Recorder).* An electronic device that records and plays back picture and sound electronically on videotape—usually reel-to-reel.

*Vertical Hold.* A control on a monitor/receiver that, when properly adjusted, holds the video image in place, preventing vertical rolls and instability.

*VDA (Video Distribution Amplifier).* A device that amplifies the video signal for distribution to a number of monitor/receivers for playback.

*Video Heads.* Tiny electromagnets on the opposite ends of a spinning bar inside the head drums, which come into direct contact with the videotape and emits electromagnetic patterns on the videotape. These patterns are reproduced as a video image.

*Video Level.* The strength of the video signal. High video levels may reflect damage to camera pick-up tubes. Low video levels affect the legibility of the image.

*Videotape.* Tape of various widths, similar to audio tape, used for recording video and audio signals.

*Videotape Formats.* Used to describe the physical width of variously sized videotapes and the methods used for recording the video signal onto the videotape.

*VU (Volume Unit).* VU meters are used to monitor audio signal and other types of levels.

*Warm Colors.* Colors that tend to flatter flesh tones like red, orange, yellow, brown, beige, and the like.

*Waveform.* The shape of the visual display of any signal being observed on such devices as waveform monitors or oscilloscopes.

*Waveform Monitor.* A device that graphically displays variations in the video signal being observed or monitored.

*White Card.* Used in front projection as a screen surface. The card should have a stiff backing and matte finish to give even illumination and to cut down on glare from the projector bulb.

*White Balance.* The control or adjustment on the camera or on the camera control unit that tells the camera's circuitry what white is, in order to establish a reference for color balancing the camera under existing light.

*Wide-Angle Lens.* This lens has a great depth of field and an extreme area of coverage.

*Wind Screen.* A foam rubber cover that fits over a microphone to cut down on wind noise.

*Wireless Microphone.* A microphone with a built-in FM transmitter that transmits to an FM receiver for amplification or recording.

*Wiring Run.* The conduit or metal-enclosed channel next to the criss-crossed bars of the lighting grid that holds the power cables and pigtailed outlets, into which the lighting units are plugged for power.

*Wrong Field Edits.* Refers to electronic edits made out of the proper field sequence.

*Y Adaptor.* An adaptor or cord that is shaped like a Y and that is used to send an output signal to two different locations simultaneously.

*Zoom.* A smooth camera lens movement toward or away from a subject. Zoom-in is a movement to a narrow angle of view, in which the scene appears closer. Zoom-out is a movement to a wide angle of view in which the scene appears farther away.

*Zoom Lens.* A variable-focal-length lens that, in one continuous move of the lens, can change from wide angle to telephoto.

# SOURCE INDEX

This is a listing of various equipment manufacturers and other companies who the authors feel deserve exposure for the help and support they have provided in the writing of this book.

*Cascom, Inc.*
707 18th Avenue South
Nashville, Tennessee 37203
(615) 329-4112

Western Region: Contact
Patsy Smiley
(213) 943-4392

Visual effects library for adding sparkle to the graphic information in film or video.

*Comprehensive Video Corporation*
148 Veterans Drive
Northvale, New Jersey 07647
(201) 767-7990

Wide assortment of video-related accessories.

*EDCOR*
16782 Hale Avenue
Irvine, California 92714
(714) 556-2740

Wireless microphones.

*Electro-Voice, Inc.*
600 Cecil Street
Buchanan, Michigan 49107
(616) 695-6831

Microphones of all types.

*Frank Wooley & Co., Inc.*
529 Franklin Street
Reading, Pennsylvania 19602
(215) 374-8335

MotionMaster makes it possible to create motion graphics using polarizing materials.

*Frezzolini Electronics, Inc.*
7 Valley Street
Hawthorne, New Jersey 07506
(201) 427-1160

Portable camera lights (Frezzi-Lite) and battery packs.

*The Great American Market*
P.O. Box 178
Woodland Hills, California 91364
(213) 883-8182

Pattern projectors, patterns to be used in ellipsoidal spots for projected backgrounds, and custom-made patterns.

*Kroy Industries, Inc.*
1728 Gervais Avenue
St. Paul, Minnesota 55109
(612) 770-7000

Low-cost lettering machines, Kroy Type 30, Kroy Type XL.

*Lee-Ray Industries, Inc.*
38 East First Avenue
Mesa, Arizona 85202
(602) 962-6806

Video equipment carts, wall brackets, and other devices to support and transport video gear.

*Lowel-Light Manufacturing, Inc.*
421 West 54th Street
New York, New York 10019
(212) 245-6744

Wide variety of portable lighting kits and accessories.

*Marshall Industries*
9674 Telstar Avenue
El Monte, California 91731
(213) 686-0141

Broad selection of tools and accessories for maintenance and repair of video systems.

*Mangum Sickles Industries, Inc.*
1200 Sickles Drive
Tempe, Arizona 85281
(602) 967-1116

Sickles Chromapro, slide camera, photographic equipment.

*Optisonics Hec Corporation*
1802 West Grant Road
Tucson, Arizona 85705
(602) 792-1040

Combined dissolve unit/sound systems for programming slide shows for front- or rear-screen presentation or transfer to videotape. Programming the slides in advance cuts down on the expense of TV studio time.

*Reynolds Letteron Co.*
6704 Valjean Avenue
Van Nuys, California 91406
(213) 994-1194

TeleDisplay Titling Systems.

*Rhoades National Corporation*
126 Nautoline Drive
Hendersonville, Tenessee 37075
(615) 824-1735

Teledapter, a device improving the audio quality from the video receiver by producing simulated stereo.

*Soper Sound*
P.O. Box 498
Palo Alto, California 94301
(415) 321-4022

A wide selection of music available for a one time purchase. No "drop" fees or royalties.

*Sound Dynamics Corporation*
161 Don Park Road
Markam, Ontario, Canada
(416) 495-0050

Speakers for use in monitoring the audio portion of the video playback.

*Uniset Corporation*
449 Avenue A
Rochester, New York 14621
(716) 544-3820

Pre-made, modular, geometric shapes that can be combined to produce three-dimensional sets for any purpose.

*Universal Fluid Heads (Aust.) Pty. Ltd.*
2A Clement Street
Rushcutters Bay
Sydney, N.S.W., Australia 2011
Cable and telegram "Unimota" Sydney

Phones: 31-8789  31-8786  A.H.: 337-1394
Fluid heads and tripods for smooth camera moves.

# INDEX

# INSTRUCTIONAL MATERIALS

**MEDIA WORKS OF ARIZONA**

### SINGLE-CAMERA
### PRODUCTION TECHNIQUES

This 30 minute videotape was designed to supplement the Single-Camera Video Production text. It teaches the viewer simple and effective production methods using a single-camera system. All of the various techniques included in the presentation are basic and easy to accomplish, using widely available devices. Each technique is shown and explained and then applied in a short vignette.

A wide variety of effects produced with 35mm slides and a dissolve unit are shown. Time-lapse photography and various types of animation, using Super-8 film, are also demonstrated, as are a variety of projection techniques for transferring slides and film to video tape. Lenses, filters, titles, other graphics, props and miniature sets — all are treated in detail.

### SERIES I
### GETTING IT ON VIDEO

The Getting It On Video series is designed to assist anyone teaching television courses or wishing to communicate through the medium of television, regardless of the quantity or type of equipment available.

The topics covered are: The Video Camera, The Videotape Recorder, Portable and Single Camera Systems, Graphics for Television, Lighting and Special Effects, and Audio for Television.

### SERIES II
### GETTING IT ON VIDEO II

The Getting It On Video II series is intended to supplement Getting It On Video. It is designed to be used by anyone teaching television production on a beginning and intermediate level.

The topics covered are: Planning a TV Production, The Ins and Outs of Video Hookups, Inexpensive Set Design for Television, Color Specifics, Troubleshooting a Video System, and Production Pointers.

### SERIES III
### SOUND: RECORDING
### AND REPRODUCTION

Sound: Recording and Reproduction is intended as an adjunct for the video series. It is designed to assist anyone teaching basic audio recording and reproduction techniques.

The topics covered are: Recording and Reproduction, Record Players and Turntables, Amplifiers and Audio Systems, Microphones and Speakers, Tape Recorders, and Mixing and Editing.

### SERIES IV
### LIGHTING FOR STILL
### AND MOTION MEDIA

The Lighting for Still and Motion Media series is designed to assist anyone teaching basic lighting techniques in any medium of production.

The topics covered are: Light and Light Metering, Existing Light and Daylight, Incandescent Lighting, Motion Picture Lighting, Television Lighting, and Flash Lighting.

## SINGLE-CAMERA
## PRODUCTION TECHNIQUES
### is available in ¾ or VHS
### Videocassette Format.
### Series I-IV are available
### in either Sound-Filmstrip or
### Videocassette Formats — ¾ or VHS.

*For further information contact:*
### MEDIA WORKS OF ARIZONA
### ROUTE 12 BOX 798
### TUCSON, ARIZONA 85715
### (602) 749-4488